THE SHADOWS OF
POWER

THE SHADOWS OF POWER

The Council on Foreign Relations And The American Decline

by
James Perloff

WESTERN ISLANDS

PUBLISHERS

APPLETON, WISCONSIN

First printing, October 1988	10,000 copies
Second printing, March 1989	5,000 copies
Third printing, June 1989	5,000 copies
Fourth printing, November 1989	25,000 copies

Published by
Western Islands
Post Office Box 8040
Appleton, Wisconsin 54913
414-749-3783

Printed in the United States of America
ISBN: 0-88279-134-6

Contents

Foreword

There is good news and there is bad news. The good news is, this book has been written. The bad news is, it's true.

Certain people in high places are going to dispute the validity of this book, they will probably try to discredit it, because they have a vested interest in concealing their activities and agenda.

But I encourage anyone who reads *The Shadows of Power* to note its painstaking documentation. This is no opinion piece; it is an assembly of hard facts that state their own conclusions.

You can check information in this book against its sources, which are noted. One thing I find interesting is that its revelations are not *new*. They have always been available — but available like a news story that is tucked under a small headline on page 183 of a Sunday newspaper. Anyone who goes to a fair-sized library can probably find copies — however dusty — of Admiral Theobald's *The Final Secret of Pearl Harbor*, or Colin Simpson's *The Lusitania*, or *From Major Jordan's Diaries*. John Toland's epic *Infamy* is on bookstore shelves today. And though it may mean microfilm, you can obtain access to the old *Congressional Record*. Lots of powerful stories are buried there, and I mean buried, because the mass media ignored them.

The book is especially unique because it not only describes scores of underreported events, but elucidates them by showing their common thread: the influence of the internationalist Establishment of the United States. If the Establishment is elusive in its identity, it certainly has a perceptible face in the Council on Foreign Relations, and that is what the author has centered on.

This is not just a book about an organization. It is a book about history. You might call it "the other side of American history from Wilson on" because it tells the "other side" of many stories that even the self-proclaimed inside information specialists, such as Jack Anderson and Bob Woodward, didn't or wouldn't report.

It has been said that *those who do not know the past are condemned to repeat it*. But how can we truly understand an incident in our American past if we are confined to the headline version, designed for public consumption in the interest of protecting the powerful and the few? *The Shadows of Power* has resurrected eight decades of censored material. Don't let anyone censor it for you now. Read the book and decide for yourself its merit. Your outlook, and perhaps your future itself, will never be the same.

James E. Jeffries
United States Congressman (Ret.)

THE SHADOWS OF POWER

Chapter 1

A Primer On The CFR

Speaking before Britain's House of Lords in 1770, Sir William Pitt declared: "There is something behind the throne greater than the king himself," thus giving birth to the phrase "power behind the throne."

In 1844, Benjamin Disraeli, England's famed statesman, published a novel entitled *Coningsby, or the New Generation*. It was well known as a thinly disguised portrayal of his political contemporaries. In it, he wrote: "[T]he world is governed by very different personages from what is imagined by those who are not behind the scenes."

Felix Frankfurter, justice of the U.S. Supreme Court, restated this in an American context when he said: "The real rulers in Washington are invisible, and exercise power from behind the scenes."[1]

Frankfurter was not alone in that assessment. During this century, the existence of a secret U.S. power clique has been acknowledged, however rarely, by prominent Americans.

On March 26, 1922, John F. Hylan, Mayor of New York City, said in a speech:

> The real menace of our republic is the invisible government which, like a giant octopus, sprawls its slimy length over our city, state and nation. At the head is a small group of banking houses generally referred to as "international bankers." This little coterie of powerful international bankers virtually run our government for their own selfish ends.[2]

3

In a letter to an associate dated November 21, 1933, President Franklin D. Roosevelt wrote:

> The real truth of the matter is, as you and I know, that a financial element in the large centers has owned the government ever since the days of Andrew Jackson . . .[3]

On February 23, 1954, Senator William Jenner warned in a speech:

> Today the path to total dictatorship in the United States can be laid by strictly legal means, unseen and unheard by the Congress, the President, or the people. . . . Outwardly we have a Constitutional government. We have operating *within* our government and political system, *another* body representing another form of government, a bureaucratic elite which believes our Constitution is outmoded and is sure that it is the winning side . . . All the strange developments in foreign policy agreements may be traced to this group who are going to make us over to suit their pleasure . . . . This political action group has its own local political support organizations, its own pressure groups, its own vested interests, its foothold within our government, and its own propaganda apparatus.[4]

The Establishment

There is, of course, in America, what we have come to call "the Establishment." This expression was popularized by English writer Henry Fairlie in an article about Britain's ruling circle. It was used in the U.S. during the Vietnam War as a term of scorn. Today it is a legitimate word in its own right, defined by the *American Heritage Dictionary* as "an exclusive group of powerful people who rule a government or society by means of private agreements and decisions." The idea of such an arrangement naturally rankles most Americans, who believe that government should be of the people at large, and not a private few.

Who or what is the American Establishment? A few books have depicted it, but these have rarely attained much circulation or publicity — perhaps for no other reason than the Establishment prefers to remain "behind the scenes."

Columnist Edith Kermit Roosevelt, granddaughter of President Theodore Roosevelt, described it as follows:

> The word "Establishment" is a general term for the power elite in international finance, business, the professions and government, largely from the northeast, who wield most of the power regardless of who is in the White House.
>
> Most people are unaware of the existence of this "legitimate Mafia." Yet the power of the Establishment makes itself felt from the professor who seeks a foundation grant, to the candidate for a cabinet post or State Department job. It affects the nation's policies in almost every area.[5]

In the public mind, the American Establishment is probably most associated with big business and with wealthy, old-line families. The sons of these families have long followed a traditional career path that begins with private schools, the most famous being Groton. From these they have typically proceeded to Harvard, Yale, Princeton, or Columbia, there entering exclusive fraternities, such as Yale's secretive Skull and Bones. Some of the brightest have traveled to Oxford for graduate work as Rhodes Scholars. From academia they have customarily progressed to Wall Street, perhaps joining an international investment bank, such as Chase Manhattan, or a prominent law firm or brokerage house. Some of the politically inclined have signed on with Establishment think tanks like the Brookings Institution and the Rand Corporation. As they have matured, a few have found themselves on the boards of the vast foundations — Rockefeller, Ford, and Carnegie. And ultimately, some have advanced into "public service" — high positions in the federal government.

For the latter, there has long been a requisite: membership in a New York-based group called the Council on Foreign Relations — CFR for short. Since its founding in 1921, the Council has been the Establishment's chief link to the U.S. government. It is the focus of this book.

5

What is the CFR?

Historian Arthur Schlesinger, Jr. has called the Council on Foreign Relations a "front organization" for "the heart of the American Establishment."[6] David Halberstam, in his acclaimed book *The Best and the Brightest,* dubbed it "the Establishment's unofficial club."[7]

Newsweek has referred to the CFR's leaders as "the foreign-policy establishment of the U.S."[8] Richard Rovere, writing in *Esquire* magazine, saw them as "a sort of Presidium for that part of the Establishment that guides our destiny as a nation."[9]

The Council describes itself as a "nonprofit and nonpartisan membership organization dedicated to improved understanding of American foreign policy and international affairs." It is headquartered in the elegant Harold Pratt House at 58 East 68th Street in New York City. As of June 1987, the CFR had 2,440 members, including many prominent persons in business, government, law, and the mass media. Membership is by invitation only.

The Council holds frequent meetings and dinners which feature a speech by a guest — usually a ranking statesman from Washington or a foreign country — followed by a discussion with members. These meetings follow a rule of "non-attribution," meaning that everything is off the record. Violation of this rule is considered grounds for dismissal from the CFR. The Council explains that its no-quote policy is to encourage candor, but economist John Kenneth Galbraith, himself a former member, has called it "a scandal." "Why," he asks, "should businessmen be briefed by Government officials on information not available to the general public, especially since it can be financially advantageous?"[10]

Pratt House also conducts fifteen to twenty study groups every year. Each is assigned a particular foreign policy topic, and meets regularly to deliberate it. The findings of a study group are customarily published, often in book form.

Five times a year, the Council puts out a journal called *Foreign Affairs.* In addition to serving as a mouthpiece for CFR members, it carries articles — some ghostwritten — by American and foreign dignitaries. Although notorious for being boring, *Foreign Affairs* is widely read by those involved with making foreign policy, and has been called by *Time* magazine "the most influential periodical in print."[11]

The CFR undertakes other activities, such as its "Corporate Program" that indoctrinates businessmen in international matters. The Council's annual budget is about $8.5 million, which is mostly funded by foundation grants, members' dues and contributions, and publication revenue. And it has affiliates called "Committees on Foreign Relations" in thirty-eight cities around the United States.

More Than Just a Club

The Council, while remaining largely unknown to the public, has exercised decisive impact on U.S. policy, especially foreign policy, for several decades. It has achieved this primarily in two ways. The first is by directly supplying personnel for upper echelon government jobs.

Few Americans know how a President chooses his administrators. The majority probably trust that, aside from an occasional political payoff, the most qualified people are sought and found. But the CFR's contribution cannot be overlooked. Pulitzer Prize winner Theodore White said that the Council's "roster of members has for a generation, under Republican and Democratic administrations alike, been the chief recruiting ground for cabinet-level officials in Washington."[12] The *Christian Science Monitor* once observed that "there is a constant flow of its members from private life to public service. Almost half of the council members have been invited to assume official government positions or to act as consultants at one time or another."[13]

Indeed, Joseph Kraft, writing in *Harper's,* called the Council a "school for statesmen."[14] David Halberstam puts it more wryly: "They walk in one door as acquisitive businessmen and come out the other door as statesmen-figures."[15]

The historical record speaks even more loudly than these quotes. Through early 1988, fourteen secretaries of state, fourteen treasury secretaries, eleven defense secretaries, and scores of other federal department heads have been CFR members.

Defenders of the Council say such enumerations are misleading because some officials are invited into the Council *after* appointment to government. However, close inspection does not reveal this to be a particularly extenuating factor. Every secretary of state since 1949 has been a member of the Council, and of these, only one, William P. Rogers, joined the CFR subsequent to appointment.

That an individual enrolls in the Council after entering public service does not purge his membership of significance, because the organization may still influence him considerably while in office.

CFR men who earn high government ranks often staff their departments with Council colleagues. As Anthony Lukas related in the *New York Times* in 1971:

[E]veryone knows how fraternity brothers can help other brothers climb the ladder of life. If you want to make foreign policy, there's no better fraternity to belong to than the Council.

When Henry Stimson — the group's quintessential member — went to Washington in 1940 as Secretary of War, he took with him John McCloy, who was to become Assistant Secretary in charge of personnel. McCloy has recalled: "Whenever we needed a man we thumbed through the roll of the Council members and put through a call to New York."

And over the years, the men McCloy called in turn called other Council members.[16]

According to the CFR itself, as of June 1987, 318 of its members were current U.S. government officials.

The second major way in which the Council affects policy is in formulating and marketing recommendations. The CFR disputes that it actually does this. Its annual report for 1986 emphatically stated: "The Council on Foreign Relations does not determine foreign policy . . ."[17] The 1987 report declared: "The Council takes no institutional position on issues of foreign policy . . ."[18]

It is true that the Council does not officially advocate policies per se; however, through its books and *Foreign Affairs* articles, ideas certainly are pushed, even if accompanied by statements that a given work only represents its author's viewpoint.

J. Robert Moskin, writing in the March 1987 issue of *Town & Country*, said the CFR "has long sought to influence U.S. foreign policy."[19] In his article for *Harper's*, Joseph Kraft noted that the Council "has been the seat of some basic government decisions, has set the context for many more . . ."[20] Indeed, it is alleged that if you want to know what the U.S. government will be doing tomorrow, just read *Foreign Affairs* today!

Admiral Chester Ward, former Judge Advocate General of the U.S. Navy, was invited into CFR membership and was shocked by what he discovered. Although he remained in the organization for nearly twenty years, he became one of its sharpest critics. In a 1975 book he coauthored with Phyllis Schlafly, Ward wrote:

> Once the ruling members of the CFR have decided that the U.S. Government should adopt a particular policy, the very substantial research facilities of CFR are put to work to develop arguments, intellectual and emotional, to support the new policy, and to confound and discredit, intellectually and politically, any opposition.[21]

The Council counters that it is a "host to many views, advocate of none."[22] In other words, it is supposedly like a professor who allows his students to thrash out all sides of an issue; he reveals no prejudice, exerts no censorship. *Foreign Affairs* has never changed a word in the disclaimer of bias that has prefaced its pages since 1922:

> The articles in FOREIGN AFFAIRS do not represent any consensus of beliefs . . . . we hold that while keeping clear of mere vagaries FOREIGN AFFAIRS can do more to inform American public opinion by a broad hospitality to divergent ideas than it can by identifying itself with one school.

The CFR claims to be pluralistic — however, because one can join only through the nomination of others already in the Council, the group naturally tends to remain homogeneous. J. Robert Moskin recounts of the CFR's early days: "Although the Council itself never took a position, its members' bias was apparent to all."[23] Richard Barnet, himself a CFR member, wrote in 1972 that "in recent years a few symbolic policy critics have actually been recruited, but failure to be asked to be a member of the Council has been regarded for a generation as a presumption of unsuitability for high office in the national security bureaucracy."[24] And even the *New York Times,* itself regarded as an Establishment organ, has acknowledged that the Council has "a uniform direction."[25]

If the CFR does possess a distinct viewpoint, Americans should know about it — because officials of the U.S. government, drawn so frequently from the Council's ranks, are apt to take that viewpoint to Washington with them.

Charges have been repeatedly leveled at the Council that it holds two particularly unwholesome doctrines.

Of Globalism

The first of these is that the CFR advocates the creation of a world government. The ultimate implication of this is that all power would be centralized in a single global authority; national identities and boundaries (including our own) would be eliminated. It is said that while the CFR does not always espouse this idea directly, it does at least insinuate it, as by suggesting measures that would serve as stepping stones toward this end.

The charge is easily substantiated. Anyone who cares to examine back issues of *Foreign Affairs* will have no difficulty finding hundreds of articles that pushed — whether zealously or by "soft sell" — this concept of globalism. But he will be hard pressed to locate even one essay opposing it. This, of course, deflates *Foreign Affairs'* claim of "a broad hospitality to divergent ideas."

According to Admiral Ward, the CFR has as a goal "submergence of U.S. sovereignty and national independence into an all-powerful one-world government." He wrote that "this lust to surrender the sovereignty and independence of the United States is pervasive throughout most of the membership . . ." And he added: "In the entire CFR lexicon, there is no term of revulsion carrying a meaning so deep as 'America First.' "[26]

Rather than stand on allegations, let us draw samples from the CFR's own works.

• An article in the inaugural issue of *Foreign Affairs* (September 1922) condemned what it called "the dubious doctrines expressed in the phrases 'safety first' and 'America first.' "[27]

• An article in the second issue (December 1922) declared:

> Obviously there is going to be no peace or prosperity for mankind so long as it remains divided into fifty or sixty independent states . . . Equally obviously there is going to be no steady progress in civilization or self-government among the more backward peoples until some kind of international system is created which will put an end to the diplomatic struggles incident to the attempt of every nation to make itself secure . . . The real problem today is that of world government.[28]

• A 1944 Council publication, *American Public Opinion and Postwar Security Commitments,* noted:

> The sovereignty fetish is still so strong in the public mind, that there would appear to be little chance of winning popular assent to American membership in anything approaching a super-state organization. Much will depend on the kind of approach which is used in further popular education.[29]

• In 1959, the Council issued a position paper entitled *Study No. 7, Basic Aims of U.S. Foreign Policy.* This document proposed that the U.S. seek to "build a new international order." The steps it cited as necessary to achieve this were:

> 1. Search for an international order in which the freedom of nations is recognized as interdependent and in which many policies are jointly undertaken by free world states with differing political, economic and social systems, and including states labeling themselves as "socialist."
> 2. Safeguard U.S. security through preserving a system of bilateral agreements and regional arrangements.
> 3. Maintain and gradually increase the authority of the U.N.
> 4. Make more effective use of the International Court of Justice, jurisdiction of which should be increased by withdrawal of reservations by member nations on matters judged to be domestic.

• In 1974, *Foreign Affairs* carried an article by Richard N. Gardner called "The Hard Road to World Order." Gardner complained that

11

"We are witnessing an outbreak of shortsighted nationalism that seems oblivious to the economic, political and moral implications of interdependence." He outlined a strategy by which " 'the house of world order' will have to be built from the bottom up rather than from the top down." He explained that "an end run around national sovereignty, eroding it piece by piece, will accomplish much more than the old-fashioned frontal assault."[30]
• And in the Fall 1984 *Foreign Affairs*, Kurt Waldheim — former Secretary-General of the UN and former Nazi — writes:

> As long as states insist that they are the supreme arbiters of their destinies — that as sovereign entities their decisions are subject to no higher authority — international organizations will never be able to guarantee the maintenance of peace.[31]

Review of the CFR's publication history unearths countless statements similar to the foregoing.

Naturally, everyone would like to see world harmony and peace. But if the United States traded its sovereignty for membership in a world government, what would become of our freedoms, as expressed in the Bill of Rights? How would the rulers of this world government be selected? And how could a single, central authority equitably govern a planet that is so diversified? These are unanswered questions that have darkened the Council's crusade for globalism.

Of Communism

A second, more controversial accusation against the Council is that it has been "soft" on Communism — so soft, in fact, that its members have often exerted their influence on behalf of the international Communist movement. This charge would appear untenable at first — considering that "the Establishment," centered on Wall Street, is conventionally regarded as the antithesis of the radical left.

But here again, review of the CFR's house organ, *Foreign Affairs*, proves very instructive. One finds that dozens of Marxists and socialists have published articles in that journal — even such titans of Communism as Leon Trotsky, Soviet Premier Nikita Khrushchev, and Yugoslavia's Josip Broz Tito. Indeed, when Trotsky died, he was eulogized in *Foreign Affairs* as follows:

> He gave us, in a time when our race is woefully in need of such restoratives, the vision of a man. Of that there is no more doubt than of his great place in history.[32]

On the other hand, if one searches *Foreign Affairs* for an American author whose name is popularly associated with patriotism or anti-Communism, he looks all but in vain.

Lenin so admired the first issue of the publication that he underscored passages in some of its articles.[33] The Council today proudly possesses Lenin's original copy.

The CFR's annual report for 1986 noted: "[W]e were intrigued to read news reports that Mr. Gorbachev himself was reading articles excerpted from *Foreign Affairs* in preparation for the meetings with President Reagan [the Geneva summit of November 1985]."[34] The Soviets were even placing ads for their airline, Aeroflot, in *Foreign Affairs*, twenty years before *glasnost*.

Affinity has always existed between Marxists and the Council. Quick proof of this is found in the yearly roster of guest speakers at Pratt House. The 1959 report, for example, listed such leftist luminaries as Fidel Castro, Anastas I. Mikoyan of the USSR, Oskar Lange of Poland's state council, Yugoslavia's Marko Nikezic, and a variety of other socialists. The 1984 report noted the following among the year's speakers: Robert Mugabe, Marxist prime minister of Zimbabwe; Daniel Ortega of Nicaragua; Guillermo Ungo, leader of the El Salvador revolutionaries; Petra Kelly of Germany's far-left Green party; and three officials from the People's Republic of China.

To be sure, many non-Communists also appear at the Council; but the hosting of Marxists shows that the CFR has no aversion to them — and vice versa.

In February 1987, a delegation of top Council members traveled to the USSR at Moscow's invitation, meeting Gorbachev and other Soviet officials. The visit was closely followed by the *New York Times*.

Perhaps nothing demonstrates the rapport between the CFR and Soviet Union more graphically than a 1961 photo appearing in *The*

Wise Men, a book published in 1986 by Simon and Schuster. The picture shows John McCloy — then chairman of the Council — and Soviet dictator Nikita Khrushchev, swimming together at the latter's private dacha on the Black Sea. A grinning Khrushchev has his arm around a grinning McCloy who, according to the text, was wearing swimming trunks loaned him by the premier himself.

The Council's defenders say the amicable exchanges with Marxists are simply an indication of its broad-minded pluralism. They point out that CFR members were among the Cold War's vanguard, and that *Foreign Affairs* has printed a multitude of articles criticizing Communism and the Soviet Union.

It is true that such articles have found space in *Foreign Affairs*, some of them sincere beyond doubt. In 1980 the periodical even ran a piece by Aleksandr Solzhenitsyn. However, in looking over the anti-Communist articles from the Cold War period (when the bulk of them appeared), it is apparent that the gist of their conclusions was this: that the best defense against Communism would be a new world order — a stronger UN, regional alliances, and other building blocks of world government. To the CFR, then, the threat of Communism seems to have been little more than a marketable rationale for its globalistic aims.

Here is how Edith Kermit Roosevelt summed it up in 1961:

> What is the Establishment's view-point? Through the Roosevelt, Truman, Eisenhower and Kennedy administrations its ideology is constant: That the best way to fight Communism is by a One World Socialist state governed by "experts" like themselves. The result has been policies which favor the growth of the superstate, gradual surrender of United States sovereignty to the United Nations and a steady retreat in the face of Communist aggression.[35]

Senator Jesse Helms, after noting the CFR's place within the Establishment, put it this way before the Senate in December 1987:

> The viewpoint of the Establishment today is called globalism. Not so long ago, this viewpoint was called the "one-world" view by its critics. The phrase is no longer fashionable among sophisticates; yet,

the phrase "one-world" is still apt because nothing has changed in the minds and actions of those promoting policies consistent with its fundamental tenets.

Mr. President, in the globalist point of view, nation-states and national boundaries do not count for anything. Political philosophies and political principles seem to become simply relative. Indeed, even constitutions are irrelevant to the exercise of power . . . .

In this point of view, the activities of international financial and industrial forces should be oriented to bringing this one-world design — with a convergence of the Soviet and American systems as its centerpiece — into being.[36]

This book contends that the accusations against the Council on Foreign Relations — the pursuit of world government, and receptiveness to Communism — are true. It further contends that due to the Council's heavy presence in Washington, these factors have acted mightily upon the course of American foreign policy in this century — a course frequently damned by disaster, that has seen the United States eroded in strength, and its allies sometimes vanquished altogether.

We have thus far quoted a number of references to the Council in well-known publications such as *Esquire* and the *New York Times*. However, mass media comment on the CFR is extremely rare. No feature article about the group appeared in any major journal or newspaper during its first thirty-six years. Today, probably not one American in five hundred can identify the CFR, despite the fact that it is arguably the most powerful political entity in the United States. This by itself should raise questions, let alone eyebrows.

Knowing the Council's record of action and influence demystifies a number of otherwise puzzling episodes in U.S. history. We shall proceed to inspect that record, but it is instructive to first know something about the people and events that led to the Council's founding in 1921.

The Council's headquarters on New York City's East 68th Street

Foreign Affairs issues from 1926 and 1986:
little change in cover or content

Foreign Affairs logo includes Latin word for "everywhere."

Richard N. Gardner calls for "an end run around national sovereignty."

Admiral Chester Ward (right) swearing in William Frankey as Assistant Secretary of the Navy. Ward, a longtime Council member, said that the CFR seeks "submergence of U.S. sovereignty and national independence into an all-powerful one-world government."

Fidel Castro and Daniel Ortega have been guests at Pratt House.

Senator Jesse Helms and Edith Kermit Roosevelt are
among those who have defined the Establishment.

Chapter 2

Background To The Beginning

International Bankers and Central Banks

An "international" banker is one who, among other things, loans money to the governments of nations. Lending to governments can be particularly profitable for several reasons. First, a government borrows far more than an individual or business; second, a government has unique tools with which it can guarantee repayment — such as the levying of taxes; third, a government may requite its debt through a medium more desirable than cash — by granting the banker certain privileges, for example, or giving him a say in policy.

No turn of events is more lucrative for an international banker than war — because nothing generates more government borrowing faster.

International banking was probably best epitomized by the Rothschilds, Europe's most famous financial dynasty. Meyer Amschel Rothschild (1743-1812) retained one of his five sons at the home bank in Germany and dispatched the other four to run offices in England, France, Austria, and Italy. The Rothschilds harvested great riches during the nineteenth century by loaning to these and other countries. Sometimes they, or their agents, financed both sides of armed conflicts — such as the Franco-Prussian War and the War Between the States. As national creditors, they earned tremendous political influence.

Essential to controlling a government is the establishment of a central bank with a monopoly on the country's supply of money and credit. Meyer Rothschild is said to have remarked: "Let me issue and control a nation's money, and I care not who writes its laws." As Gary Allen related in his bestseller *None Dare Call It Conspiracy:*

19

The Bank of England, Bank of France and Bank of Germany were not owned by their respective governments, as everyone imagines, but were privately owned monopolies granted by the heads of state, usually in return for loans.[1]

Georgetown professor Dr. Carroll Quigley, who was himself close to the Establishment, dealt extensively with central banks in his 1966 book *Tragedy and Hope*. He wrote:

It must not be felt that these heads of the world's chief central banks were substantive powers in world finance. They were not. Rather, they were technicians and agents of the dominant investment bankers of their own countries, who had raised them up and were perfectly capable of throwing them down.[2]

Quigley further noted:

[T]he powers of financial capitalism had another far-reaching aim, nothing less than to create a world system of financial control in private hands able to dominate the political system of each country and the economy of the world as a whole. This system was to be controlled in a feudalist fashion by the central banks of the world acting in concert, by secret agreements arrived at in frequent private meetings and conferences.[3]

The Rothschilds, as the foremost "power behind the throne" of Europe's central banks, savored the thought of a similar arrangement in the United States. According to Gustavus Myers in his *History of the Great American Fortunes:*

Under the surface, the Rothschilds long had a powerful influence in dictating American financial laws. The law records show that they were the power in the old Bank of the United States.[4]

However, the Bank of the United States (1816-36), an early attempt to saddle the nation with a privately controlled central bank, was abolished by President Andrew Jackson. He declared:

The bold effort the present bank had made to control the government, the distress it had wantonly produced . . . are but premonitions of the fate that awaits the American people should they be deluded into a perpetuation of this institution or the establishment of another like it.[5]

America heeded Jackson's warning for the remainder of the century. The tide began to turn, however, with the linking of European and U.S. banking interests, and the growth in power of America's money barons, such as J. P. Morgan, John D. Rockefeller, and Bernard Baruch.

In 1902, German banker Paul Warburg, an associate of the Rothschilds, migrated to the United States. He soon became a partner in America's most powerful banking firm: Kuhn, Loeb and Company. He was married to the daughter of Solomon Loeb, one of its founders. The head of Kuhn, Loeb was Jacob Schiff, whose family ties with the Rothschilds went back a century.

While earning an annual salary of $500,000 — a tidy sum even by today's standards — Paul Warburg lectured widely and published pamphlets on the need for an American central banking system.

The Panic of 1907 was artificially triggered to elicit public acceptance of this idea. Snowballing bank runs began after J. P. Morgan spread a rumor about the insolvency of the Trust Company of America.

In 1949, historian Frederick Lewis Allen reported in *Life* magazine:

[C]ertain chroniclers have arrived at the ingenious conclusion that the Morgan interests took advantage of the unsettled conditions during the autumn of 1907 to *precipitate* the panic, guiding it shrewdly as it progressed so that it would kill off rival banks and consolidate the preeminence of the banks within the Morgan orbit.[6]

Allen himself did not accept this explanation, but he noted: "The lesson of the Panic of 1907 was clear, though not for some six years

21

was it destined to be embodied in legislation: the United States gravely needed a central banking system."

Congressman Charles Lindbergh, Sr., father of the famous aviator, declared in 1913: "The Money Trust[*] caused the 1907 panic, and thereby forced Congress to create a National Monetary Commission. . . ."[7] Heading the Commission was Senator Nelson Aldrich. Aldrich was known as the international bankers' mouthpiece on Capitol Hill. His daughter married John D. Rockefeller, Jr.; his grandson, Nelson Aldrich Rockefeller, who became Vice President in 1974, was named for him.

After the Commission spent almost two years studying central banking in Europe, Aldrich met secretly with Paul Warburg and top representatives of the Morgan and Rockefeller interests. This took place at Morgan's hunting club on Jekyll Island, off the coast of Georgia. There the plan was formulated for America's central bank: what would come to be known as the Federal Reserve.

One of those in attendance at Jekyll Island was Frank Vanderlip, president of the Rockefellers' National City Bank. Twenty-five years later, Vanderlip wrote in the *Saturday Evening Post*:

[T]here was an occasion, near the close of 1910, when I was as secretive — indeed as furtive — as any conspirator . . . . I do not feel it is any exaggeration to speak of our secret expedition to Jekyl [sic] Island as the occasion of the actual conception of what eventually became the Federal Reserve System . . . .

We were told to leave our last names behind us. We were told further that we should avoid dining together on the night of our departure. We were instructed to come one at a time and as unobtrusively as possible to the terminal of the New Jersey littoral of the Hudson, where Senator Aldrich's private car would be in readiness, attached to the rear end of the train for the South.

Once aboard the private car, we began to observe the taboo that had been fixed on last names.

---

*The term "Money Trust," in popular use at the time, referred to the coterie of finance monopolists based on Wall Street. It included, among others, Rockefeller, Morgan, Warburg, and Schiff.

Discovery, we knew, simply must not happen, or else all our time and effort would be wasted.[8]

After the Jekyll Island meeting, Senator Aldrich proposed the plan to Congress. His connections to the banking establishment raised enough suspicion that the Aldrich bill did not pass, but a similar measure, under another name, was subsequently pushed through. The Federal Reserve became law in December 1913. Ostensibly, the system was to act as guardian of reserves for banks; it was granted control over interest rates and the size of the national money supply. The public was induced to accept the Fed by claims that, given these powers, it would stabilize the economy, preventing further panics and bank runs. It did nothing of the kind. Not only has our nation suffered through the Great Depression and numerous recessions, but inflation and federal debt — negligible problems before the Fed came into existence — have plagued America ever since.

Congressman Lindbergh was one of the most forthright opponents of the Federal Reserve Act. He warned the Congress:

> This act establishes the most gigantic trust on earth . . . . When the President signs this act the invisible government by the money power, proven to exist by the Money Trust investigation, will be legalized . . . .
> The money power overawes the legislative and executive forces of the Nation and of the States. I have seen these forces exerted during the different stages of this bill . . . .
> This is the Aldrich bill in disguise . . .[9]

Later, Congressman Louis McFadden, who chaired the House Committee on Banking and Currency from 1920 to 1931, would declare:

> When the Federal Reserve Act was passed, the people of these United States did not perceive that a world banking system was being set up here.
> A super-state controlled by international bankers and international industrialists acting together to enslave the world for their own pleasure.

Every effort has been made by the Fed to conceal its powers but
the truth is — the Fed has usurped the government.[10]

The average American probably does not know — or even think
— very much about our Federal Reserve System, but a few things
should be noted about it.

- Although it is called "Federal," it is privately owned.
- It has never received a meaningful audit from an independent
source.
- It makes its own policies and is not subject to the President or
the Congress. Private banks within the system select two-thirds of
the directors of the twelve Federal Reserve banks; the Federal Reserve Board chooses the rest.
- As to the Federal Reserve Board itself, its members *are* appointed
by the President and approved by the Senate, but, once in office,
they serve fourteen-year terms. Fed Chairmen have routinely come
from the New York banking community, on its recommendations,
and the great majority have been members of the CFR. Paul Warburg was appointed to the original board, and Benjamin Strong of
the Morgan interests, who had been at Jekyll Island with him,
headed the New York Fed, the system's nucleus.

How did the Federal Reserve benefit the financiers who secretly
designed it? First, in its capacity as overseer and supplier of reserves,
it gave their banks access to public funds in the U.S. Treasury,
enhancing their capacity to lend and collect interest.

Furthermore, by staffing the Federal Reserve's management with
themselves or their associates, the international bankers gained
effective control over the nation's money supply and interest rates
— and thus over its economic life. Indeed, the Fed is authorized to
create money — and thus inflate — at will. According to the Constitution, only Congress may issue money or regulate its value. The
Federal Reserve Act, however, placed these functions in the hands
of private bankers — to their perpetual profit. Congressman Lindbergh explained:

The new law will create inflation whenever the trusts want inflation.
It may not do so immediately, but the trusts want a period of inflation,

because all the stocks they hold have gone down . . . Now, if the trusts can get another period of inflation, they figure they can unload the stocks on the people at high prices during the excitement and then bring on a panic and buy them back at low prices . . . .

The people may not know it immediately, but the day of reckoning is only a few years removed.[11]

That day of reckoning, of course, came in 1929, and the Federal Reserve has since created an endless series of booms and busts by the strategic tightening and relaxation of money and credit.

Finally, the Fed was empowered to buy and sell government securities, and to loan to member banks so that they might themselves purchase such securities, thus greatly multiplying the potential for government indebtedness to the banking community.

However, if Washington was to incur debts, it had to have some means of paying them off. The solution was income tax. Prior to 1913, there was no income tax in America (except during the War Between the States and early Reconstruction period). The U.S. government survived on other revenue sources, such as tariffs and excise taxes. As a result, it could neither spend nor borrow heavily.

Because income tax had been declared unconstitutional by the Supreme Court in 1895, it had to be instituted by constitutional amendment. The man who brought forward the amendment in Congress was the same senator who proposed the plan for the Federal Reserve — Nelson Aldrich.

Why did the American people consent to income tax? Initially, it was nominal: a mere one percent of income under $20,000 — a figure few made in those days. Naturally, there were assurances that it would never increase!

Another pitch used to sell the tax was that, being graduated, it would "soak the rich." But Senator Aldrich's backing of the amendment implied that "the rich" *desired* it. America's billionaire elite, of course, are notorious for sidestepping the IRS. The Pecora hearings of 1933, for example, revealed that J. P. Morgan had not paid any income tax in 1931-32. When Nelson Rockefeller was being confirmed as Vice President under Gerald Ford, the fact arose that he had not paid any income tax in 1970.

One of the leading devices by which the wealthy dodge taxes is the channeling of their fortunes into tax-free foundations. The major foundations, though commonly regarded as charitable institutions, often use their grant-making powers to advance the interests of their founders. The Rockefeller Foundation, for example, has poured millions into the Council on Foreign Relations, which in turn serves as the Establishment's main bridge of influence to the U.S. government. By the time the income tax became law in 1913, the Rockefeller and Carnegie foundations were already operating.

Income tax didn't soak the rich, it soaked the middle class. Because it was a graduated tax, it tended to prevent anyone from rising into affluence. Thus it acted to consolidate the wealth of the entrenched interests, and protect them from new competition.

The year 1913 was an ominous one — there now existed the means to loan the government colossal sums (the Federal Reserve), and the means to exact repayment (income tax). All that was needed now was a good reason for Washington to borrow.

In 1914, World War I erupted on the European continent. America eventually participated, and as a result her national debt soared from $1 billion to $25 billion.

Many historians would have us believe that this trio of events — the income tax, the Federal Reserve, and the war — was a coincidence. But too often history has been written by authors financed by foundations, in books manufactured by Establishment publishing houses.

Many more "coincidences" were yet to trouble the American people in this century.

Wilson and House

In 1913, Woodrow Wilson became President. His book, *The New Freedom,* was published that same year. In it, he wrote:

> Some of the biggest men in the United States, in the field of commerce and manufacture, are afraid of something. They know that there is a power somewhere so organized, so subtle, so watchful, so interlocked, so complete, so pervasive, that they had better not speak above their breath when they speak in condemnation of it.[12]

Wilson knew this force — intimately.

His predecessor, Republican President William Howard Taft, had been against a central bank, saying he would veto a bill proposing one. For this reason, the international bankers sought to replace Taft with a submissive candidate. Woodrow Wilson was rocketed from president of Princeton University to governor of New Jersey in 1911, to the Democratic Presidential nominee in 1912. Among his weighty financial backers were Cleveland Dodge of the Rocke-fellers' National City Bank; Jacob Schiff of Kuhn, Loeb; and Ber-nard Baruch.

According to one eyewitness, Baruch brought Wilson to Demo-cratic Party headquarters in New York in 1912, "leading him like one would a poodle on a string." Wilson received an "indoctrination course" from the leaders convened there, during which he agreed, in principle, to do the following if elected:

• support the projected Federal Reserve;
• support income tax;
• lend an ear to advice should war break out in Europe;
• lend an ear to advice on who should occupy his cabinet.[13]

Polls showed incumbent President Taft as a clear favorite over the stiff-looking professor from Princeton. So, to divide the Repub-lican vote, the Establishment put money behind Teddy Roosevelt on the Progressive Party ticket. J. P. Morgan and Co. was the financial backbone of the Roosevelt campaign.[14]

The strategy succeeded. Republican ballots were split between Taft and Roosevelt, and Woodrow Wilson became President with only forty-two percent of the popular vote.

During his White House terms, Wilson was continuously guided by a front man for the international banking community, Colonel Edward M. House (House did not serve in the military; his title was strictly honorary). The President's top advisor, he was called "As-sistant President House" by *Harper's Weekly*.

So close was the relationship between the two that Wilson said of House:

> Mr. House is my second personality. He is my independent self. His
> thoughts and mine are one. If I were in his place I would do just as

27

he suggested . . . . If anyone thinks he is reflecting my opinion by whatever action he takes, they are welcome to the conclusion.[15]

Under House's watchful eye, Wilson paid off as arranged. House was reported to have handpicked his cabinet. At Wilson's first cabinet meeting, Franklin K. Lane introduced himself, saying: "My name is Lane, Mr. President. I believe I am the Secretary of the Interior."[16]

Wilson's first year in office, 1913, saw institution of both income tax and the Federal Reserve, although the former slightly preceded his inauguration.

According to Charles Seymour, House's biographer, the Colonel was "the unseen guardian angel" of the Federal Reserve Act. He was regularly in touch with Paul Warburg while the legislation was being written and maneuvered through Congress.

In light of President Wilson's dependence on his advisor, it is instructive to know something about House's convictions. According to another of his biographers, Arthur D. Howden Smith, House believed that

the Constitution, product of eighteenth-century minds and the quasi-classical, medieval conception of republics, was thoroughly outdated; that the country would be better off if the Constitution could be scrapped and rewritten. But as a realist he knew that this was impossible in the existing state of political education.[17]

House wrote a novel, published anonymously in 1912, entitled *Philip Dru: Administrator*. Later, he acknowledged the book as his own. The novel's hero, Philip Dru, rules America and introduces a variety of radical changes. Among these are a graduated income tax and a central bank.

George Viereck, in *The Strangest Friendship in History* (1932), wrote of *Philip Dru:*

Out of this book have come the directives which revolutionized our lives . . . The Wilson administration transferred the Colonel's ideas from the pages of fiction to the pages of history.[18]

What may seem surprising is that the character Philip Dru was attempting to install what he called "Socialism as dreamed of by Karl Marx." This becomes less incongruous when one realizes that income tax and central banking were both called for by Marx in his *Communist Manifesto*, which laid out a ten-plank plan for establishing a Communist state. Plank two was "A heavy progressive or graduated income tax." Plank five was "Centralization of credit in the hands of the State, by means of a national bank with state capital and an exclusive monopoly."

Thus, in 1913, America adopted two of Marx's precepts. This is certainly not to imply that House and Wilson were Communists; however, it does once again demonstrate that finance capitalism has a great deal in common with the ideology that is supposedly its opposite.

World War I and the League of Nations

Another objective specified in *Philip Dru* was a "league of nations." This, of course, was precisely the name given to the world body created at Woodrow Wilson's suggestion during the 1919 Paris Peace Conference. Just as the 1907 Panic was employed to justify a central bank, so was World War I used to justify world government.

It is certainly true that a number of America's money barons, including Wilson campaign backers, profited from the war. The President appointed Bernard Baruch head of the War Industries Board, a position never authorized by Congress. As such, Baruch became the economic czar of the United States, having dictatorial power over the nation's businesses. He, like the Rockefellers, is said to have reaped some $200 million from the war.[19] Top Wilson backer Cleveland Dodge shipped munitions to the allies, and J. P. Morgan supplied them with hundreds of millions in loans — which, of course, U.S. entry into the war helped protect.

But profit was not the only evident motive behind our participation in the conflict. Well before our declaration of war, the idea of a world government to ensure peace was being promoted in America.

In the 1950's, U.S. government investigators examined old records of the powerful Carnegie Endowment for International Peace, a long-time promoter of globalism. They discovered that, several years before the outbreak of World War I, Carnegie trustees had hoped to involve the United States in a general war to set the stage for world government.[20]

Prior to 1917, America had stayed clear of European wars. George Washington, in his Farewell Address, had warned the nation against entangling foreign alliances. This counsel was heeded only too happily by the American people, millions of whom had come to this country to escape oppression overseas. And naturally, no one wanted to fight in a war of dubious origins.

It was therefore necessary to devise an incident that would supply provocation. This occurred when a German submarine sank the British ocean liner *Lusitania*, on its way from New York to England. 128 Americans on board perished, and this tragedy, more than any other event, was used to arouse anti-German sentiment in the United States.

Certain facts, however, were denied the public. Thanks to the work of British author Colin Simpson in his book *The Lusitania*, much of the truth is known today.

The *Lusitania* was transporting six million rounds of ammunition, plus other war munitions, to Britain, which is why the Germans sank it (internal explosions caused the ship to go down in just eighteen minutes after a single torpedo hit[21]). This information was suppressed at subsequent hearings that investigated the sinking. Woodrow Wilson ordered the ship's original manifest — which listed the munitions — to be hidden away in Treasury archives.[22]

Even more pertinent is evidence that the ship was deliberately sent to disaster. Before the incident, Winston Churchill — then head of the British Admiralty — had ordered a report done to predict the political impact if a passenger ship was sunk carrying Americans.[23] And the following conversation took place between Colonel House and Sir Edward Grey, the British Foreign Minister.

> Grey: What will America do if the Germans sink an ocean liner with American passengers on board?
>
> House: I believe that a flame of indignation would sweep the United States and that by itself would be sufficient to carry us into the war.[24]

The British had cracked Germany's naval code and knew the approximate whereabouts of all U-boats in the vicinity of the British Isles. According to Commander Joseph Kenworthy, then in British Naval Intelligence: "The *Lusitania* was deliberately sent at considerably reduced speed into an area where a U-boat was known to be waiting and with her escorts withdrawn."[25]

It should be noted that the Germans had taken out large ads in the New York papers in an effort to dissuade Americans from boarding the *Lusitania*. Their navy was attempting to stop war supplies from reaching England — just as the British navy was doing to them! Who was the real aggressor in the war is a matter of debate. Had America not participated, the belligerents of Europe would probably have reached a settlement, as those nations had been doing for centuries.

Woodrow Wilson was reelected in 1916 on the slogan "He kept us out of war," but those words proved short-lived. Colonel House, in England, had already negotiated a secret agreement committing us to join the conflict.[26] When war was declared, propaganda went full tilt: all Huns were fanged serpents, and all Americans against the war were traitors. The U.S. mobilization broke the battlefield stalemate, leading to Germany's surrender.

The Paris Peace Conference of 1919 settled the aftermath of the war. It resulted in the Versailles Treaty, which required Germany to pay the victors severe reparations — even the pensions of allied soldiers. This devastated the German economy in the 1920's and paved the way for Adolph Hitler's rise.

Woodrow Wilson brought to the conference his famous "fourteen points." It was the fourteenth point that carried the payload: a proposal for a "general association of nations." From this sprang the League of Nations. It was the first step toward the ultimate goal of the international bankers: a world government — supported, no doubt, by a world central bank.

The concept of the league did not originate with Wilson. Ray Stannard Baker, Wilson's official biographer, said that "practically nothing — not a single idea — in the Covenant of the League was original with the President." It was Colonel House who had written the Covenant. According to Charles Seymour, President Wilson "ap-

31

proved the House draft almost in its entirety, and his own rewriting of it was practically confined to phraseology."[27] In 1917, House had assembled a group in New York called "the Inquiry," consisting of about one hundred men. Under the direction of House's brother-in-law, Sidney Mezes, they developed plans for the peace settlement. Some twenty members of the Inquiry went with Wilson to Paris in 1919, as did House and bankers Paul Warburg and Bernard Baruch.

The League of Nations was successfully instituted; a number of countries that enrolled had powerful internationalist forces operating within them. But the United States could not join unless the Versailles Treaty received Senate ratification — a condition that the U.S. Constitution stipulates for any treaty.

The Senate balked. It was clear that the League couldn't guarantee peace any more than marriage guarantees that spouses won't quarrel. For the League to be strong enough to enforce world security, it would also have to be strong enough to threaten our national sovereignty — and freedom-loving Americans wanted none of that. They had done their part to help win the war, and saw no reason why they should further entwine their fate with the dictatorships and monarchies of the Old World.

John D. Rockefeller in 1911

The elder J. P. Morgan in 1904

Charles Lindbergh, Sr.,
an outspoken opponent
of the Federal Reserve

Nelson Aldrich was among
those to attend the secret
Jekyll Island meeting.

The original Federal Reserve Board. Paul Warburg (top left) was willing to forfeit an annual salary of $500,000 to secure a position on it. Frederic Delano is at bottom right.

Although Woodrow Wilson ran as an opponent of the Money Trust, his 1912 campaign was financed by Wall Street bankers such as Jacob Schiff (above with wife at Wilson inaugural).

President Wilson, Mrs. Wilson, and "Colonel" House

The doomed *Lusitania*

Chapter 3

The Council's Birth And Early Links To Totalitarianism

Well before the Senate's vote on ratification, news of its resistance to the League of Nations reached Colonel House, members of the Inquiry, and other U.S. internationalists gathered in Paris. It was clear that America would not join the realm of world government unless something was done to shift its climate of opinion. Under House's direction, these men, along with some members of the British delegation to the Conference, held a series of meetings. On May 30, 1919, at a dinner at the Majestic Hotel, it was resolved that an "Institute of International Affairs" would be formed. It would have two branches — one in the United States, one in England.

The American branch became incorporated in New York as the Council on Foreign Relations on July 29, 1921.

As a note of interest, the British branch became known as the Royal Institute of International Affairs (RIIA). Its leadership was controlled by members of the Round Table — a semi-secret internationalist group headquartered in London. The RIIA is the CFR's counterpart, and has been dominant in British politics for over half a century. Were it the subject of this book, a great deal could be said about it. The CFR and RIIA were originally intended to be affiliates, but became independent bodies, although they have always maintained close informal ties.

In 1922, the Council stated its purpose as follows:

The Council on Foreign Relations aims to provide a continuous conference on the international aspects of America's political, economic and financial problems. . . . It is simply a group of men concerned in spreading a knowledge of international relations, and, in particular, in developing a reasoned American foreign policy.[1]

This self-description is quite similar to many others the Council has issued over the years — invariably conveying the idea that the CFR is merely a chatty foreign affairs club whose aims are innocuous and whose outlook is blandly impartial. If this is all the Council amounts to, it is curious that the Establishment has expended tens of millions of dollars on it.

One does not have to look very hard to determine that the CFR in the 1920's was very unobjectively lobbying for American participation in the League of Nations. An article in the first issue of *Foreign Affairs* was entitled "The Next American Contribution to Civilization." Can we all guess what that was to be?

Our government should enter heartily into the existing League of Nations, take a sympathetic share in every discussion broached in the League, and be ready to take more than its share in all the responsibilities which unanimous action of the nations constituting the League might impose.[2]

Of course, not every article in *Foreign Affairs* openly boosted world government, which would have overstated the case. But typically the journal printed one or two that did, mixed in with dry dissertations on a variety of international topics. No conspiracy lurked behind such titles as "Singapore's Mineral Resources" or "The Soya Bean in International Trade." However, many of the particularized articles did present solutions pointing toward globalism.

Colonel House, of course, was one of the CFR's founding members. As to the others, Robert D. Shulzinger, in *The Wise Men of Foreign Affairs: The History of the Council on Foreign Relations,* noted that "nearly all of them were bankers and lawyers."[3] This stereotype was unchanged fifty years later. John Franklin Campbell wrote in *New York* magazine in 1971 that membership in the CFR "usually means that you are a partner in an investment bank or law firm — with occasional 'trouble shooting' assignments in government."[4] This raises a question: Why should foreign affairs lie almost exclusively in the province of these two professions?

The CFR's founders were specialized in yet another way: association with J. P. Morgan and Company. Dr. Carroll Quigley, referred to earlier, had unique insight into the Council's founding. He was very close to members of the Round Table, which was the core of the CFR's counterpart group in Britain. In the early 1960's, he was allowed to inspect its secret records. Quigley termed the CFR "a front group for J. P. Morgan and Company in association with the very small American Round Table Group."[5]

The founding president of the CFR was John W. Davis, who was J. P. Morgan's personal attorney and a millionaire in his own right. Founding vice-president was Paul Cravath, whose law firm also represented the Morgan interests. Morgan partner Russell Leffingwell would later become the Council's first chairman. A variety of other Morgan partners, attorneys and agents crowded the CFR's early membership rolls.

Conscious of such uniformity, the Council's steering committee moved to distinguish the roster by adding college professors. However, most of these had been members of Colonel House's Inquiry. Furthermore, they hailed from campuses beholden to J. P. Morgan. As Dr. Quigley observed: "The Wall Street contacts with these professors were created originally from Morgan's influence in handling large academic endowments."[6]

Bolshevik Connections

Another denominator common to many of the early CFR members was support — material or moral — for the Bolsheviks in Russia.

A revolution, like any other substantive undertaking, cannot succeed without financing. The 1917 Russian Revolution was no exception. It is now well known that the Germans helped Lenin — who had been exiled by the Czar — into Russia in a sealed train, carrying some $5 million in gold. The Germans, of course, had an ulterior motive: Czarist Russia was fighting them on the side of the Allies, and a successful revolution would mean one less adversary for Germany to contend with.

Less widely known is the U.S. contribution. Probably the best reference on this is *Wall Street and the Bolshevik Revolution* by Antony Sutton, former fellow at Stanford University's Hoover Institution. It is based on assiduous research, including a deep probe into State Department files. While Sutton's focus is not on the CFR, comparing his findings with the Council's early rosters proves revealing indeed. His book was actually part of a trilogy, the other two volumes examining Wall Street's links to Franklin D. Roosevelt and to Nazi Germany.

Just when American patronage of the Bolsheviks began is probably unknown. But an excerpt from Colonel House's prophetic *Philip Dru* is not a bad place to start the story.

> Sometimes in his day dreams, Dru thought of Russia in its vastness, of the ignorance and hopeless outlook of the people, and wondered when her deliverance would come. There was he knew, great work for someone to do in that despotic land.[7]

Leon Trotsky, who was living in New York City at the time Czar Nicholas abdicated, was able to return to Russia only because Woodrow Wilson intervened to secure him an American passport.[8] On November 28, 1917, with the Bolsheviks newly in power, House cabled Wilson that any newspaper accounts describing Russia as a new enemy should be "suppressed."[9] On that same day, Wilson declared there should be no interference with the revolution. Although the Bolsheviks' atrocities prevented the U.S. from officially recognizing their new government, Wilson continued to express his support for them, to the shock of many people.

Jacob Schiff, the head of Kuhn, Loeb and Co., heavily bankrolled the revolution. This was reported by White Russian General Arsene de Goulevitch in his book *Czarism and the Revolution*. The *New York Journal-American* stated on February 3, 1949:

> Today it is estimated even by Jacob's grandson, John Schiff, a prominent member of New York Society, that the old man sank about

$20,000,000 for the final triumph of Bolshevism in Russia. Other New York banking firms also contributed.

Schiff died before the CFR's incorporation, but his son Mortimer, and his partner, Federal Reserve architect Paul Warburg, both became founding Council members.

By "founding member" we refer to anyone who appeared on the Council's original 210-man membership roll in 1922. Examination of that list unveils a rogues' gallery of Bolshevik supporters.

• In the summer of 1917, to the city of Petrograd — nerve center of the Russian Revolution — came one of the strangest Red Cross missions in history. It consisted of fifteen Wall Street financiers and attorneys, led by Federal Reserve director William Boyce Thompson, plus a small contingent of doctors and nurses. The medical team, discovering that they were but a front for political activities, returned home in protest after one month. The businessmen remained in Petrograd.[10]

The mission supplied financing, first for the socialist regime of Aleksandr Kerensky, and then for the Bolsheviks who supplanted him. In his biography of William Boyce Thompson, Hermann Hagedorn produced photographic evidence that J. P. Morgan cabled Thompson $1 million through the National City Bank branch in Petrograd — the only bank in Russia the Bolsheviks did not nationalize.

What became of the $1 million? The *Washington Post* of February 2, 1918, supplies the answer. Under the headline "GIVES BOLSHE-VIKI A MILLION," it noted:

> William B. Thompson, who was in Petrograd from July until November last, has made a personal contribution of $1,000,000 to the Bolsheviki for the purpose of spreading their doctrine in Germany and Austria.
>
> Mr. Thompson had an opportunity to study Russian conditions as head of the American Red Cross Mission, expenses of which also were largely defrayed by his personal contributions. . . .
>
> Mr. Thompson deprecates American criticism of the Bolsheviki. He believes they have been misrepresented . . .[11]

Thompson also authored a pamphlet praising the Soviets that was published in the United States.

Three of the Wall Streeters in the Petrograd Red Cross mission — Thompson, Alan Wardwell, and Robert Barr — went on to become founding members of the CFR; three others — Henry Davison, Thomas Thacher, and Harold Swift — joined the Council in subsequent years.

• In May 1918, Thompson helped found the American League to Aid and Cooperate with Russia. Three of the group's executives — Oscar Straus, Charles Coffin, and Maurice Oudin — became CFR founding members. The League's president, Frank Goodnow, entered the Council in 1925.

• In June 1918, the State Department received a memorandum from a committee of the War Trade Board advocating "closer and more friendly commercial relations between the United States and Russia."[12] The committee consisted of three individuals: Thomas Chadbourne (CFR founder), John Foster Dulles (CFR founder), and Clarence Woolley (CFR 1925). State Department files reveal that later in 1918, Chadbourne was instrumental in securing $10,000 for George Lomonossoff, a Soviet emissary sent to the United States.[13]

Among the other Bolshevik abettors in the CFR's original membership were the following:

• Morgan partner Thomas Lamont, who helped persuade the British government to accept the new Soviet regime, and whose family became a financial backer of extreme left-wing organizations, including the Communist Party;

• Paul Cravath, the aforementioned vice president of the CFR, who urged recognition of the Bolsheviks in Foreign Affairs,[14] and whose law firm helped make that goal an eventual reality;[15] and

• Ivy Lee, the public relations man who spruced up the Soviets' image in the USA.

In 1923, the Council signed on Averell Harriman. A pioneer in trading with the Russian Communists, Harriman formed a joint shipping firm with them, obtained a multi-million dollar concession from them to operate the manganese mines of the Caucasus Mountains, and nearly swung a deal to float $42 million in Bolshevik bonds — until the U.S. government stepped in.[16] Years later, he would become our ambassador to the Soviet Union and a confidante of its rulers.

We should not overlook Archibald Cary Coolidge, editor of *Foreign Affairs*. In the periodical's first issue, he wrote an article about Russia, under the simple pseudonym "K," which chided the United States for being "coldly aloof, haughtily refusing to recognize the Soviet government or to have any dealings with it except in dispensing charity."

Coolidge acknowledged the brutality of the Bolsheviks, but reasoned:

> Shall we refuse to sell sorely needed farm instruments to the Russian peasants because we dislike the Moscow Soviet? To recognize the government of a country does not imply that we admire it . . .

Despite claims to the contrary, it is evident that Wall Street and the CFR enjoyed an early love affair with the Bolsheviks. Perhaps the best testimony came from one of Moscow's own representatives — Ludwig Martens of the Soviet Bureau in New York. In 1919, he was brought before a Senate committee investigating Soviet influence in America. The *New York Times* reported:

> According to Martens, instead of carrying on propaganda among the radicals and the proletariat he has addressed most of his efforts to winning to the side of Russia the big business and manufacturing interests of this country . . . . Martens asserted that most of the big business houses of the country were aiding him in his effort to get the government to recognize the Soviet government.[17]

The Strange Partnership

More than once, this book has noted the alignment of Wall Street's highest circles with Communism. This, of course, is hardly the orthodox outlook. We have always been told that Marxists and capitalists are sworn enemies. But this is frequently contradicted by their record.

Probably no name symbolizes capitalism more than Rockefeller. Yet that family has for decades supplied trade and credit to Communist nations. After the Bolsheviks took power, the Rockefellers' Standard Oil of New Jersey bought up Russian oil fields, while Standard Oil of New York built the Soviets a refinery and made an arrangement to market their oil in Europe. During the 1920's the Rockefellers' Chase Bank helped found the American-Russian Chamber of Commerce, and was involved in financing Soviet raw material exports and selling Soviet bonds in the U.S.[18]

The Rockefeller perspective in more recent years hasn't changed. The *New York Times* of January 16, 1967 carried the headline "Eaton Joins Rockefellers To Spur Trade With Reds." The ensuing story noted that the Rockefellers were teaming up with tycoon Cyrus Eaton, Jr., who was financing for the Soviet bloc the construction of a $50 million aluminum plant and rubber plants valued at over $200 million. During the 1970's, American technology helped the Soviets construct the $5 billion Kama River truck factory. It is the world's largest producer of heavy trucks and has been successfully converted by the Kremlin to military purposes, such as the manufacture of vehicles for the war on Afghanistan. The Soviets built the factory mostly on loans from the U.S.; the chief private source of this credit was the Chase Manhattan Bank, chaired by David Rockefeller. The Chase, which maintains a branch office at 1 Karl Marx Square in Moscow, has gained notoriety for financing projects behind the Iron Curtain.

We note parenthetically that while the J. P. Morgan interests dominated the CFR in its early days, the center of influence gradually shifted to the Rockefellers. Indeed, David Rockefeller was chairman of the CFR from 1970 to 1985.

Now the question that must arise is why this unexpected — and unpublicized — harmony exists between the super-rich and the Reds. If the Communists were obedient to their creed, they would be spitting at the "capitalist bosses," not climbing in bed with them.

The explanation materializes when we define, or perhaps redefine, certain concepts. Communism, *in practice,* is a system where government has total power — not only political power, but power over the economy, education, communications, etc. Socialism is essentially a lesser form — a little brother — of Communism: the government controls the means of production and distribution, but is not as pervasive in its authority.

The American free enterprise system, as originally set up, was much the opposite of Communism. The Constitution forced the government to remain "laissez faire"; it could exert virtually no influence on business, education, religion, and most other features of national life. These were left in the private hands of the people.

It is natural enough to suppose that rich capitalists, who made their fortunes through the free market, would be proponents of that system. This, however, has not been the case historically. Free enterprise means competition: it means, in its purest form, that everyone has an equal opportunity to make it in the marketplace. But John D. Rockefeller, J. P. Morgan, and other kingpins of the Money Trust were powerful monopolists. A monopolist seeks to *eliminate* competition. In fact, Rockefeller once said: "Competition is a sin." These men were not free enterprise advocates.

Their coziness with Marxism (it is well to remember that Marx's coauthor, Friedrich Engels, was a wealthy businessman) becomes more comprehensible when we realize that Communism and socialism are themselves forms of monopoly. The only difference is that in this case, the monopoly is operated by the government. But what if an international banker, through loans to the state, manipulation of a central bank, campaign contributions, or bribes, is able to achieve dominion over a government? In that case, he would find socialism welcome, for it would serve him as an instrument to control society.

Frederick C. Howe laid out the strategy of utilizing government in his book *Confessions of a Monopolist* (1906):

> This is the story of something for nothing — of making the other fellow pay. This making the other fellow pay, of getting something for nothing, explains the lust for franchises, mining rights, tariff privileges, railway control, tax evasions. All these things mean monopoly, and all monopoly is bottomed on legislation.[19]

Howe further explained:

These are the rules of big business. They have superseded the teachings of our parents and are reducible to a simple maxim: Get a monopoly; let society work for you; and remember that the best of all business is politics, for a legislative grant, franchise, subsidy or tax exemption is worth more than a Kimberly or Comstock lode, since it does not require any labor, either mental or physical, for its exploitation.[20]

Robber barons of the nineteenth century, such as Jay Gould and Cornelius Vanderbilt, grew rich partly by bribing government officials. "Regulation," traditional scourge of the businessman, has another face: it can be used to acquire exclusive monopolies and feed on tax revenues. The early railroad magnates were able to get public funds to foot the bill for constructing their lines. The very first U.S. regulatory agency — the Interstate Commerce Commission — was created at the petition of railroad owners, not railroad users. When the Federal Reserve was under consideration in 1912, J. P. Morgan partner Henry Davison (later a CFR member) told Congress: "I would rather have regulation and control than free competition."[21] Antony Sutton, in *Wall Street and FDR,* reviews a succession of corporate notables who have espoused socialism in speeches and books.

A modern illustration of how big business uses government for its own ends is the Export-Import Bank. This federal bank was established to "promote trade." Here is how it can work. An American manufacturer wants to sell his products to, say, Poland — but the Poles have no cash to put up. So the Export-Import Bank theoretically loans Poland money to buy the goods. We say "theoretically" because in practice this step is cut out as unnecessary — the money goes straight to the manufacturer. The Poles then pay off the Export-Import Bank in installments — but at a low rate subsidized by American taxpayers. And what if the Poles default? We taxpayers pick up the whole tab! The manufacturer makes the transaction at no risk to himself, through the medium of a federal agency.

There is nothing on earth more powerful than government, a fact long ago recognized by international bankers. Regulation, socialism, and Communism are simply different gradations of monopoly. Who cares if the government is running things, if you run the government? In Communist countries, it bears observing, the people do not run the government. There are either no elections or sham elections. Just as many captains of Wall Street ride falsely under the banner of free enterprise, so do the Communists have their own public relations myths. They are supposedly champions of the people — the "masses." Yet, from Petrograd to Phnom Penh, genocide has been the stamp of Communist takeover. What kind of government is it that erects walls and barbed wire to keep the people in? Such a country is not a "workers' paradise" but a prison. In the final analysis, there is little difference between the goals of Marxism and capitalist monopolism. And both, along with the Council on Foreign Relations, share a common final objective: one-world government.

The CFR and Germany

To help pay off the harsh reparations forced upon it by the Versailles Treaty, Germany printed outrageous quantities of paper money, leading to one of the most disastrous inflations in history. It was so severe that 100 million marks could not buy a box of matches.

The potential for profit in this situation beckoned to the instincts of the international bankers (and they had done much to precipitate it through their influence at the Paris Peace Conference). *Foreign Affairs* articles in the early 1920's called for reform in the German reparations program. In 1923, the Council began a study group on the subject.

The Dawes Plan (1924) and the abortive Young Plan (1930) were the international measures adopted to solve Germany's payment troubles. J. P. Morgan had a heavy hand in both. The plans were named after the two American bankers who headed the committees that originated them. How much the CFR contributed to the plans conceptually is arguable, but it should be noted that both Charles Dawes and Owen Young were Council members, Dawes joining in 1927 and Young as a founder. Both programs were hailed in *Foreign Affairs* with no dissenting views proffered.

Not surprisingly, the Dawes Plan called for massive loans to Germany. Dr. Carroll Quigley said of the undertaking:

It is worthy of note that this system was set up by the international bankers and that the subsequent lending of other people's money to Germany was very profitable to these bankers.[22]

David Lloyd George, who had been British Prime Minister from 1916 to 1922, stated:

The international bankers dictated the Dawes reparation settlement . . . They swept statesmen, politicians and journalists to one side and issued their orders with the imperiousness of absolute monarchs who knew that there was no appeal from their ruthless decrees.[23]

Profit and arrogance, however, were overshadowed by a far more sinister aspect to the new reparations program. Three German cartels in particular were beneficiaries of credit under the Dawes Plan. This trio became the industrial backbone of the Nazi war machine, and the financial backbone of Adolph Hitler's rise to power in Germany.

Of the three cartels, the chemical enterprise I. G. Farben stands out. The Farben company received significant assistance under the Dawes Plan, including a flotation of $30 million from the Rockefellers' National City Bank. I. G. Farben grew to be the largest chemical concern in the world.

After World War II, an investigation by the U.S. War Department noted:

Without I. G.'s immense productive facilities, its intense research, and vast international affiliations, Germany's prosecution of the war would have been unthinkable and impossible . . .[24]

This is entirely supported by statistics. In 1943, for example, Farben produced one hundred percent of Germany's synthetic rubber, one hundred percent of its lubricating oil, and eighty-four percent of its explosives.[25] It even manufactured the deadly Zyklon B gas, used to exterminate human beings in Hitler's concentration camps.[26]

I. G. Farben also supplied forty-five percent of the election funds used to bring the Nazis to power in 1933.[27]

What is particularly odious is that certain American companies did robust business with I. G. Farben, which hired Ivy Lee (CFR) to handle its public relations in the U.S. In 1939, on the eve of blitzkrieg, the Rockefellers' Standard Oil of New Jersey sold $20 million in aviation fuel to the firm.[28] I. G. Farben even had an American subsidiary called American I. G. Among the directors of the latter were the ubiquitous Paul Warburg (CFR founder), Herman A. Metz (CFR founder), and Charles E. Mitchell, who joined the CFR in 1923 and was a director of both the New York Federal Reserve Bank and National City Bank. There were also several Germans on the board of American I. G.; after the war, three of them were found guilty of war crimes at the Nuremburg trials. But none of the Americans were ever prosecuted.

This story of American ties to German fascism has been avoided like the plague by the major U.S. media. However, several books on the subject have appeared in recent years. Of these, Sutton's *Wall Street and the Rise of Hitler* probably remains the definitive study.

Morgan partner Russell Leffingwell (at right, leaving Senate hearing chamber with Morgan) was the CFR's first chairman.

Founding CFR president John W. Davis (right) was J. P. Morgan's personal attorney. Above, Morgan and Davis confer during Senate inquiry into the banking practices of the Morgan corporation. Thomas Lamont, Morgan partner and founding Council member, is at left.

Attorney Paul Cravath, who also represented the Morgan interests, was the Council's first vice-president.

Antony C. Sutton documented Wall Street's early ties to the Soviet Union.

Kuhn, Loeb's Jacob Schiff helped bankroll the Russian Revolution.

William Boyce Thompson, a founding CFR member, was leader of the odd Red Cross mission to Petrograd. 1920 photo.

At ceremonies marking the opening of the Council's East 65th Street headquarters in 1930, speakers included (left to right) secretary-treasurer Edwin F. Gay, honorary president Elihu Root, and president John W. Davis. Root stated in his address that, to attain its objectives, the Council would have to emulate the brick-by-brick construction of the building, engaging in "steady, continuous, and unspectacular labor."

The rise of Adolph Hitler and the Nazis depended largely on I. G. Farben — and the Dawes plan.

Averell Harriman (above, between Churchill and Stalin),
one of many Council members who, although
wealthy capitalists, enjoyed high harmony with the Bolsheviks.

The platitude that capitalists and Communists are archenemies has
long been discredited, however quietly, by figures such as the
Rockefellers. Above, Nelson Rockefeller greets Soviet premier Nikita
Khrushchev in 1959.

Chapter 4

The CFR And FDR

The Council on Foreign Relations exerted only limited influence on Washington during the 1920's. The American people had wearied of Wilsonian policy, with its attendant war, debt, taxation, and inflation. In 1920, Republican Warren Harding was elected President with over sixty percent of the popular vote. A resolute opponent of both Bolshevism and the League of Nations, Harding was anathema to the CFR and international bankers, a factor that should not be overlooked when considering the evil reputation some historians have assigned him.

Under Harding and his successor, Calvin Coolidge, the United States enjoyed unprecedented prosperity in an atmosphere of world peace. It was a happy era of spirited accomplishments, remembered for the introduction of radio and talkies, Lindbergh's transatlantic flight, and Babe Ruth's home runs. Some eight billion dollars were even sliced off the federal deficit accrued under Wilson. This atmosphere was apparently not to the liking of the Money Trust. They sought to oust the new Republican dynasty from the White House and install someone more cooperative — Franklin D. Roosevelt.

Ever since his first Presidential campaign, FDR has been touted as a "man of the little people," a knight on a white horse who stood up to Wall Street. This image is just that — an image.

Roosevelt was himself a prototypic Wall Streeter. His family had been involved in New York banking since the eighteenth century. His uncle, Frederic Delano, was on the original Federal Reserve Board. FDR had a customary Establishment education, attending Groton and Harvard. During the 1920's he pursued a career on Wall Street, working as a bond writer and corporate promoter, and or-

53

ganizing speculation enterprises. He was on the board of directors of eleven different corporations.[1]

In 1928, millionaire John Raskob, vice president of both Du Pont and General Motors, became chairman of the Democratic National Committee. He approached Roosevelt, whose family name carried distinction and political clout, about running for governor of New York — a traditional stepping stone for Presidential candidates. Roosevelt declined, explaining that he owed $250,000 in connection with his polio resort at Warm Springs, Georgia. However, after Raskob and other men of wealth wrote out checks liquidating the debt, he agreed to run, and was elected New York's governor that year.[2]

We mentioned earlier the maxim that what appears in *Foreign Affairs* today becomes foreign policy tomorrow. It would be an exaggeration to say that we can predict who the next President will be by noting which politicians are writing in *Foreign Affairs,* but history suggests that, at strategic times, the candidates favored by the Establishment, or who at least seek its favor, contribute to the journal.

In the July 1928 *Foreign Affairs*, some two months before Raskob approached him, FDR had published a piece entitled "Our Foreign Policy: A Democratic View." In it, he recalled how Woodrow Wilson "brought home to the hearts of mankind the great hope that through an association of nations the world could in the days to come avoid armed conflict and substitute reason and collective action for the age-old appeal of the sword." He gave clear signals to the Establishment that he was ready to play ball in the game of world government:

> The United States has taken two negative steps. It has declined to have anything to do with either the League of Nations or the World Court . . . .
>
> Even without full membership we Americans can be generous and sporting enough to give the League a far greater share of sympathetic approval and definite official help than we have hitherto accorded . . . .
>
> The time has come when we must accept not only certain facts but many new principles of a higher law, a newer and better standard in international relations.

FDR's bonds to the Council were affirmed by his son-in-law, Curtis Dall. Dall, a regular visitor at the Roosevelt home, eventually wrote a book entitled *FDR: My Exploited Father-In-Law.* He wrote therein:

> For a long time I felt that FDR had developed many thoughts and ideas that were his own to benefit this country, the U.S.A. But, he didn't. Most of his thoughts, his political "ammunition," as it were, were carefully manufactured for him in advance by the CFR-One World Money group. Brilliantly, with great gusto, like a fine piece of artillery, he exploded that prepared "ammunition" in the middle of an unsuspecting target, the American people — and thus paid off and retained his internationalist political support.[3]

In 1929 the Council on Foreign Relations purchased new quarters for itself at 45 East 65th Street in New York City. By a remarkable "coincidence," this address was next door to the house of Franklin D. Roosevelt, who had just become governor of the state. Thus, throughout the years preparatory to his White House tenure, FDR lived literally under the CFR's shadow.

The '29 Bust: FDR's Boom

Tragedy is the mother of new directions. The Panic of 1907 spawned the Federal Reserve, the sinking of the *Lusitania* led us toward World War I, and the war itself nearly brought us into the League of Nations. What happened in late October of 1929 would also rechart our destiny.

Establishment historians present the '29 stock market crash as they do most events: an accident, evolved from erroneous policies, not from deliberate planning. We have all heard how foolish speculation bid stock prices high, but that the bubble finally burst, plunging brokers out of windows and America into the Depression.

That version is correct enough, but has several missing parts. The free enterprise system has been the traditional scapegoat for the Crash. In reality, however, the Federal Reserve prompted the speculation by expanding the money supply a whopping sixty-two percent between 1923 and 1929. When the central bank became law in 1913, Congressman Charles Lindbergh had warned: "From now on, depressions will be scientifically created."[4] Like two con men working a mark, the Fed made credit easy while Establishment newspapers hyped what riches could be made in the stock market.

Louis McFadden, chairman of the House Banking Committee, declared of the Depression: "It was not accidental. It was a carefully contrived occurrence. . . . The international bankers sought to bring about a condition of despair here so that they might emerge as rulers of us all."[5]

Curtis Dall, himself a syndicate manager for Lehman Brothers, was on the floor of the New York Stock Exchange on the day of the Crash. He said of the calamity:

> Actually, it was the calculated "shearing" of the public by the World-Money powers triggered by the planned sudden shortage of call money in the New York money market.[6]

It must be understood that an expedient existed on the New York exchange called a "24 hour broker call loan." In those days, one could purchase stock on extensive credit. He could lay down, say, $100, and borrow $900 from a bank through his broker, to purchase $1000 in securities. If the stock increased just ten percent in value, he could sell it, repay the loan, and walk away with his original investment doubled.

The only problem was that such a loan could be called at any time — and if it was, the investor had to pay it off within twenty-four hours. For most, the only way to do so was to sell the stock. One can imagine the impact on the market if a great multitude of these loans were called simultaneously.

In *The United States' Unresolved Monetary and Political Problems,* William Bryan explains what occurred during the '29 Panic:

> When everything was ready, the New York financiers started calling 24 hour broker call loans. This meant that the stock brokers and the customers had to dump their stock on the market in order to pay the loans. This naturally collapsed the stock market and brought a banking collapse all over the country because the banks not owned by the oligarchy were heavily involved in broker call claims at this time, and

bank runs soon exhausted their coin and currency and they had to close. The Federal Reserve System would not come to their aid, although they were instructed under the law to maintain an elastic currency.[7]

Plummeting stock prices ruined small investors, but not the top "insiders" on Wall Street. Paul Warburg had issued a tip in March of 1929 that the Crash was coming.[8] Before it did, John D. Rockefeller, Bernard Baruch, Joseph P. Kennedy, and other money barons got out of the market. According to John Kenneth Galbraith in *The Great Crash, 1929*, Winston Churchill appeared in the visitors' gallery of the New York Stock Exchange during the frenzy of the panic.[9] It has been said that Bernard Baruch brought him there, perhaps to show him the power of the international bankers.

Early withdrawal from the market not only preserved the fortunes of these men: it also enabled them to return later and buy up whole companies for a song. Shares that once sold for a dollar now cost a nickel. Joseph P. Kennedy's worth reportedly grew from $4 million in 1929 to $100 million in 1935.[10] Not everyone was selling apples during the Depression!

FDR now rode an open highway to the Presidency, fueled by such men as Bernard Baruch. The latter's assistant, Hugh Johnson, said of the campaign: "Every time a crisis came, B. M. [Baruch] either gave the necessary money, or went out and got it."[11] In the meantime, the Republicans were issued a death sentence. Newspapers blamed President Herbert Hoover for the Crash and Depression. The Federal Reserve, instead of moving to stimulate growth and recovery, contracted the money supply by more than one third between 1929 and 1933, thus sustaining the Depression and giving no relief to the thousands of banks dying from runs.

President Hoover had a plan to bail out the banks, but he needed backing from the Democratic Congress. After losing the 1932 election, the lame duck President appealed to Roosevelt: Would he issue a statement encouraging Congressional support, and thus help end the crisis? FDR gave no reply, later claiming that he had written one, but that due to an oversight it was not sent.[12] The banks were allowed to go on collapsing right until his inauguration, thus attaching maximum stigma to the Republican Party. Ironically, when the new President announced emergency banking measures, he used the very plan drawn up by Hoover's Treasury Secretary.[13]

Roosevelt in the White House

FDR did much to indulge his mentors. In his first year in office, he granted recognition to the Soviet Union, fulfilling an objective long promulgated by *Foreign Affairs*.

In 1934, he took America off the gold standard, setting the stage for unrestrained expansion of the money supply, leading to decades of inflation — and decades of credit revenues for his friends in finance. With his Treasury Secretary, Henry Morgenthau, Jr. (the son of a founding CFR member), he arbitrarily jacked up the price of gold from $20 per ounce to $35, yielding untold profits for the international banking community.*

FDR is probably best remembered for the New Deal, with its vast tangle of tri-lettered bureaus and agencies. Of course, since a large portion of the work force was unemployed, there was not enough tax revenue to pay for these programs. So the government turned to its other source — borrowing. In effect, the international bankers, having created the Depression, now loaned America the cash to recover from it. Naturally, the interest on these loans would be borne on the backs of taxpayers for years to come. But many impoverished Americans were only too ready to accept the money dangled by FDR, without any deep contemplation of its origins or consequences.

While thousands went hungry, the President's Agricultural Adjustment Administration (AAA) paid farmers to destroy their crops and livestock to "raise prices." Even a child could see the madness of these actions, which demonstrated the dangers inherent in granting excessive power to government. What the New Deal really gave America was a thick dose of socialism, or government monopoly. This, of course, was precisely what the international bankers sought. To this day, many Americans do not perceive that when they accept federal aid, they almost invariably surrender a degree of freedom

---

*For a detailed account of the results of this maneuver, see Martin A. Larson, *The Federal Reserve and our Manipulated Dollar* (Old Greenwich, Conn.: Devin-Adair, 1975).

THE CFR AND FDR

or control. Sunsets may be an exception to the old saw, "You can't get something for nothing," but government benefits are not.

Top Wall Streeters were pleased with the creation of the Export-Import Bank in 1934, but the New Deal agency they probably liked most was the National Recovery Administration (NRA), which was designed to regulate the country's businesses.

The essence of the plan for the NRA was laid out by Bernard Baruch in a speech on May Day in 1930. As chairman of the War Industries Board during World War I, Baruch had possessed government-granted autocratic power over America's businesses. He now savored the idea of the same arrangement in peacetime. Roosevelt appointed Baruch's protégé, Hugh Johnson, to run NRA. Assisting Johnson were Gerard Swope, president of General Electric and a member of the CFR; Walter Teagle, chairman of the board of Standard Oil of New Jersey and a director of I. G. Farben's American subsidiary; and Louis Kirstein, vice president of Filene's of Boston. Thus the bureau was administered by the captains of industry — the very people who, myopic historians tell us, regarded the New Deal as a dreaded scourge. It is notable that when FDR operated on Wall Street, his office had been at the same address as the offices of Baruch and Swope — 120 Broadway.[14]

The NRA collaborated with business to set prices, wages, and working conditions. The trick was that the largest companies had the most say. For example, in establishing NRA guidelines for the iron and steel industry, U.S. Steel was allotted 511 votes, while Allegheny Steel, a small firm, had only seventeen; Continental Steel had but sixteen. This meant that giant corporations could dictate the operating standards in their respective fields, strangling small competitors out of existence. In the iron and steel industry alone, there were more than sixty complaints of such oppression in early 1934.[15]

This book is not intended to vindicate Herbert Hoover, who sometimes compromised with the international bankers, and even joined the CFR in 1937. But it should be observed that Wall Street had attempted to force NRA on him while he was President. He refused, and paid for it. In his memoirs, Hoover wrote:

Among the early Roosevelt fascist measures was the National Industry Recovery Act (NRA) . . . The origins of this scheme are worth repeating. These ideas were first suggested by Gerard Swope . . . Following this, they were adopted by the United States Chamber of Commerce. During the campaign of 1932, Henry I. Harriman, president of that body, urged that I agree to support these proposals, informing me that Mr. Roosevelt had agreed to do so. I tried to show him that this stuff was pure fascism; that it was merely a remaking of Mussolini's "corporate state" and refused to agree to any of it. He informed me that in view of my attitude, the business world would support Roosevelt with money and influence. That for the most part, proved true.[16]

The police-state power of NRA was perhaps best illustrated by the case of Jack Magid, a New Jersey tailor. Magid pressed a suit for thirty-five cents, whereas the NRA code for tailors stipulated forty cents. For this "crime," Magid was fined and thrown in jail.

Luckily for America, the Supreme Court ruled the NRA and AAA unconstitutional. Roosevelt retaliated by sending a bill to Congress that would enable him to appoint as many as six additional Supreme Court justices. This became known as the famous "court-packing" scheme. But even the President's friends on Capitol Hill could not stomach such an assault on the checks and balances of power, and the measure failed.

The Council on Foreign Relations played a significant role in the Roosevelt administration, although its influence did not peak until World War II. After being nominated at the 1932 Democratic convention, FDR traveled to Colonel House's home to pay his respects. House had an article published in the January 1933 *Foreign Affairs* laying out what some of the new Washington regime's aims should be. Among the officials Roosevelt drew from the ranks of the CFR were Secretary of State Edward Stettinus (former board chairman of U.S. Steel and the son of a Morgan partner), Assistant Secretary of State Sumner Welles, and War Secretary Henry Stimson. Wall Street banker Norman H. Davis, who served as the Council's president from 1936 to 1944, was FDR's close friend and went on missions abroad for him. James P. Warburg (CFR), the son of Paul Warburg, became a member of the President's "brain trust." It was James Warburg who would later tell a Senate committee: "We shall have world government whether or not you like it — by conquest or consent." Other CFR men held various positions in the Roosevelt government.

The Establishment also sought control of the Republican Party, which the Crash had broken. The Republican Presidential nominee in 1940 was Wendell Willkie. Certainly no one could call Willkie a party traditionalist. Until the year he ran, he had been a registered Democrat. A rabid internationalist, he wrote a book entitled *One World* and later became a CFR member. Seven weeks before the nominating convention, a poll showed that only three percent of Republicans favored Willkie. But thanks to some mass media magic, he emerged as "the" candidate. Congressman Usher Burdick had this to say about it before the House:

> We Republicans in the West want to know if Wall Street, the utilities, and the international bankers control our party and can select our candidate?
>
> I believe I am serving the best interests of the Republican Party by protesting in advance and exposing the machinations and attempts of J. P. Morgan and the New York utility bankers in forcing Wendell Willkie on the Republican Party . . . .
>
> There is nothing to the Willkie boom for President except the artificial public opinion being created by newspapers, magazines, and the radio. The reason back of all this is money. Money is being spent by someone, and lots of it.[17]

Wendell Willkie lost the election, but that was of no concern to the insiders of Wall Street; they were supporting both candidates. Willkie soon became an international emissary for FDR.

Wall Street district during the Crash of '29.
Conventional accounts have some missing pieces.

Franklin D. Roosevelt publicly decried Wall Street, but turned to
banking insider Bernard Baruch for campaign financing. Above,
the President-elect poses with Baruch following their conference
in Warm Springs, Georgia in January 1933.

Baruch with his lieutenant, Hugh Johnson, leaving the White House in 1934. The President made Johnson head of the NRA.

Roosevelt's relationship to the Council was described by his son-in-law, Curtis Dall. Above, Dall leaves the White House after a visit with FDR in 1939.

Wendell Willkie (with arms outstretched), the "instant" Republican.

Chapter 5

A Global War With Global Ends

In September 1939, Hitler's troops invaded Poland. Britain and France declared war on Germany; World War II had begun.

Less than two weeks later, Hamilton Fish Armstrong, editor of *Foreign Affairs*, and Walter Mallory, the CFR's executive director, met in Washington with Assistant Secretary of State George Messersmith. They proposed that the Council help the State Department formulate its wartime policy and postwar planning. The CFR would conduct study groups in coordination with State, making recommendations to the Department and President. Messersmith (a Council member himself) and his superiors agreed.[1] The CFR thus succeeded, temporarily at least, in making itself an adjunct of the United States government. This undertaking became known as the War and Peace Studies Project; it worked in secret and was underwritten by the Rockefeller Foundation. It held 362 meetings and prepared 682 papers for FDR and the State Department. Consultation, however, soon became encroachment. Harley Notter, assistant chief of the division of special research in the State Department, wrote a letter of resignation to his superior (a CFR member), explaining that his dissatisfaction stemmed from

relations with the Council on Foreign Relations. I have consistently opposed every move tending to give it increasing control of the research of this Division, and, though you have also consistently stated that such a policy was far from your objectives, the actual facts already visibly show that Departmental control is fast losing ground.[2]

64

While the Council was digging a niche in our government, FDR, like Woodrow Wilson, was basing his reelection campaign on pledges to stay out of war. In a speech on October 30, 1940, he declared, "I have said this before, but I shall say it again and again and again: Your boys are not going to be sent into any foreign wars."[3]

But Roosevelt was planning just the opposite. It is noteworthy that when the *Lusitania* went down, Winston Churchill was head of the British admiralty, and FDR — his distant cousin — Assistant Secretary of the U.S. Navy. This conjured up a haunting sense of *déjà vu* twenty-five years later, as the two men, now heads of state, conferred. In 1940, at the American embassy in London, a code clerk named Tyler Kent discovered secret dispatches between Churchill and FDR, revealing the latter's intention to bring the U.S. into the war. Kent tried to smuggle some of the documents out of the embassy, hoping to alert the American people, but he was caught and confined to a British prison for the duration of the war.[4]

The President's closest advisor was Harry Hopkins, who lived in the White House and enjoyed a relationship with him that some have likened to the House-Wilson kinship. According to Winston Churchill in *The Grand Alliance*, Hopkins visited him in January 1941 and said, "The President is determined that we shall win the war together. Make no mistake about it. He has sent me here to tell you that at all costs and by all means he will carry you through, no matter what happens to him. . . ."[5] William Stevenson noted in *A Man Called Intrepid* that American-British military staff talks began that same month under "utmost secrecy," which, he clarified, "meant preventing disclosure to the American public."[6] Even Robert Sherwood, the President's friendly biographer, once said: "If the isolationists had known the full extent of the secret alliance between the United States and Britain, their demands for the President's impeachment would have rumbled like thunder through the land."[7]

CFR members were interested in exploiting the Second World War — as they had the first — as a justification for world government. This, of course, later became reality in the crude form of the United Nations, which was predominantly their creation. However, to involve America in such a body would first require involving it in the war itself. *Foreign Affairs* preached rearmament; in 1940, a group of Council members wrote an appeal that ran in newspapers across the nation asserting that "the United States should immediately declare that a state of war exists between this country and Germany."[8] The globalists hoped to use the Axis threat to force the U.S. and England into a permanent Atlantic alliance — an intermediate step toward world government. Ads in *Foreign Affairs* pushed Clarence Streit's book *Union Now*, while the journal's contributors hailed the same objective. In the last issue before Pearl Harbor, the lead article typically maintained:

> [H]ope for the world's future — the only hope — lies in the continued collaboration of the oceanic Commonwealth of Free Nations.
>
> To the overwhelming majority of Englishmen, and to very many thousands of Americans, this recognition by both nations of their common needs and common responsibilities is the great good that is coming out of the war, just as for their fathers (and the thought is a warning) the League of Nations was the offset that could be made against the misery of the last war.[9]

However, a 1940 Gallup poll found eighty-three percent of Americans against participation in the European conflict. The U.S. wasn't about to go to war — unless there was an incident even more insufferable than the *Lusitania* affair.

While there is no denying the belligerence and atrocities of the Axis powers, it is certainly true that FDR dealt them incitements to attack. Despite our neutrality, and without Congressional approval, he shipped fifty destroyers to Great Britain. This idea originated with the Century Group, an ad hoc organization formed by CFR members.[10] Roosevelt also sent hundreds of millions of ammunition rounds to Britain; ordered our ships to sail directly into the war zone; and closed all German consulates. The U.S. occupied Iceland and depth-charged U-boats. But the Germans avoided retaliation, knowing that America's entry into the war would turn the tide against them, as it had in 1917.

Provocation was also given Japan. Henry Stimson, War Secretary and a patriarch of the CFR, wrote in his diary after meeting with the President: "We face the delicate question of the diplomatic fencing to be done so as to be sure Japan is put into the wrong and makes the first bad move — overt move."[11] After a subsequent meeting, he recorded: "The question was how we should maneuver them [the Japanese] into the position of firing the first shot . . ."[12] The Council's War and Peace Studies Project sent a memorandum to Roosevelt recommending a trade embargo against Japan, which he eventually enacted.[13] In addition, Japan's assets in America were frozen, and the Panama Canal closed to its shipping. On November 26, 1941 — just eleven days before Pearl Harbor — the U.S. government sent an ultimatum to the Japanese demanding, as prerequisites to resumed trade, that they withdraw all their troops from China and Indochina, and in effect abrogate their treaty with Germany and Italy. For Tokyo, that proved to be the final slap in the face.

Double Infamy at Pearl Harbor

Over the years, a number of books have documented that Franklin D. Roosevelt had foreknowledge of the surprise attack on Pearl Harbor. Of these, the most recent and authoritative is *Infamy: Pearl Harbor and Its Aftermath* (1982) by Pulitzer-Prize winner John Toland.

The author of *The Shadows of Power* summarized at length the details of this matter in the December 8, 1986 issue of *The New American*. We review them here briefly.

American military intelligence had cracked the radio code Tokyo used to communicate with its embassies. As a result, Japanese diplomatic messages in 1941 were known to Washington, often on a same-day basis. The decoded intercepts revealed that spies in Hawaii were informing Tokyo of the precise locations of the U.S. warships docked in Pearl Harbor; collectively, the messages suggested an assault would come on or about December 7. These intercepts were routinely sent to the President and to Army Chief of Staff General George Marshall. In addition, separate warnings about the attack — with varying specificity as to its time — were transmitted to these two men by or through various officials, including Joseph Grew, our ambassador to Japan; FBI Director J. Edgar Hoover; Senator Guy Gillette, who was acting on a tip from the Korean underground; Congressman Martin Dies; Brigadier General Elliot Thorpe, the U.S. military observer in Java; Colonel F. G. L. Weijerman, the Dutch military attaché in Washington; and other sources. Captain Johan Ranneft, the Dutch naval attaché in Washington, recorded that U.S. naval intelligence officers told him on December 6 that Japanese carriers were only 400 miles northwest of Honolulu.[14]

Despite all of this, no alert was passed on to our commanders in Hawaii, Admiral Husband Kimmel and General Walter C. Short. Kimmel's predecessor, Admiral Richardson, had been removed by FDR after protesting the President's order to base the Pacific Fleet in Pearl Harbor, where it was quite vulnerable to attack. Roosevelt and Marshall stripped the island of most of its air defenses shortly before the raid, and allotted it only one third of the surveillance planes needed to reliably detect approaching forces. Perhaps to preserve his station in history, Marshall sent a warning to Hawaii that arrived a few hours after the attack, which left over two thousand Americans dead, and eighteen naval vessels sunk or heavily damaged.

FDR appointed a commission to investigate what had happened. Heading it was Supreme Court justice Owen Roberts, an internationalist friendly with Roosevelt. Two of the other four members were in the CFR. The Roberts Commission absolved Washington of blame, declaring that Pearl Harbor had been caught off guard due to "dereliction of duty" by commanders Kimmel and Short. The two officers long sought court-martials so they might have a fair hearing. This was finally mandated by Congress in 1944. At the court-martials, attorneys for the defendants dug up some of Washington's secrets. The Roberts verdict was overturned: Kimmel was exonerated; Short received a small reprimand; and the onus of blame was fixed squarely on Washington. But the Roosevelt administration suppressed these results, saying public revelation would endanger national security in wartime. It then conducted "new" inquiries in which several witnesses were persuaded to change their testimony. Incriminating memoranda in the files of the Navy and War departments were destroyed. The court-martial findings were buried in a forty-volume government report on Pearl Harbor, and few Americans ever learned the truth.

We noted introductively that the CFR has been accused of fondness for Communism and globalism. In light of this, it may be in-

68

structive to observe that these two systems were the prime beneficiaries of World War II.

Gains for Communism

When World War I ended, millions of French, German, British,
and American soldiers lay dead. What was it all for? What was truly
won for their great sacrifice? Although the war had supposedly been
fought "to make the world safe for democracy," it did not achieve
that. But one group did profit significantly — the Communists. They
used the chaos of the war to enflame Russia with revolution, and
captured the largest country on earth.

World War II had a similar denouement. Millions of French, German, British, and American soldiers again lay dead. And for what?
Yes, the threat of fascism had been valorously eliminated, but this
was gain in the negative sense. Only the Communists *acquired* something from World War II: Eastern Europe, and a foothold in Asia.
The war had a commonly overlooked irony. It was begun to save
Poland from conquest by Germany. Yet when it was over, Poland
had been conquered anyway — by the Soviets. This brought no tears
from CFR men like John Scott, who wrote in 1945: "When Russia
disappoints us, as in Poland, we must not indulge our tendency to
moralize and say that we cannot deal with the Bolsheviks."[15]

During World War II, the United States and USSR were allies.
Ostensibly this was an expedient forced by the threat of Hitler. But,
as we have already seen, the growth of German fascism and armed
might were made possible by the Dawes plan, a brainchild of the
international bankers that had the CFR's blessing.

Soviet dictator Joseph Stalin was a strange choice for an ally. Like
Hitler, he had slaughtered millions of his own people, including some
six million during the Ukrainian genocide (1932-33) alone. And like
Hitler, Stalin was an international aggressor. Few recall that the
1939 invasion of Poland was a joint venture by the Germans and
Soviets, who had signed a pact that year. In 1939-40, Stalin also
invaded Finland, occupied the Baltic States of Lithuania, Latvia,
and Estonia, and annexed part of Romania. Nevertheless, FDR
called him "Uncle Joe," and the American press built him up as an
anti-fascist hero after Germany attacked Russia in 1941. And more

than adulation was offered in support. During the war, America bestowed over $11 billion in lend-lease aid on the USSR.

Overseeing these shipments was FDR's top advisor, Harry Hopkins, a zealous admirer of the Bolsheviks. Not everything Hopkins sent was for the record. After the war, two Congressional hearings examined evidence that he had also given Moscow nuclear materials and purloined blueprints for the atomic bomb. Hopkins didn't face charges — he was dead. But the facts of the case were chronicled and preserved by George Racey Jordan, a lend-lease expediter, in his book *From Major Jordan's Diaries.*

Under lend-lease, the Soviets received, among other things, 14,000 aircraft; almost half a million tanks, trucks, and other vehicles; and over 400 combat ships.[16] Without this massive infusion of materiel, it is doubtful that they could have turned back the German military. America thus saved from extinction what is today regarded as its greatest threat — Soviet Communism.

The U.S. government also cooperated in Stalin's territorial aggrandizement. At the "Big Three" conferences attended by Stalin, Churchill, and Roosevelt, FDR made concession after concession to the Red ruler. At Teheran, it was agreed that armies of the Western allies would strike at Germany through France — not the Balkans — which preserved Eastern Europe for Soviet engulfment. It was agreed that Stalin would control eastern Poland, liberate Prague, and maintain possession of the Baltic states. And it was agreed that all would support Tito in Yugoslavia, rather than the anti-Communist Draja Mihailovich.

At the Yalta Conference, an ailing President Roosevelt brought along as advisor Alger Hiss, the Soviet spy who was later discovered and convicted. Hiss, a member of the CFR, claimed that "it is an accurate and not immodest statement to say that I helped formulate the Yalta agreement to some extent."[17] At Yalta, it was conceded that the Soviets would have three votes in the General Assembly of the United Nations (which has been the official reality since the UN started operating — all other countries have only one vote). In the Pacific theater, the Soviets were given control of the Kurile Islands, the southern half of Sakhalin Island, and the Manchurian ports of Dairen and Port Arthur. And it was agreed that all Russians "displaced" by the war — that is, who had fled from Stalin's tyranny westward into Europe — would be repatriated by the Allies. This plan was in fact carried out: after the war, at least two million Russian nationals were rounded up by reluctant American and British army units and forced into boxcars that returned them to the Soviet Union, where they faced brutal reprisals. Many committed suicide rather than go. This outrage was suppressed from the American public's knowledge and has become better known only recently, thanks to such books as Julius Epstein's *Operation Keelhaul*. It is little wonder that William C. Bullitt, former U.S. ambassador to the Soviet Union, said of the Yalta agreement: "No more unnecessary, disgraceful and potentially disgraceful document has ever been signed by a President of the United States."[18]

Gains for Globalism

Most Americans believe the UN was formed after World War II as a result of international revulsion at the horrors of the war. Actually, it originated in CFR intellects, and the term "United Nations" was in use as early as 1942.

In January 1943, Secretary of State Cordell Hull formed a steering committee composed of himself, Leo Pasvolsky, Isaiah Bowman, Sumner Welles, Norman Davis, and Myron Taylor. All of these men — with the exception of Hull — were in the CFR. Later known as the Informal Agenda Group, they drafted the original proposal for the United Nations. It was Bowman — a founder of the CFR and member of Colonel House's old "Inquiry" — who first put forward the concept. They called in three attorneys, all CFR men, who ruled that it was constitutional. They then discussed it with FDR on June 15, 1944. The President approved the plan, and announced it to the public that same day.[19]

The UN founding conference took place in San Francisco in 1945. More than forty of the American delegates attending were CFR members. Preeminent among them was Soviet agent Alger Hiss, who was Secretary-General of the conference and helped draft the UN Charter.

The Senate had rejected the League of Nations largely because the legislators had been able to study the issue before it came to a vote. This time, however, no chances were taken. Alger Hiss flew directly from San Francisco to Washington with the Charter locked in a small safe. After glib assurances from delegates to the conference, the Senate ratified the document without significant pause for debate. Senator Pat McCarran later said: "Until my dying day, I will regret voting for the UN Charter."

But the United Nations was now law, and America, for the first time, part of a world government. Using an $8.5 million gift from John D. Rockefeller, Jr., the UN purchased land on New York's East River for its headquarters.

In the meantime, the CFR found a new home of its own, moving into the Harold Pratt House on East 68th Street, where it remains to this day. Curiously, the Soviets established their United Nations mission in a building across the street.

Since the United Nations' founding, the CFR and its mouthpiece *Foreign Affairs* have consistently lobbied to grant that world body more power and authority. That this has not been meaningfully achieved is not from lack of effort on their part; it is thanks to counter-efforts by distrustful Americans who have valued national self-determination.

Toward More Centralized Banking

If the key to controlling a nation is to run its central bank, one can imagine the potential of a *global* central bank, able to dictate the world's credit and money supply. The roots for such a system were planted when the International Monetary Fund (IMF) and World Bank were formed at the Bretton Woods Conference of 1944. These UN agencies were both CFR creations. The idea for them hatched with the Economic and Finance Group, one of the units of the Council's War and Peace Studies Project. This group proposed the IMF and World Bank in a series of increasingly sophisticated memos to the President and State Department during 1941-42. After Bretton Woods, the two institutions were touted in *Foreign Affairs*.

A. K. Chesterton, the distinguished British author, declared: "The final act of Bretton Woods, which gave birth to the World Bank and International Monetary Fund . . . and many similar assemblies of hand-picked functionaries were not incubated by hard-pressed Governments engaged in waging war, but by a Supra-national Money Power which could afford to look ahead to the shaping of a post-war world that would serve its interest."[20]

The IMF was ostensibly set up to control international exchange rates and "stabilize currencies," but is the framework for a central bank of issue. It is noteworthy that at Bretton Woods, Federal Reserve Board governor Mariner Eccles observed: "An international currency is synonymous with international government."[21] John Maynard Keynes, the leading British figure at the Conference, proposed a world currency which he called *bancor*, but this plan was rejected as too radical to gain international acceptance. However, this goal has not been abandoned. Dr. Johannes Witteveen, former head of the IMF, said in 1975 that the agency should become "the exclusive issuer of official international reserve assets."[22] In the Fall 1984 *Foreign Affairs*, Richard N. Cooper laid out a modern plan for international currency. He wrote:

> A new Bretton Woods conference is wholly premature. But it is not premature to begin thinking about how we would like international monetary arrangements to evolve in the remainder of this century. With this in mind, I suggest a radical alternative scheme for the next century: *the creation of a common currency for all the industrial democracies, with a common monetary policy and a joint Bank of Issue to determine that monetary policy.* (Emphasis in the original.)

Given the prophetic tendency of *Foreign Affairs,* and the increasing uniformity of Europe's currencies, we must regard Cooper's proposal as having more than trivial significance.

The IMF's sister, the World Bank, was supposedly established to help postwar reconstruction and development. It is an international lending agency, but what it lends more than anything else is dollars from the U.S. taxpayer.

Who is the ultimate beneficiary? The World Bank hierarchy has traditionally been closely linked to the Rockefellers' Chase Manhattan Bank. As Congressman John Rarick once explained: "[A]id to the poor countries usually ends up as seed money or loans to the wealthy industrialists from the developed countries to further their

73

overseas operations in competition with the people whose country they claim to represent."[23] The *Los Angeles Times* elaborated in 1978: "Ostensibly to encourage agriculture and rural development, World Bank loans go overwhelmingly to build an infrastructure — from roads to dams — that enriches local and foreign contractors and consultants."[24] *Barron's* put it succinctly that same year: "There's a saying that the Bank takes tax money from poor people in rich nations to give to rich people in poor nations." And, *Barron's* noted: "To make matters worse, many of the social reforms that the Bank is funding involve fostering the spread of socialism and Communism."[25]

Perhaps no one has summarized the strategy of the international bankers better than Senator Jesse Helms, who stated in 1987:

> [I]t is no secret that the international bankers profiteer from sovereign state debt. The New York banks have found important profit centers in the lending to countries plunged into debt by Socialist regimes. Under Socialist regimes, countries go deeper and deeper into debt because socialism as an economic system does not work. International bankers are sophisticated enough to understand this phenomenon and they are sophisticated enough to profit from it.
>
> Because the public debt is sovereign debt, the bankers have calculated that they will always be able to collect. If there is too much risk in the private debt side, it is a simple matter to get Socialist governments to nationalize banks, industrial enterprises, and agricultural holdings. In this way, private debt is converted to sovereign state debt which the bankers have believed will always be collectable.
>
> The New York banks find the profit from the interest on this sovereign debt to be critical to their balance sheets. Up until very recently, this has been an essentially riskless game for the banks because the IMF and World Bank have stood ready to bail the banks out with our taxpayer's money.[26]

Bretton Woods marked neither the first nor last time that the international bankers would devise a means of using other people's money to obtain profits — both monetary and political — in the name of humanitarianism.

Foreign Affairs editor Hamilton Fish Armstrong helped build bridges between the Council and Washington.

Henry Stimson: "The question was how we should maneuver them into the position of firing the first shot . . ."

In his 1982 best seller *Infamy*, historian John Toland (left) enumerated the numerous warnings Washington received about Pearl Harbor through such individuals as Senator Guy Gillette (right). Earlier books that dealt with the controversy included: *Pearl Harbor* by George Morgenstern; *Perpetual War for Perpetual Peace*, edited by Harry Elmer Barnes; *The Final Secret of Pearl Harbor* by Admiral Robert Theobald; and *Admiral Kimmel's Story* by Husband Kimmel.

Admiral Kimmel (left) and General Short (right) were made scapegoats after the attack, which sank or heavily damaged eighteen naval vessels, destroyed 188 planes, and left over two thousand dead.

The Roberts Commission. Its verdict pleased Washington.

At the "Big Three" conferences, Stalin won
a steady stream of concessions.

1943: Major George Racey Jordan (right) is decorated by Colonel A. N. Kotikov, head of USSR lend-lease mission. Jordan and other witnesses later testified that Presidential advisor Harry Hopkins had shipped the Soviets uranium as well as the secret plans for the atomic bomb.

Harry Hopkins

Isaiah Bowman

Of the American delegates at the founding UN conference in
San Francisco, more than forty belonged to the CFR. Above,
Hamilton Fish Armstrong proposes an amendment, June 15, 1945.

Alger Hiss shakes hands with Harry Truman at UN founding
conference. Hiss, a Council member later exposed as a
Soviet spy, was Secretary-General of the conference.

UN PHOTO

March 1947: John D. Rockefeller III, on behalf of his father, presents
UN Secretary-General Trygve Lie with an $8.5 million
check to purchase land for the UN's headquarters.

Chapter 6

The Truman Era

Franklin D. Roosevelt died on April 12, 1945, and was succeeded by Vice President Harry Truman. Truman, a former senator from Missouri, had risen in politics through the backing of the notorious Pendergast machine, which was later extensively prosecuted for vote fraud.

The acclaimed new book *The Wise Men*, by Walter Isaacson and Evan Thomas, centers on six statesmen whose careers peaked during the Truman era. They were: Dean Acheson (a Truman Secretary of State), Robert Lovett (Under Secretary of State and later Secretary of Defense), Averell Harriman (various positions), John McCloy (High Commissioner to Germany), George Kennan (State Department advisor and Ambassador to the Soviet Union) and Charles Bohlen (State Department advisor). The book calls these men "architects of the American century" who "left a legacy that dominates American policy to this day." As chance would have it, all six were members of the CFR, and their backgrounds, for the most part, were typically Establishment.

Harry Truman did not fit their mold by breeding; he did not hail from Harvard, Wall Street, or the CFR. After Roosevelt's death, some of the "wise men" descended on the White House and began what Isaacson and Thomas call "the education of Harry Truman."[1]

The Marshall Scam
Certainly one of the foremost highlights of the eventful Truman years was the Marshall Plan, a massive package of economic aid the U.S. bestowed on Western Europe. General George Marshall, who was now Secretary of State, proposed it in a Harvard commencement

speech in 1947. Conventional history presumes Marshall initiated the concept, which, not surprisingly, had its actual birth at the Council on Foreign Relations.

In their study of the CFR, *Imperial Brain Trust*, Laurence Shoup and William Minter reported:

> In 1946-1947 lawyer Charles M. Spofford headed a [CFR study] group, with banker David Rockefeller as secretary, on Reconstruction in Western Europe; in 1947-1948 that body was retitled the Marshall Plan. The Council's annual report for 1948 explained that even before Secretary of State George C. Marshall had made his aid to Europe proposal in June 1947, the Spofford group had "uncovered" the necessity for aid to Europe and "helped explain the needs for the Marshall Plan and indicated some of the problems it would present for American foreign policy. Moreover, a number of members of the 1947-1948 group, through their connections with . . . governmental bodies were in constant touch with the course of events."[2]

Originally, it was to be called the Truman Plan, but this was scrapped because it was felt that the name of Marshall — who was Chief of Staff during the war — could elicit more bipartisan Congressional support.[3] Thus was Marshall selected to introduce the proposal publicly.

The Marshall Plan, overseen by the Economic Cooperation Administration (ECA), transferred $13 billion from the U.S. taxpayers to Western Europe. But where did the dollars end up? In 1986, Tyler Cowen observed in *Reason* magazine: "[A]ll of the aid channeled through the ECA was linked to purchases of particular US goods and services. In this regard, the Marshall Plan subsidized some US businesses at the expense of the American taxpayer."[4] Cowen entitled his article "The Great Twentieth-Century Foreign-Aid Hoax." Firms that could not get Americans to buy their products now *forced* them to pay through surrogate European consumers. Some of the goods sent were overstocked, overpriced, or inferior in quality — but the Europeans took what the ECA stipulated. And why not? For them, it was free.

The Marshall Plan was originally presented as a humanitarian undertaking. But many U.S. congressmen, whose approval was needed to secure the appropriations, were turning thumbs down. Some called it a "New Deal for Europe." So a different marketing appeal was used: the aid, it was said, would prevent Soviet aggression.

Isaacson and Thomas quote John McCloy:

> "People sat up and listened when the Soviet threat was mentioned," he later said. It taught him a valuable lesson: One way to assure that a viewpoint gets noticed is to cast it in terms of resisting the spread of Communism.[5]

"Acheson," they relate, "concluded that the anti-Communist rhetoric was necessary to win support for the British package."[6]

Harry Truman had set the pace in March 1947, when he enunciated the so-called Truman Doctrine: that America would support democracies around the world against aggression.

The Wise Men claims, however, that "Truman did not really mean what he said":[7]

> "It seemed to General Marshall and me that there was a little too much flamboyant anti-Communism in that speech," Bohlen later recalled. Marshall and Bohlen sent a cable back to Washington asking that it be toned down. The reply came back from Truman: without the rhetoric, Congress would not approve the money.[8]

Each of the six CFR "wise men" played unique roles in instituting the Marshall Plan: Harriman became the program's administrator in Europe; Bohlen was PR man; Lovett testified daily to Congress about the Soviet menace; Acheson, on temporary leave from public service, formed the Citizens' Committee for the Marshall Plan; John McCloy became president of the World Bank, floating loans to Europe.

George Kennan — wittingly or not — supplied the intellectual rationale when he authored the most famous article ever to appear in *Foreign Affairs*. Called "The Sources of Soviet Conduct" and anonymously bylined "X," it was partially reprinted in *Life* and *Reader's Digest*. In it, Kennan submitted that the U.S. should "contain" Communism, an idea which became the keystone of American Cold War strategy. *Foreign Affairs* ran the piece in July 1947, the month following Marshall's address. Kennan had summarized his thoughts in a speech at Pratt House, after which editor Hamilton Fish Armstrong asked him for a written essay. Not insignificantly, the same issue carried a lead article by Armstrong suggesting aid to Europe.

Given a hard sell in terms of prohibiting Soviet expansionism, Congress now approved the plan — even Joe McCarthy voted for it. But insiders knew the score. Charles L. Mee, in his book *The Marshall Plan*, quoted Pierre Mendès-France, French executive director of the World Bank:

> "The Communists are rendering a great service. Because we have a 'Communist danger,' the Americans are making a tremendous effort to help us. We must keep up this indispensable Communist scare."[9]

None of this means there was no Soviet threat — Stalin had subjugated half of Europe. What it does help confirm, however, is that when CFR members have professed anti-Communism, they have often done so for ulterior motives.

NATO and Other Alliances

It was Winston Churchill who first warned of the "iron curtain" in a speech at Fulton, Missouri in 1946. What is not well remembered, however, is the solution he advocated: a "fraternal association of the English-speaking peoples."

The North Atlantic Treaty Organization (NATO), formally established in 1949, has always been explained to Americans as an anti-Communist alliance. But the CFR's definition is far less narrow. It regards all regional organizations as building blocks of world government. This frame of reference was expressed in *Foreign Affairs* as early as 1926, when Eduard Beneš wrote:

> Locarno [a European collective security agreement] represents an attempt to arrive at the same end by stages, — by treaties and local

regional pacts which are permeated with the spirit of the Geneva Protocol, — these to be constantly supplemented, until at last, within the framework of the League of Nations, they are absorbed by one great world convention guaranteeing world security and peace by the enforcing of the rule of law in inter-state life.[10]

In April 1948, when Under Secretary of State Robert Lovett was secretly arranging the NATO alliance, *Foreign Affairs* noted:

[A] regional organization of nations, formed to operate within the framework of the United Nations, can only strengthen that organization.[11]

Shortly after American entry into NATO was ratified by the U.S. Senate, in a pamphlet called "The Goal is Government of All the World," Elmo Roper of the CFR mused:

But the Atlantic Pact (NATO) need not be our last effort toward greater unity. It can be converted into one more sound and important step working toward world peace. It can be one of the most positive moves in the direction of One World.[12]

For NATO, then, as for the Marshall Plan, anti-Communism was apparently just a selling point. The original plan called for Western Europe to consolidate her forces into one army, but this was rejected by the nations themselves — an alliance such as NATO was as far as they would go. The pressure for European unity, however, has never ceased. Through such associations as the Common Market (established in 1957) and the European Parliament (which held its first popular elections in 1979), Europe has become an increasingly collective global unit.

NATO, of course, is not unique. In 1964, in his *Foreign Affairs* article "The World Order in the Sixties," Roberto Ducci explained:

Pending the formation of such wider and more responsible political units, encouragement should be given to regional organizations, of the type recognized by the U.N. Charter. They should be strengthened

85

so as to make them able to keep the peace in their respective areas: NATO in the North Atlantic and the Council of Europe in the European regions, O.A.S. in the Americas, O.A.U. in Africa, SEATO in Southeast Asia.[13]

For decades, the CFR pushed this ascending approach to world government, with *Foreign Affairs* carrying such titles as "Toward European Integration: Beginnings in Agriculture," "Toward Unity in Africa," "Toward a Caribbean Federation," and so on.

Within the North Atlantic context, both the Marshall Plan and NATO may be understood as facets of the attempt to use the threat of Soviet Communism to push America and Europe into a binding alliance, as a halfway house on the road to world order. The Marshall Plan created the economic footing for this alliance, while NATO represented the military component. The political bond — the final and most crucial stage — was supposed to come to life in an Atlantic commonwealth the globalists whimsically dubbed "Atlantica." An organization called the Atlantic Union Committee, dominated by CFR members, was formed to promote this concept. It did so diligently during the 1950's and 60's, and through the lobbying efforts of it and its successor, the Atlantic Council, several resolutions were actually brought before Congress that would have authorized a convention to lay the foundations of an Atlantic union. These, however, were consistently rejected by the elected representatives of the American people.

The Fall of China

In 1949, the Communists took over the most populous nation on earth. An intense controversy erupted over this in the United States. Substantial evidence, now all but forgotten, implicated American diplomacy in the debacle.

The story began with the Yalta Conference, when it was arranged that the Russians would march into China, presumably to battle the Japanese forces there. Stalin had maintained a nonaggression treaty with Tokyo during the war, but said he would break it — provided that we equip his army for the job. Roosevelt consented. Without consulting the Chinese, it was also promised that the Soviets would receive control of the Manchurian ports of Dairen and Port Arthur, as well as joint operation of Manchuria's railways with the Chinese.

This agreement was disgraceful for at least two reasons: first, Japan's defeat was already imminent, nullifying any need to invite Stalin — a known aggressor — into the Pacific theater; second, Roosevelt had no right to cede the territory of a sovereign nation to a third country.

The Russians entered the Pacific war, all right — just days before it ended. The atomic bomb had already pounded Hiroshima. The Soviets confiscated Japan's surrendered munitions in Manchuria, collecting the spoils without expending the effort. They then turned these, as well as American lend-lease supplies, over to China's Communist rebels, led by Mao Tse-tung.

For the next four years, the land was ablaze as Mao fought to overthrow the Nationalist regime of Chiang Kai-shek. Chiang, a faithful ally of the United States, was trying to establish a constitutional republic. He had been criticized in *Foreign Affairs* as far back as 1928, shortly after his struggle with the Communists had begun.

In late 1945, President Truman dispatched General Marshall to China as a special ambassador to mediate the conflict. Marshall had been an obscure colonel until the reign of FDR, who boosted him past dozens of senior officers to Chief of Staff. Marshall was never listed on the CFR's roster, but he was chronically in the company of its members, and once wrote the introduction to the Council's annual volume, *The United States in World Affairs*.

In China, Marshall demanded that Chiang accept the Communists into his government or forfeit U.S. support. He also negotiated truces that saved the Reds from imminent defeat, and which they exploited to regroup and seize more territory. Finally, Marshall slammed a weapons embargo on the Nationalist government, as the Communists had been urging him to do.

He returned home and was appointed Secretary of State. It became the official line of the CFR-dominated State Department that Chiang Kai-shek was a corrupt reactionary and that Mao Tse-tung was not a Communist but an "agrarian reformer." This propaganda was extensively disseminated to the public by the now-defunct Institute of

Pacific Relations (IPR). The CFR was the parent organization of the IPR, which had no less than forty Council members in its ranks. The Institute, like the Council, was heavily funded by Establishment foundations.

An FBI raid on the offices of *Amerasia*, a magazine produced by IPR's leaders, uncovered 1800 stolen government documents. Later, the Institute was investigated by the Senate Committee on the Judiciary, which declared in 1952:

> The Institute of Pacific Relations was a vehicle used by the Communists to orient American Far Eastern policies toward Communist objectives. Members of the small core of officials and staff members who controlled IPR were either Communist or pro-Communist . . .[14]

The situation in China became desperate. Thanks to the U.S. embargo, the Nationalists were running out of ammunition, while the Communists remained Soviet-supplied. In 1948, Congress voted $125 million in military aid to Chiang. But the Truman administration held up implementation for nine months with red tape, while China collapsed.[15] In contrast, after the Marshall Plan had passed, the first ships set sail for Europe within days.

Chiang and the Nationalists fled to Taiwan. The IPR myth that he was the heavy and Mao the hero fell apart: Taiwan emerged as a bastion of freedom, and out-produced the world trade of the entire mainland; Mao, on the other hand, instituted totalitarian Communism, and slaughtered tens of millions of Chinese in purges lasting over two decades.

On January 25, 1949, a young congressman declared before the House of Representatives: "Mr. Speaker, over this weekend we have learned the extent of the disaster that has befallen China and the United States. The responsibility for the failure of our foreign policy in the Far East rests squarely with the White House and the Department of State. The continued insistence that aid would not be forthcoming, unless a coalition government with the Communists were formed, was a crippling blow to the National Government." He reaffirmed this in a speech five days later, concluding: "This is the tragic story of China, whose freedom we once fought to preserve.

88

What our young men had saved, our diplomats and our President have frittered away."[16] The young congressman was John F. Kennedy.

The Strange War in Korea

The Second World War and Vietnam have overshadowed the war sandwiched between them. The Korean conflict, like the loss of China, had roots in World War II diplomacy. When Harry Hopkins visited Stalin in May 1945, they agreed that Korea, a protectorate of Japan, should be ruled by a postwar international trusteeship. A *Foreign Affairs* article had proposed this in April 1944, recommending that

> a trusteeship for Korea will be assumed not by a particular country, but by a group of Powers, say, the United States, Great Britain, China and Russia.[17]

In fact, Korea was divided in half, its disposition similar to Germany's. The U.S. occupied the South below the 38th parallel, and the Soviets the North, which they converted into a Marxist satrapy under Kim Il Sung. It is not unreasonable to say that there never would have been a Communist regime in North Korea, nor would there ever have been a Korean War, had American negotiations and lend-lease shipments not brought the USSR into the Pacific theater.

The Soviets trained a 150,000-man North Korean army, supplying it with tanks and fighter planes. But when the U.S. evacuated the South, we left only a constabulary force of 16,000 Koreans equipped with small arms. General Albert C. Wedemeyer, sent by Truman to evaluate the military situation in the Far East, reported that North Korea represented a distinct military threat to the South, which he recommended arming; but his warning was ignored, and his report suppressed from public knowledge. (Dismayed by the negligence that led to the war, Wedemeyer became an outspoken critic of American foreign policy after retiring from active service in 1951; his revealing book, *Wedemeyer Reports!*, was widely read.)

In January 1950, Kim Il Sung proclaimed in a New Year's Day statement that this would be Korea's "year of unification," and called for "complete preparedness for war." What was the U.S. reponse to this saber-rattling? Two weeks later, Dean Acheson, now Truman's Secretary of State, declared that South Korea lay outside the "defensive perimeter" of the United States. This gave a clear signal to Kim, who invaded the South that June under Soviet auspices.

Like Pearl Harbor, the invasion shocked the average American; but it is hard to believe that it shocked Truman, Acheson, or other high foreign policy officials who had watched these events unfolding.

To review the war's course very concisely, the North Koreans had initial success. But General Douglas MacArthur's troops, after a brilliant landing at Inchon, drove them back across the 38th parallel, liberating nearly all of Korea up to the Yalu River, which marks the border of China. At this point, Communist Chinese armies entered the fray, pushing MacArthur's forces back. The war finally ended in stalemate, with the North-South frontier remaining close to what it had been.

The war, like its prelude, had a number of anomalies. First, American soldiers were fighting as part of a UN police force (even though they made up ninety percent of it).

Constitutionally, only the U.S. Congress is authorized to declare war. But in the case of Korea, the President by-passed declaration of war. We had ratified the UN Charter and were subject to *its* statutes.

In 1944, the CFR had prepared a confidential memorandum for the State Department that prophetically anticipated this circumstance. It noted:

> [A] possible further difficulty was cited, namely, that arising from the Constitutional provision that only Congress may declare war. This argument was countered with the contention that a treaty would override this barrier, let alone the fact that our participation in such police action as might be recommended by the international security organization need not necessarily be construed as *war*.[18]

One of the remarkable ironies of the Korean episode was that the Soviets, by simple exercise of their veto in the Security Council, could have easily prevented the UN's intervention on behalf of South

Korea. But they staged a walkout, allegedly over the failure of the UN to seat Red China. They did not return until after the Korea vote, even though UN Secretary General Trygve Lie expressly invited them to attend. Why would the Soviets pass up a conspicuous opportunity to protect their surrogate operation in Korea? This raises the possibility that their "blunder" was intentional.

No less strange than the Soviets' conduct was Washington's prosecution of the war. American armed forces were required to fight under restrictions never before known in military annals.

Establishment historians have always faulted General MacArthur for China's entry into the war, saying that the field commander's cockiness caused him to underestimate the risks of pushing to the Yalu. They ignore the consequences of the declaration issued by Harry Truman, two days after the North Koreans' invasion:

> . . . I have ordered the Seventh Fleet to prevent any attack on Formosa. As a corollary of this action, I am calling upon the Chinese Government on Formosa to cease all air and sea operations against the mainland. The Seventh Fleet will see that this is done.[19]

During the war, under the pretext of not inciting Peking, the U.S. Navy was ordered to protect the mainland from Chiang Kai-shek's troops on Taiwan (Formosa). This freed up the Communist Chinese armies for their strike across the Yalu. Chiang also offered us his men for direct use on the Korean front. As a member of the UN, Taiwan presumably had a perfect right to partake in this UN action. But the proposition was rejected by General Marshall (whom Truman had now appointed Secretary of Defense).

To halt the Chinese Communists' advance across the Yalu, MacArthur ordered the river's bridges bombed. Within hours, his order was countermanded by General Marshall. MacArthur said of this:

> I realized for the first time that I had actually been denied the use of my full military power to safeguard the lives of my soldiers and the safety of my army. To me, it clearly foreshadowed a future tragic situation in Korea, and left me with a sense of inexpressible shock.[20]

American planes were forbidden to hit supply depots on the other side of the Yalu, or to pursue attacking MIGs whenever they retreated behind the Chinese border. All of this was purportedly to avoid "a wider war."

But it was precisely due to these restrictions, coupled with the blockade of Taiwan, that China felt bold enough to attack. General Lin Piao, commander of the Chinese forces, later said:

> I never would have made the attack and risked my men and my military reputation if I had not been assured that Washington would restrain General MacArthur from taking adequate retaliatory measures against my lines of supply and communication.[21]

Probably thousands of American GI's died needlessly thanks to Washington's meddling in the methodology of warfare. General Mark Clark, who later signed the Korean armistice, said it was "beyond my comprehension that we would countenance a situation in which Chinese soldiers killed American youth in organized, formal warfare and yet we would fail to use all the power at our command to protect those Americans."[22]

This, then, was the new concept of "limited war." We were not really in it to win, but merely, as George Kennan put it, to "contain" Communism. Of course, in an activity as desperate as combat, victory requires all-out effort. One does not win a fight by shackling his own arms and donning a blindfold. In World War II, the U.S. spared no available tool, not even the atomic bomb, to ensure triumph. "Unconditional surrender" was demanded of Germany and Japan, but no such terms were applied to the Communists in Korea.

Did the CFR know something the American public did not? As early as 1942, *Foreign Affairs* had been confidently forecasting Allied victory in the Second World War and discussing what should be done with postwar Europe. However, *Foreign Affairs* made no predictions of success for the Korean effort, and afterwards the Council published a book, *Korea: A Study of United States Policy in the United Nations,* which mocked the idea of victory in war.

Did a secret purpose lie in the shadows of Korea? Dean Acheson later said: "The only reason I told the President to fight in Korea was to validate NATO."[23] Validating the *UN* was probably more to the point. In 1952, *Foreign Affairs* ran a lead article entitled "Korea in Perspective," in which the author summed up thus:

> The burden of my argument, then, based on the meaning of our experience in Korea as I see it, is that we have made historic progress toward the establishment of a viable system of collective security.[24]

CFR members had already used anti-Communist pretenses to manipulate the United States into the Marshall Plan and NATO. A fair question then arises — in light of all the strange policies that induced the Korean conflict and governed its progress — if the war was a sick-minded contrivance to "prove" that the UN (world government) could effectively prevent aggression and should thus be granted more power. If so, it was a sorry joke on the American and Korean people.

Men may be willing to die for their country, they may be willing to die for freedom, but who — as author James Burnham asked — wants to die for "containment"? One man who comprehended this was Douglas MacArthur. In April 1951, Truman fired him without a hearing, supposedly because his dissent with Washington had been made public, but more probably because he was determined to win rather than settle for stalemate. Replacing MacArthur in Korea was General Matthew Ridgway, whom David Halberstam called "a military extension of Kennan," and who later joined the CFR.

The dismissal outraged Americans. Within forty-eight hours, 125,000 telegrams were sent to the White House. MacArthur returned home to the largest ticker tape parades in U.S. history. Before Congress he declared that there is "no substitute for victory."

The Truman administration was finished.

Harry Truman with two of his "wise men,"
John McCloy (center) and Dean Acheson (right)

More than twenty years later, Acheson and McCloy would still
be advising the White House. Above, they flank President
Richard Nixon. Figure closest to camera is Henry Kissinger.

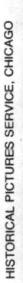

George Marshall and Robert Lovett testify before Congress about the need for the Marshall Plan. Only by addressing the Soviet threat — arousing the anti-Communist instincts of a Christian America — could the billions sought be obtained. This posturing helped give the Establishment its illusive veneer of conservatism.

George Kennan in June 1947

94th CONGRESS
1st Session

H. J. RES. 606

IN THE HOUSE OF REPRESENTATIVES

JULY 30, 1975

Mr. FINDLEY (for himself, Mr. ZABLOCKI, Mr. FRENZEL, Mr. NIX, Mr. YATRON, Mr. HARRINGTON, Mr. RYAN, Mr. CHARLES WILSON of Texas, Mr. RIEGLE, Mrs. COLLINS of Illinois, Mrs. MEYNER, Mr. BIESTER, Mr. ADAMS, Mr. ANDERSON of Illinois, Mr. BOLLING, Mr. LUJAN, Mr. MATSUNAGA, Mr. MURPHY of Illinois, Mr. PEYSER, Mr. PRICE, Mr. QUIE, Mr. ROONEY, Mr. SCHNEEBELI, Mr. SISK, and Mrs. SULLIVAN) introduced the following joint resolution, which was referred to the Committee on International Relations

JOINT RESOLUTION

To Call an Atlantic Convention

Whereas a more perfect union of the Atlantic Community consistent with the United States Constitution and the Charter of the United Nations gives promise of strengthening common defense, assuring more adequate energy resources, providing a stable currency to improve commerce of all kinds, and enhancing the economic prosperity, general

One of the many Atlantic Union resolutions brought before Congress. All were rejected.

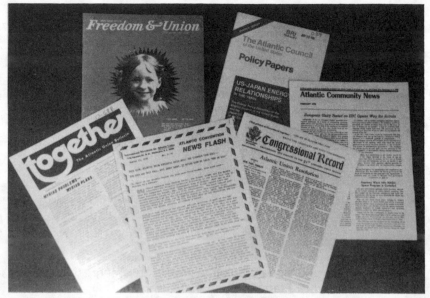

Literature promoting the Atlantic Union

The Marshall Mission aided the Communist victory in China. Left to right: Chou En-lai, Marshall, Chu Teh, Cheng Kai-min, Mao Tse-tung.

As Marshall looks on, Chou En-lai signs the cease-fire
agreement he does not intend to honor.

The Chinese Communists executed millions.

The Forrestal Case

Truman tapped former CFR member James Forrestal to be Defense
Secretary. Forrestal stunned the Establishment, however, with overtly
anti-Communist activities. His initiative was largely responsible for
preventing a Communist takeover in Italy in 1948. Discerning the true
intent of Establishment foreign policy, he stated with revulsion:
"Consistency has never been a mark of stupidity. If the diplomats
who have mishandled our relations with Russia were merely stupid,
they would occasionally make a mistake in our favor." He resolved to
counteract treason within the government. Truman fired him in March
1949. Forrestal then planned to buy the *New York Sun* and convert it
into an anti-Communist citadel — an undertaking sure to mean
steamy revelations about Washington. He never had the chance.
Five days after his dismissal, he was taken to Bethesda Naval
Hospital (for "fatigue"), where he was heavily drugged and held
incommunicado for seven weeks. All visitors except immediate family
were denied. Forrestal's diaries — undoubtedly explosive — were
meanwhile confiscated by the White House. His priest, Monsignor
Maurice Sheehy, finally prevailed upon Navy Secretary John Sullivan
to authorize his release. On May 22, 1949, Forrestal was scheduled
for discharge. But at 2 AM that morning, he fell from a window near
his sixteenth-floor room. His bathrobe cord was found knotted around
his neck. The death was declared suicide. Forrestal's brother Henry
called it murder. The tragedy, subsequent cover-up, and
contradictions in the "suicide" verdict were canvassed by Cornell
Simpson in his 1966 book *The Death of James Forrestal*.

Chinese soldiers crossed the Yalu under Washington's aegis, without which Chinese general Lin Piao (above) acknowledged he would not have attacked.

U.S. fighters hunt for MIGs over North Korea. American pilots in Korea operated under restraints unheard of in war.

The determined anti-Communism of Douglas MacArthur and Chiang Kai-shek brought the wrath of the American Establishment on both.

The dismissal of MacArthur proved not his undoing, but Truman's.

TELEGRAMS FOR TRUMAN
9

LETTERS FOR MacA.
3,940

MacARTHUR

TELEGRAMS FOR MacA.
1,836

LETTERS FOR TRUMAN
67

Congressman Joseph Martin surveys some of the public response.

Chapter 7

Between Limited Wars

Eisenhower and the CFR

It was clear in 1952 that the Republicans would return to the White House. Harry Truman had more problems than the Alger Hiss scandal. "Containment" was simply not working. Since the concept's origination, hundreds of millions of people had fallen under Communist domination. Americans sensed the need for a strong new leader who could stand up to the Soviets. The favorite of the GOP's rank and file was Senator Robert Taft of Ohio, the son of the former President, and an outspoken foe of Communism. Douglas MacArthur openly supported Taft, who entertained plans to make the general his running mate. It was the Establishment's aversion to this candidacy that brought Dwight D. Eisenhower forward.

In 1941, the year we went to war, Eisenhower, or "Ike," was a lieutenant colonel who had never seen a battle in his life. Yet by late 1943 he had become a four-star general and supreme commander of Allied forces in Western Europe. Eisenhower's meteoric rise has been popularly ascribed to his performance in Louisiana war maneuvers, and his efficiency as General Marshall's chief of operations in Washington. But Robert Welch, in his critical biography *The Politician*, noted that the extraordinary rash of promotions was preceded by a dinner in Seattle where Ike met FDR's daughter Anna, leading to a White House interview.[1]

After the war, Eisenhower commanded U.S. occupation forces in Germany. He returned home to become U.S. Chief of Staff. According to Ike's adulatory biographer, Stephen Ambrose, "The elite of the Eastern Establishment moved in on him almost before he occupied his new office."[2] The general and his wife, says Ambrose,

101

spent their evenings and vacation time with Eisenhower's new, wealthy friends. When they played bridge in the thirties, it was with other majors and their wives; in the forties, it was with the president of CBS, or the chairman of the board of U.S. Steel, or the president of Standard Oil.[3]

Bernard Baruch became a close acquaintance. Although he had no academic background, Eisenhower was made president of Columbia University in 1948. He joined the Council on Foreign Relations, was on the editorial advisory board of *Foreign Affairs*, and chaired a Council study group on aid to Europe. Joseph Kraft, in *Harper's*, quoted one CFR member as saying: "Whatever General Eisenhower knows about economics, he learned at the study group meetings."[4] In 1950 he was appointed supreme commander of the globalists' baby, NATO.

The Establishment knew that to divest Taft and MacArthur of the Republican nomination, they would have to present a candidate who looked credibly tough and anti-Communist. General Eisenhower, who was still wearing an aura of World War II glory, became their choice.

By no stretch of the imagination was Ike a Republican traditionalist. In fact, until he ran, he had no party affiliation. The Democrats tried to draft him in 1948, and Harry Truman had even approached him about running on the same ticket.[5] Nonetheless, when Eisenhower beckoned to GOP ears during the 1952 campaign, he began mouthing the same things Taft and MacArthur were saying. He condemned the Yalta agreement, even though it was Ike himself who had executed a number of its provisions: during the war, he held his troops back, allowing the Soviets to conquer Prague and Berlin; and as commander of postwar occupation forces, he authorized Operation Keelhaul, repatriating at least two million Soviet nationals to the USSR against their will.[6]

The Establishment machine worked at full throttle for Eisenhower. Even the *New York Times* modestly noted:

> There is some degree of similarity between the Willkie drive and the movement to nominate General of the Army Dwight D. Eisen-

hower. The same financial and publishing interests or their counterparts are behind the Eisenhower movement.[7]

Human Events (January 23, 1952) told how certain bankers applied pressure

> on businessmen who favor Taft but have the misfortune to owe money
> to these Eastern bankers. We have, on investigation, spotted several
> cases in which businessmen . . . have received communications from
> their New York creditors, urging them to join pro-Eisenhower committees and to raise or contribute funds thereto.[8]

At the Republican nominating convention, "dirty tricks" abounded. The rules for selecting delegates were changed; Taft delegations from Georgia, Louisiana, and Texas were thrown out and replaced by Eisenhower supporters.

Here is how Taft himself explained the lost nomination:

> First, it was the power of the New York financial interests and a
> large number of businessmen subject to New York influence, who
> selected General Eisenhower as their candidate at least a year ago. . . .
> Second, four-fifths of the influential newspapers in the country were
> opposed to me continuously and vociferously and many turned themselves into propaganda sheets for my opponent.[9]

In the lead article of the October 1952 *Foreign Affairs,* McGeorge Bundy exulted over the nominations of Ike and his Democratic opponent, Adlai Stevenson (also a member of the CFR). Once again, the Establishment had succeeded in controlling both parties. Bundy candidly acknowledged:

> Contemplating this remarkable result, many were tempted simply
> to thank their lucky stars; but it was not all luck. These two nominations were not accidental. . . .
> The fundamental meaning of the Eisenhower candidacy can best be
> understood by considering the nature of the forces he was drafted to
> stop — for fundamentally he was the stop-Taft candidate . . .

As President, Eisenhower drew his staff from the Establishment's club. His first choice for Secretary of State was John McCloy, who had served in the Roosevelt and Truman administrations. McCloy, however, declined — he was busy in 1953, becoming chairman of both the Council on Foreign Relations and Chase Manhattan Bank.

Winding up as Secretary of State was John Foster Dulles. Dulles had been one of Woodrow Wilson's young protégés at the Paris Peace Conference. A founding member of the CFR, he had contributed articles to *Foreign Affairs* since its first issue. He was an in-law of the Rockefellers, and chairman of the board of the Rockefeller Foundation. He was also board chairman of the Carnegie Endowment for International Peace, where his choice for president of that body had been Alger Hiss.[10] An inveterate internationalist, he had been a delegate to the founding UN conference. Also a member of Truman's State Department, he had none of the earmarks one would expect of a Republican. Nevertheless, before the election, he began to parrot conservative slogans, just as Eisenhower did. So great was the disparity between Dulles' words and his personal reality that one of his biographies was entitled *The Actor*.

Dulles died in 1959. Eisenhower replaced him with Christian Herter, who had also been with Wilson at the Paris Peace Conference. Herter married into the Standard Oil fortune, and joined the CFR in 1929. A rabid proponent of the Atlantic Union, he wrote a book entitled *Toward an Atlantic Community*, and elaborated his views in a *Foreign Affairs* article called "Atlantica."[11]

For CIA director, Ike selected Allen Dulles, John Foster's brother. He, too, had been at the Paris Peace Conference. He joined the CFR in 1926 and later became its president.

Among the other administrators that Eisenhower drew from the Council were: Treasury Secretary Robert Anderson; Commerce Secretary Lewis Strauss; National Security Adviser Gordon Gray; HEW Under Secretary Nelson Rockefeller; Under Secretary of State for Economic Affairs, Douglas Dillon; and many others who held lesser positions.

Of course, Ike's choice for Vice President was Richard Nixon, about whom we will say more later.

The Eisenhower Years

The Eisenhower Presidency was what one would expect from a CFR administration.

• Ike did not reverse the Democratic trend of big spending and big government. His cumulative deficits were nearly five times greater than Harry Truman's, and the giant Department of Health, Education, and Welfare was added to the federal bureaucracy.

• In 1953, a measure known as the Bricker Amendment was introduced in Congress. It stipulated that no treaty signed by the U.S. could override the Constitution or infringe on the rights guaranteed Americans. It was born out of the painful retrospect of Yalta and the UN Charter. *Foreign Affairs*, that great paragon of "hospitality to divergent views," ran a 19-page denunciation of the Bricker Amendment as its lead article for October 1953. President Eisenhower toed the CFR line, calling the amendment's backers "nuts and crackpots."[12] Biographer Ambrose writes: "Eisenhower used all his persuasive powers — in stag dinners, at meetings, in private, in correspondence, even on the golf course — to kill the amendment."[13] And killed it was.

• Also in 1953, Congress established the Reece Committee to investigate tax-free foundations. For what was probably the first and last time, the CFR came under official scrutiny.

The Committee's findings stated:

> In the international field, foundations, and an interlock among some of them and certain intermediary organizations, have exercised a strong effect upon our foreign policy and upon public education in things international. This has been accomplished by vast propaganda, by supplying executives and advisers to government and by controlling much research in this area through the power of the purse. The net result of these combined efforts has been to promote "internationalism" in a particular sense — a form directed toward "world government" and a derogation of American "nationalism."[14]

The report also observed that major foundations "have actively supported attacks upon our social and government system and financed the promotion of socialism and collectivist ideas." The Com-

105

mittee declared that the CFR was "in essence an agency of the United States Government" and that its "productions are not objective but are directed overwhelmingly at promoting the globalist concept."[15]

Through political string-pulling and the mass media, the Establishment moved to wreck and discredit the Reece Committee. Congressman Wayne Hays set about disrupting its proceedings. René Wormser, counsel to the Committee, stated that "Mr. Hays told us one day that 'the White House' had been in touch with him and asked him if he would cooperate to kill the Committee."[16] Wormser summarized the Committee's discoveries and ordeals in his book *Foundations: Their Power and Influence.*

● 1954 marked the decline in influence of Joe McCarthy, who has been portrayed ever since as the vilest of slanderers. But even his critics, if they stopped to think about it, would have to acknowledge that no American has received more disparagement in this century than McCarthy himself. He has been reviled by nearly every Establishment journal in or out of print not because he denounced some minor government employees as subversive. The international bankers would not lose sleep over such people whether they were innocent or not. McCarthy was crucified because he discovered that there was more than a tip to the iceberg.

As Anthony Lukas explained in his *New York Times* article on the CFR:

> Though his nominal targets were Communists in Government, by the fifties few Communists retained important positions, and as McCarthy bulled ahead it became clear that his real target was the Eastern Establishment, which had run the nation's foreign policy for decades . . .
>
> McCarthy never explicitly attacked the Council (as he did the closely allied Institute of Pacific Relations). But many of those he denounced were or had been Council members: Frederick Vanderbilt Field, Alger Hiss, Lauchlin Currie, Owen Lattimore, Philip Jessup, Charles Bohlen and Dean Acheson.[17]

Stephen Ambrose notes that Eisenhower "was determined to destroy McCarthy."[18] But he left it to his subordinates, such as his confidante Paul Hoffman (CFR) and White House Chief of Staff Sherman Adams, to pressure Congress to censure the senator. Anyone who really believes McCarthy made wild accusations should read his exposé of George Marshall, *America's Retreat From Victory*, in which he scrupulously documented every charge, or read James J. Drummey's informative catechism about McCarthy in the May 13, 1987 issue of *The New American*.*

● In 1955, Eisenhower became the first President to attend a peacetime summit with the Soviets. While the meeting accomplished nothing for the West, it was a propaganda coup for the USSR. Photos of Eisenhower clinking cocktail glasses with Soviet leaders would be useful to demoralize the captive citizens of Eastern Europe, who looked to the U.S. as their hope for liberation.

These people, however, trusted in Eisenhower's anti-Communist rhetoric, which was occasionally broadcast over Radio Free Europe and expressed support for their cause.

The Poles revolted in June 1956, but were subdued by tanks. In late October of that year, the Hungarians succeeded in driving out the Soviets, and rejoiced in freedom for five days. Then the Soviets returned to the Hungarian border with 2,000 tanks, and the world looked to see if Eisenhower would act.

Ohio Congressman Michael Feighan later explained what happened next:

> Then the State Department, allegedly concerned about the delicate feelings of the Communist dictator Tito, sent him the following cabled assurances of our national intentions in the late afternoon of Friday, November 2, 1956: "The Government of the United States does not look with favor upon governments unfriendly to the Soviet Union on the borders of the Soviet Union."
>
> It was no accident or misjudgment of consequences which led the imperial Russian Army to reinvade Hungary at 4 a.m. on the morning of November 4, 1956. The cabled message to Tito was the go ahead

---

*The Drummey article factually corrects numerous distortions and falsehoods about Senator McCarthy that were spread to discourage further inquiry into the true nature of the Establishment. The article is highly commended and is available in reprint form for $2.00 from: Reprints, The New American, Post Office Box 8040, Appleton, Wisconsin 54913.

signal to the Russians because any American school boy knows that Tito is Moscow's Trojan Horse. It took less than 48 hours for him to relay this message of treason to his superiors in the Kremlin. All the world knows the terrible consequences of that go ahead signal.[19]

The Hungarians radioed: "Help us, not with advice, not with words, but with action! With soldiers and arms! Our ship is sinking, the light vanishes, the shades grow darker." Eisenhower, however, only gave them words.

A group of heroic Spanish pilots wanted to fly supplies to the freedom fighters. This plan required refueling in West Germany. Prince Michel Sturdza, former foreign minister of Romania, wrote in his book *Betrayal by Rulers:* "The Eisenhower government intervened immediately in Madrid and Bonn, with all the means of pressure at its command, demanding that the German government cancel the authorization already granted . . ."[20] The planes did not get through.

Soviet rule was bloodily restored to Hungary. Rebellion then died out in Eastern Europe for many years. Some commentators said it was because the USSR had liberalized its grip, and the people were now happy. Quite to the contrary, their spirit of rebellion was broken because they now knew that the West would never help them.

• Perhaps the greatest shame of the Eisenhower administration was allowing Fidel Castro to transform Cuba into the Soviets' first outpost in the Western Hemisphere. Despite reasonable evidence, some of the President's apologists long contended that Castro had not been a Communist when he originally took power. The controversy was ultimately dispelled by the dictator himself in his 1977 interview with Barbara Walters, when he said that he had been a Communist since his university days.

Of course, no hint of this was communicated to the American people. In 1957, Herbert L. Matthews (CFR) made the rebel Castro out to be the George Washington of Cuba in a series of *New York Times* articles that began with the front page of a Sunday edition. Castro also received plenty of favorable coverage and interviews on prime time TV. The public was given the "Chiang and Mao" treatment all over again. Cuban President Fulgencio Batista was suddenly depicted as a corrupt tyrant, while Castro was — in Matthews' words — "a man of ideals" with "strong ideas of liberty, democracy, social justice . . ."[21]

Former U.S. Ambassador to Cuba Earl E. T. Smith stated in a letter published in the *New York Times* in 1979:

> To the contrary, Castro could not have seized power in Cuba without the aid of the United States. American Government agencies and the United States press played a major role in bringing Castro to power. . . . As the U.S. Ambassador to Cuba during the Castro-Communist revolution of 1957-59, I had first-hand knowledge of the facts which brought about the rise of Fidel Castro. . . . The State Department consistently intervened — positively, negatively, and by innuendo — to bring about the downfall of President Fulgencio Batista, thereby making it possible for Fidel Castro to take over the Government of Cuba.[22]

While Castro's supporters overseas sent him modern military supplies, the U.S. government embargoed arms to Batista, whose troops fought with obsolescent weapons — many of them dating to World War I. On December 17, 1958, Ambassador Smith, acting on instructions from the Eisenhower State Department, asked Batista to step down.[23] He abdicated two weeks later.

In 1959, Castro, the new ruler of Cuba, was a guest speaker at Pratt House. Those who warned that he was a Communist were scoffed at. But three years later, he had Soviet missiles pointing at the USA.

JFK and the CFR

In 1960, John F. Kennedy was elected President. His family had long flirted at the outskirts of the Establishment. Arthur Schlesinger, Jr. noted in *A Thousand Days:*

> The New York Establishment had looked on Kennedy with some suspicion. This was mostly because of his father, whom it had long since blackballed as a maverick in finance and an isolationist in foreign

109

policy . . . . Now that he was President, however, they were prepared
to rally round . . .[24]

The Kennedys' relationship with the Establishment was loosely
fictionalized in *Captains and the Kings*, Taylor Caldwell's novel
about an Irish immigrant who seeks to make his son the first Cath-
olic President. The book, which was dramatized as a TV miniseries,
depicted a secret, conspiratorial power clique it called the "Committee for Foreign Studies." It is worth reading the book's somber
foreword, in which Caldwell warned that the Committee really exists, under another name.

Whether or not Kennedy belonged to the CFR has been disputed.
As a senator, he stated that he was a member — yet, strangely, his
name never appeared on the Council's official roster.

Like Franklin D. Roosevelt, John F. Kennedy was given an Establishment education, attending prep school and then Harvard.
And, like Roosevelt, he made an apparent play for Establishment favor
by writing an article for *Foreign Affairs* (October 1957) with a similar
title to FDR's: "A Democrat Looks at Foreign Policy." In it, Kennedy
referred to "distinguished individuals" who had served under Harry
Truman. Among those he named were John McCloy and Robert Lovett.
These were the two men whom Schlesinger, in *A Thousand Days*,
specified as the "present leaders" of "the American Establishment."[25]

As David Halberstam relates in the opening pages of *The Best
and the Brightest*, it was Lovett that President-elect Kennedy turned
to for counsel on his cabinet selection. In fact, JFK wanted Lovett
himself, offering him his choice of Secretary of State, Treasury, or
Defense. The aging "wise man" declined, but advised Kennedy on
who should fill the three positions. *Without exception,* Lovett's recommendations materialized in Kennedy's actual cabinet.

JFK spoke of a "New Frontier," but that term did not apply to his
administration. Some of the faces were new to Washington, but they
were dredged up from the same old breeding place — the Council
on Foreign Relations.

Like Eisenhower, Kennedy chose for Secretary of State the chairman of the Rockefeller Foundation — now Dean Rusk. Rusk had
not only been suggested by Lovett and Dean Acheson, but he had

written an article for the April 1960 *Foreign Affairs* on how a President should conduct foreign policy. That, presumably, just about cinched it. An old protégé of George Marshall in the Truman State Department, Rusk had been in the CFR since 1952.

The Council would dominate Rusk's staff. Anthony Lukas reported in the *New York Times*:

> Of the first 82 names on a list prepared to help President Kennedy staff his State Department, 63 were Council members. Kennedy once complained, "I'd like to have some new faces here, but all I get is the same old names."[26]

Some of the other CFR members Kennedy appointed to high stations were:

Douglas Dillon, Secretary of the Treasury
McGeorge Bundy, National Security Adviser
Walt Rostow, Deputy National Security Adviser
John McCone, CIA Director
Roswell Gilpatric, Deputy Secretary of Defense
Paul Nitze, Assistant Secretary of Defense
Henry Fowler, Under Secretary of the Treasury
George Ball, Under Secretary of State
Averell Harriman, Assistant Secretary of State for Far Eastern Affairs
Arthur Schlesinger, Jr., Special Assistant to the President
Jerome Wiesner, Special Assistant to the President
Angier Duke, Chief of Protocol
John McCloy, Chief of U.S. Disarmament Administration

John Kenneth Galbraith said: "Those of us who had worked for the Kennedy election were tolerated in the government for that reason and had a say, but foreign policy was still with the Council on Foreign Relations people."[27]

The Kennedy Years

Cuba was almost thematic to Kennedy's Presidency; it even seemed to haunt him at death, as investigators of his assassination

111

have periodically stumbled across links to Cuba, consequential or not. The Caribbean island marked what is usually regarded as Kennedy's greatest failure (the Bay of Pigs) and his greatest triumph (the Missile Crisis). But a degree of mythology has gathered around both of these events. The first was characterized by "blunder" and the second by "coincidence," the two favorite words of Establishment historiography.

The Bay of Pigs invasion (April 1961) was an attempt by a group of expatriate Cubans to return to their homeland and liberate it. They had been trained into an efficient brigade by the U.S. military. The mission ended in grievous defeat — owing to eleventh-hour decisions in Washington.

. The operation had two parts. First, there were to be three preliminary air strikes by Cuban pilots, based in Nicaragua, flying old B-26 bombers. The air raids were designed to destroy the Communists' small air force. Thanks to superb U.S. reconnaissance photos, the location of every Castro plane was known. There were to be three raids, and a total of forty-eight sorties.[28]

However, orders from the White House eventually reduced this to one raid with eight sorties. This inflicted some damage, but still left Castro with a viable air force.

Kennedy did not cancel the last of the air strikes until the brigade had already set sail, accompanied by the U.S. Navy. He made the decision at the urging of his CFR advisors (Rusk, Bundy, Adlai Stevenson)[29] and over the objections of his military consultants, who warned it would doom the mission. The official reason later given for the cancellations was that the bombings demonstrated too much U.S. "involvement" and might adversely affect "world opinion."

The invaders landed before dawn, and announced to rejoicing inhabitants that they had come to free Cuba. They penetrated far inland. The better part of a Communist militia regiment defected to their side. Then, to their shock and dismay, Castro's jets appeared in the sky, blasting away with guns and rockets. Two of the brigade's offshore supply vessels were sunk, and the others were forced to withdraw.

Kennedy could still have salvaged the mission by ordering nearby aircraft carriers to intervene. Richard Bissell (CIA) and Admiral

Arleigh Burke urged him to do so, but the Rusk group again prevailed.[30] The President did nothing.

After the Kennedy era, two books emerged as the authorities on that period: Ted Sorenson's *Kennedy* and Schlesinger's *A Thousand Days*. Both authors had been Kennedy advisors, both joined the CFR. And their books both downplayed the significance of the aborted bombing strikes, which in fact had been the crux of the invasion plan's success.

As in Hungary, anti-Communist freedom fighters were abandoned. And as in Korea, civilian advisors overruled the military in the conduct of warfare — with catastrophic results.

The Cuban Missile Crisis (October 1962) has been called JFK's "finest hour." We are told of how, after U.S. reconnaissance planes spotted Soviet missiles in Cuba, Kennedy blockaded the island, stood up to the Russians and made them back down.

Of course, there never would have been a missile crisis if the Bay of Pigs invasion had gone off unhindered. This and a few other points have been commonly overlooked.

Nineteen Soviet ships passed the vaunted blockade unimpeded.[31] Only one vessel was ever halted and inspected — the *Marcula*, an American-built ship of Lebanese registry, sailing under Soviet charter.

Little attention has been given to the concessions Kennedy made to get the nuclear weapons out of Cuba. Columnist Walter Lippmann — a founding member of the CFR who had been in Colonel House's old "Inquiry" — suggested that the United States dismantle its missile bases in Turkey as an exchange. Two days later, Soviet dictator Nikita Khrushchev made the same proposal. In the end, the United States removed all of its intermediate-range missiles, not only from Turkey, but from England and Italy as well. The public was told that this was a coincidence, that the weapons were obsolete and due for withdrawal anyway. General Curtis LeMay, former head of the Strategic Air Command, sharply contradicted this in his book *America Is in Danger*, pointing out that the missiles had just become operational!

A further concession made by Kennedy was a pledge of no more invasion attempts against Cuba. The White House ordered that anti-

Castro militants in the U.S. be rounded up, and their guns and boats confiscated.

The President originally demanded on-site UN inspection of the Soviet missile withdrawal, but later backed down, settling for Moscow's promise. To this day, no one knows with certainty if the missiles were really evacuated or simply shifted into caves and underground facilities.

Kennedy's "finest hour" was, on balance, a greater triumph for the Soviets: it set the stage for the strategic nuclear superiority they would later enjoy in Europe, and it guaranteed the preservation of their Cuban colony.

In handling the crisis, Kennedy relied not only on his usual staff, but called upon the services of Lovett, McCloy, and Acheson. The final agreement was worked out by McCloy at his home in Stamford, Connecticut, where he hosted the Soviet Deputy Foreign Minister, Vasily Kuznetsov.[32]

Whatever we may say about John F. Kennedy, he remains one of the most esteemed U.S. Presidents. A man with an independent streak, he was apparently never a true "insider." Some have even speculated that his assassination, still clothed in mystery, may have resulted from an attempt to break with the Establishment. Though it may have no significance, both McCloy and Allen Dulles — the chairman and former president of the CFR — served on the Warren Commission investigating the President's death.

The Establishment's fear of Robert Taft
(at right, with Representative Fred Hartley)
generated the candidacy of Dwight Eisenhower.

Nixon and Eisenhower exult at
the 1952 Republican National Convention.

Ike with Bernard Baruch

The President with a few of the many CFR men in his administration.
Left to right, Eisenhower, Secretary of State John Foster Dulles,
Security Adviser Dillon Anderson (joined the Council subsequent to
appointment), and Commerce Secretary Lewis Strauss.

116

The Reece Committee. The Establishment
sought to abort the investigation.

October 31, 1956: Hungarian freedom fighters
take aim at Communist secret police.

Former Ambassador to Cuba Earl E. T. Smith (left) recounted the U.S. help given Castro (right) during his climb to power.

Lovett and President-elect Kennedy after their meeting

Kennedy's Secretary of Defense, Robert McNamara (left),
and Secretary of State, Dean Rusk (center),
were both chosen on Lovett's recommendation.

Bay of Pigs invaders were denied
the critical air support they had been promised.
Above, captured invaders are marched off to prison in Havana.

Chapter 8

The Establishment's War In Vietnam

The Vietnam War is a dismal remembrance to its veterans, many of whom still ask why we went and why we lost. No single event has brought America more social transformation. We are prone to accept that transformation as the unintended by-product of a war that was a blunder. But as we have seen, historical "blunders," from the Great Crash to Pearl Harbor to Cuba, have a convenient way of serving the interests of the backstage globalists who run our country.

French control of Indochina ended in 1954. CFR chronicler Robert Shulzinger notes that the Council's "study groups on Southeast Asia, meeting in 1953-54, prepared the ground for the United States to take over France's role as the outside power waging war against local leftist insurrection."[1] The groups stressed the importance of Southeast Asia to American interests.

After the Geneva Conference artificially divided Vietnam into North and South, the U.S. government helped depose Emperor Bao Dai — symbol of Vietnamese unity — and backed Ngo Dinh Diem as the South's prime minister. Eventually Washington turned on Diem as well; the Kennedy administration's collusion in the coup that overthrew him (and ultimately resulted in his brutal murder) is now widely documented.

In Vietnam, as in Korea, we engaged in war without declaring it. C. L. Sulzberger stated in the *New York Times* in 1966:

Dulles fathered SEATO with the deliberate purpose, as he explained to me, of providing the U.S. President with legal authority to intervene in Indochina. When Congress approved SEATO it signed the first of a series of blank checks yielding authority over Vietnam policy.[2]

Later, President Lyndon Baines Johnson obtained the power to escalate the war from Congress through the Tonkin Gulf Resolution. This transpired after an alleged assault on U.S. destroyers by North Vietnamese torpedo boats — an incident whose authenticity many later questioned. Doubts intensified after it was revealed that the Johnson administration had drafted the resolution before the skirmish took place.

The matter has since been settled rather decisively by Admiral James Stockdale, a former navy fighter pilot, in his 1984 book *In Love & War*. Stockdale, a Congressional Medal of Honor winner who spent more than seven years as a POW in North Vietnam, had been on the scene during the supposed Tonkin Gulf attack. Although both destroyers were firing rounds, Stockdale did not detect any Vietnamese boats in the vicinity during an hour and a half of overflight.

It was now the nuclear age. At a televised dinner of the Council on Foreign Relations (January 12, 1954), John Foster Dulles had declared that, thanks to our nuclear arsenal, we could deter Soviet aggression with the threat of "massive retaliation." But this new trend in U.S. policy had a corollary: if we exasperated the Soviets, it was claimed, they too might push the button. Wars against Communism would therefore have to be limited and not aimed at winning. Thus, in Establishment dogma, the idea of victory in war was now not only an anachronism: it was a liability.

As James E. King, Jr. wrote in *Foreign Affairs* in 1957:

> Moreover, we must be prepared to fight limited actions ourselves. Otherwise we shall have made no advance beyond "massive retaliation," which tied our hands in conflicts involving less than our survival. And *we must be prepared to lose limited actions*. No limitation could survive our disposition to elevate every conflict in which our interests are affected to the level of total conflict with survival at stake. Armed conflict can be limited only if aimed at limited objectives and fought

with limited means. If we or our enemy relax the limits on either objectives or means, survival *will* be at stake, whether the issue is worth it or not.[3] (First emphasis added.)

In Korea, where the Establishment's interest was in accrediting the UN's police powers, stalemate had been considered an acceptable substitute for victory; now that we were outside of a UN context, however, defeat itself was acceptable. This was not explained to the brave Americans who fought and bled in Vietnam. They found out the hard way.

Mismanaging the War

In Vietnam, as in Korea, extraordinary restrictions were placed on the U.S. military. These, known as the "rules of engagement," were not declassified until 1985, when twenty-six pages in the *Congressional Record* were required to summarize them.

• The Air Force was repeatedly refused permission to bomb those targets that the Joint Chiefs of Staff deemed most strategic.

• U.S. troops were given a general order not to fire at the Vietcong until fired upon.

• Vehicles more than two hundred yards off the Ho Chi Minh Trail could not be bombed. (Enemy supply trucks, forewarned of approaching U.S. planes, had only to temporarily divert off the trail to escape destruction.)

• A North Vietnamese MIG could not be struck if spotted on a runway; only if airborne and showing hostile intent.

• Surface-to-air missile sites could not be bombed while under construction; only after they became operational.

• Enemy forces could not be pursued if they crossed into Laos or Cambodia. This gave the Communists a safe sanctuary just fifty miles from Saigon. Even the brief incursion into Cambodia that Richard Nixon authorized in 1970 was hamstrung by a variety of rules and regulations authored in Washington.

Lieutenant General Ira C. Eaker observed:

> Our political leaders elected to fight a land war, where every advantage lay with the enemy, and to employ our vast sea and air superiority in very limited supporting roles only.

Surprise, perhaps the greatest of the principles of war . . . was deliberately sacrificed when our leaders revealed our strategy and tactics to the enemy. . . .

The enemy was told . . . that we would not bomb populated areas, heavy industry, canals, dams, and other critical targets — and thus sanctuaries were established by us along the Chinese border and around Haiphong and Hanoi. This permitted the enemy to concentrate antiaircraft defenses around the North Vietnamese targets that our Air Force *was* permitted to attack — greatly increasing our casualities. Missiles, oil and ammunition were permitted to enter Haiphong harbor unmolested and without protest.[4]

Such restrictions were equaled in perfidy by the indirect support the United States provided North Vietnam by boosting trade with the Soviet Bloc (which furnished some eighty percent of Hanoi's war supplies).

This commerce was one of the Establishment's pet projects. Zbigniew Brzezinski, writing in *Foreign Affairs*, had called for economic aid to Eastern Europe as early as 1961.[5] The journal even featured an article by Ted Sorenson bluntly titled "Why We Should Trade with the Soviets."[6]

The actualization of such trade seems to have begun with David Rockefeller's trip to Moscow in 1964. The *Chicago Tribune* reported on September 12 of that year:

David Rockefeller, president of Chase Manhattan bank, briefed President Johnson today on his recent meeting with Premier Nikita S. Khrushchev of Russia.

Rockefeller told Johnson that during the two-hour talk, the Red leader said the United States and the Soviet Union "should do more trade." Khrushchev, according to Rockefeller, said he would like to see the United States extend long-term credits to the Russians.

On October 7, 1966 — with the war now at full tilt — Johnson stated:

We intend to press for legislative authority to negotiate trade agreements which could extend most-favored-nation tariff treatment to European Communist states . . .

We will reduce export controls on East-West trade with respect to hundreds of non-strategic items.[7]

Six days later the *New York Times* told its readers:

The United States put into effect today one of President Johnson's proposals for stimulating East-West trade by removing restrictions on the export of more than four hundred commodities to the Soviet Union and Eastern Europe.

Among the "non-strategic items" cleared for export were: petroleum, aluminum, scrap metal, synthetic rubber, tires, air navigation equipment, ground and marine radar, rifle cleaning compounds, diethylene glycol (used in the manufacture of explosives), computers, electric motors, rocket engines, diesel engines, diesel fuel, and various truck and automobile parts.[8] Almost anything short of a weapon itself was classified "non-strategic." In times of war, however, few commodities are truly *not* strategic — even food, seemingly innocuous, is vital for an army to prosecute war.

Did the Johnson administration's easing of restrictions influence the flow of goods from Warsaw Pact nations to Hanoi? Two weeks after the announcement, the *New York Times* reported (October 27, 1966):

The Soviet Union and its allies agreed at the conference of their leaders in Moscow last week to grant North Vietnam assistance in material and money amounting to about one billion dollars.

Bombing the Ho Chi Minh Trail to interdict the enemy's supplies made no sense when we were enriching the source of those supplies. Trade that would have been labeled "treason" in World War II was called "building bridges" during the Vietnam War. This, along with the self-destructive restrictions on the military, were two of the reasons why we could not defeat tiny North Vietnam, whereas it had taken us less than four years to overcome the combined might of the German and Japanese empires.

Why Did We Go to Vietnam?

Analysts such as David Halberstam believe John F. Kennedy increased our commitment in Vietnam as an antidote to humiliation: that after the Bay of Pigs and a bullying Khrushchev gave JFK in Vienna, the President wanted to show the Russians — if not his right-wing critics — that he had backbone.

But if Kennedy really wanted to atone for the Bay of Pigs, he didn't have to go to Vietnam — all he had to do was send our armed forces against Fidel Castro, and it is doubtful that the tin-pot dictator's fledgling regime would have lasted another day.

If you wanted to fight Communism, Vietnam was a terrible place to pick. Our supply lines had to stretch halfway around the world. There were no fronts; the enemy was nearly invisible, not only due to the jungle terrain, but because the Vietcong, who wore no uniforms, looked like ordinary villagers. A glance at the map shows Vietnam is a narrow country whose extensive border with Laos and Cambodia always ensured the Communists of nearby refuge. The French had not been able to hold out there with 300,000 troops, which hardly imbued the enterprise with optimism. And the government of South Vietnam, thanks in part to U.S. meddling, was unstable, fraught with coups and corruption. No, Vietnam was not a utopian battlefield on which to confront Communism.

In dissecting the Establishment psyche that produced our Vietnam entanglement, it should first be noted that the Establishment was, in the early 1960's, under heavy fire. Traditionally, the American people seem to be more wary of the loyalty of our public servants during Democratic administrations. Under Truman, there was an uproar concerning the State Department. Not long after Alger Hiss's conviction, Joe McCarthy made his famous Wheeling, West Virginia speech. Four months later, however, Truman sent U.S. soldiers to battle the North Koreans. This tended to deflect, temporarily at least, criticism that his administration was soft on Communism.

From 1953 to 1961, the Oval Office housed a Republican — albeit a nominal one — and conservatives' scrutiny of Washington became largely inert. But, after the reinstatement of the Democrats under Kennedy, the American right experienced a renaissance.

• In 1961, the largest anti-Communist rally in American history was held at the Hollywood Bowl, and J. Edgar Hoover's *Masters of Deceit* hit the best-seller list.

• In 1962, three exposés of the Council on Foreign Relations were published: *The Invisible Government*, by former FBI man Dan Smoot; *The Welfare Staters*, by Colonel Victor J. Fox; and *America's Unelected Rulers: The Council on Foreign Relations*, by Kent and Phoebe Courtney.

• Also in 1962, the American Legion passed a resolution condemning the CFR "as being actively engaged in destroying the Constitution and sovereignty of the United States of America," and the Daughters of the American Revolution adopted a resolution petitioning Congress to investigate the Council.

• *American Mercury* magazine was regularly blasting both the CFR and the international bankers linked to it.

• The recently formed John Birch Society was using its educational program to counteract Communism and its Establishment sympathizers.

• And the Goldwater movement was picking up, striving to restore the GOP to its tradition.

Newsweek and the *New York Times* may have ignored it, but Americans were at war with the Establishment, especially those figures in the Kennedy administration. The decision to go to Vietnam took much of the steam out of these movements. Those who hated Communism were now given a war against it — but it was an endless, no-win war, one that would be dragged out until the nation at large renounced ever fighting Communism again.

The Manipulators

We have noted a number of times in this book that the Establishment is not "conservative," despite PR to the contrary. In *The Strawberry Statement: Notes of A College Revolutionary*, James Kunen quoted a fellow student radical's report about a 1968 SDS convention:

Also at the Convention, men from Business International Round-tables — the meetings sponsored by Business International — tried to buy up a few radicals. These men are the world's leading industrialists and they convene to decide how our lives are going to go. . . .
They offered to finance our demonstrations in Chicago.
We were also offered Esso (Rockefeller) money. They want us to make a lot of radical commotion so they can look more in the center as they move to the left.[9]

Yet it was members of this same Establishment who were at the helm during the Vietnam War. All of our ambassadors to Saigon from 1963 to 1973 — Henry Cabot Lodge, Maxwell Taylor, and Ellsworth Bunker — were members of the Council. LBJ sought John McCloy for that particular job, but he turned it down.

One of the chief engineers of the Vietnam fiasco was Walt Rostow, chairman of the State Department's policy planning council from 1961 until 1966, when he became National Security Adviser. The *Washington Post* of August 10, 1966, called him "the Rock of Johnson's Viet Policy." But was Rostow a hawk? A conservative right-winger? Like his equally prominent brother, Eugene Victor Debs Rostow (named for the Socialist Party leader Eugene Debs), Walt Rostow had been a member of the CFR since 1955. He was rejected for employment in the Eisenhower administration three times because he could not pass security checks. In 1960, in his book *The United States in the World Arena*, Rostow declared that:

it is a legitimate American national objective to see removed from all nations — including the United States — the right to use substantial military force to pursue their own interests. Since this residual right is the root of national sovereignty and the basis for the existence of an international arena of power, it is, therefore, an American interest to see an end to nationhood as it has been historically defined.[10]

Not exactly the words of a die-hard patriot. Rostow called for unilateral disarmament and an international police force. In 1962, there was a stir in Washington when Congress learned of a secret State Department report Rostow had produced entitled "Basic National Security Policy." It discussed our "overlapping interests" with Communist nations, called for recognition of Red China and East Germany, and said we should bar assistance to freedom fighters behind the Iron Curtain.

Robert Strange McNamara, who was Secretary of Defense during the first half of the war, was hardly a militarist. Schlafly and Ward, in their book *The Betrayers*, summarized McNamara's impact on U.S. defense capabilities. By the time he left office in 1968 he had:

... reduced our nuclear striking force by 50% while the Soviets had increased theirs by 300%.

... caused the U.S. to lose its lead in nuclear delivery vehicles.

... scrapped ¾ of our multimegaton missiles.

... cut back the originally planned 2,000 Minutemen to 1,000.

... destroyed all our intermediate and medium-range missiles.

... cancelled our 24-megaton bomb.

... scrapped 1,455 of 2,710 bombers left over from the Eisenhower Administration.

... disarmed 600 of the remaining bombers of their strategic nuclear weapons.

... frozen the number of Polaris subs at 41, refusing to build any more missile-firing submarines.

... refused to allow development of any new weapons systems except the TFX (F-111).

... cancelled Skybolt, Pluto, Dynasoar and Orion [missile systems].

It was aptly noted that McNamara, who even called for the abolition of our armed forces reserves, had inflicted more damage on America's defenses than the Soviets could have achieved in a nuclear first strike! He continually exasperated the Joint Chiefs on Vietnam policy, forbidding sorties against strategic targets and keeping our troops in short supply. After resigning, he stated, "I am a world citizen now," and was appointed president of the World Bank. During his tenure there, the Bank's annual lending grew from $1 billion to $11.5 billion; in 1978 he oversaw a $60 million loan to Communist Vietnam. More recently, CFR member McNamara has been appearing on television as a peacenik, and has coauthored articles for

Foreign Affairs opposing the construction of SDI (the Strategic Defense Initiative).

Averell Harriman served as Kennedy's Assistant Secretary of State for Far Eastern Affairs, and was later chief negotiator at the Paris peace talks. Harriman, as we have noted, was a trailblazer of trade with the Bolsheviks. He was instrumental in bringing the Communists to power in Romania.[11] Soviet Ambassador Anatoly Dobrynin customarily attended Harriman's birthday parties, and even vacationed with him in Florida.[12]

Another critical Establishment figure was William Bundy, appointed Assistant Secretary of State for Far Eastern Affairs in 1964, the same year he became a director of the CFR. The Pentagon Papers later exposed him as a major architect of our Vietnam policy. It was he who "prematurely" drafted the Tonkin Gulf Resolution. And it was his brother, McGeorge Bundy (CFR) who, as National Security Adviser, oversaw the mission that resulted in the Tonkin incident. McGeorge went on to become president of the Ford Foundation.

William Bundy was certainly no flag-waving anti-Communist. He had once donated $400 to the Alger Hiss defense fund.[13] In 1972, David Rockefeller chose him as the new editor of *Foreign Affairs*, replacing Hamilton Fish Armstrong, who was retiring after fifty years of service. Under Bundy's guidance, *Foreign Affairs* began to repudiate Cold War attitudes. J. Robert Moskin, writing in *Town & Country*, notes that "Bundy surprised his critics by publishing articles in *Foreign Affairs* that questioned the wisdom of American intervention in Southeast Asia."[14]

Thus a grand paradox crystallized. Bundy had helped get us into the no-win war; now he edited a journal suggesting that Vietnam proved the futility of challenging Communism. His apologists believe that he was being penitent after realizing his errors in Vietnam. But there remains another possibility: that it was planned this way.

Further insight can be derived by tracing the career of Bundy's father-in-law — Dean Acheson.

Acheson and the "Wise Men"

Acheson, like Bundy, attended Groton, Yale, and Harvard Law School. At the latter he became a protégé of the leftist professor

Felix Frankfurter, who got him a job in Washington. Even before the Soviet Union was recognized by the U.S., Joseph Stalin hired Acheson to represent Bolshevik interests in America. During the Roosevelt and Truman administrations, he alternated between private law practice and public service. In 1945, he told a Madison Square Garden rally of the Soviet-American Friendship Society: "We understand and agree with the Soviet leaders that to have friendly governments along her borders is essential both for the security of the Soviet Union and for the peace of the world."[15] This attitude was reflected in Acheson's diplomacy. While Under Secretary of State, he approved a $90 million loan for Poland, even though our ambassador to that country, Arthur Bliss Lane, protested because of the Communist government's severe human rights abuses. To secure the loan, the Poles had retained Acheson's law firm, which made over $50,000 on the deal.[16]

Donald Hiss, brother of Soviet spy Alger Hiss, was Acheson's law partner. In the State Department, Acheson helped Alger himself, as well as several other men later identified as spies or security risks (John Stewart Service, John Carter Vincent, Lauchlin Currie) to high positions. He promoted Service even after the FBI had caught him passing secrets to Communist agents. It was this Acheson clique that helped push China into Mao Tse-tung's hands, causing a furor in the U.S. When Ambassador Lane heard that Acheson had been appointed Secretary of State, he said: "God help the United States!"[17] Acheson became a byword to many Americans. On December 15, 1950, the Republicans in the House of Representatives resolved *unanimously* that he be removed from office.

He was — by the voters' repudiation of the Truman administration in 1952. And many breathed a sigh of relief. But although his public career was over, his influence was not. Acheson's law offices were strategically located across Lafayette Park from the White House. He became an unofficial advisor to the Kennedy, Johnson, and Nixon administrations. Nixon even had a phone installed in Acheson's winter home in Antigua.[18]

Acheson had a crucial role in bringing about the Vietnam escalation. The meaning of this must be weighed in light of his past, even though some claimed his views on Communism hardened in old age.

Lyndon Baines Johnson, it should be noted, had inherited the Presidency after John F. Kennedy's death in 1963. He also inherited Kennedy's Establishment advisors, with whom he did not harmonize well. Unlike JFK, he had little in common with these men. He was not a Harvard-CFR intellectual. A graduate of Southwest Texas State Teacher's College, he had risen to prominence in Congress. Kennedy chose him as his running mate in 1960 for his capacity to win Southern votes and his influence within the Senate. When Johnson sought to retain the Presidency in the 1964 election, the Establishment backed him to the hilt: Barry Goldwater was the Republican nominee and, as such, was the first GOP Presidential candidate in decades it had not controlled. Indeed, Goldwater represented nearly everything the Establishment was against. For that reason, the mass media was arrayed against him, and he was falsely characterized as a fanatic who would start a nuclear war and snatch social security checks from the elderly. These scare tactics sufficed to give Johnson a landslide victory. Nevertheless, relations remained shaky between LBJ and the Establishment administrators surrounding him. He resented their arrogance, but also admired their intellects. In any case, he probably trusted that they would not do anything deliberately contrary to America's interests.

During the Vietnam War, Johnson met periodically with an advisory group he himself called "the Wise Men" — fourteen VIP's, twelve of whom were CFR members. Acheson was chief among these. McCloy, Lovett, and Harriman were included in the gatherings.

In 1965, Johnson was reluctant to heighten our role in Vietnam any further, and explained his reasons before the assembled patriarchs. The Isaacson and Thomas book, *The Wise Men*, which is intended as a tribute to some of these men, relates:

> Acheson fidgeted impatiently as he listened to Johnson wallow in self-pity. Finally, he could stand it no longer. "I blew my top and told him he was wholly right on Vietnam," Acheson wrote [to Truman], "that he had no choice except to press on, that explanations were not as important as successful action."

131

Acheson's scolding emboldened the others. "With this lead my colleagues came thundering in like the charge of the Scots Greys at Waterloo," Acheson exulted to the former President. "They were fine; old Bob Lovett, usually cautious, was all out."[19]

In effect, the Wise Men seized Johnson by the collar, kicked his butt, and told him to escalate. They were almost unanimous in this exhortation. William Bundy said that this was the occasion when "America committed to land war on the mainland of Asia. No more critical decision was made."[20]

Each year, as the war intensified, Johnson consulted the Wise Men, who told him to push on.

But in private they felt differently. Halberstam notes: "As early as May 1964 Dean Acheson stopped a White House friend at a cocktail party and said he thought Vietnam was going to turn out much worse than they expected, that it was all much weaker than the reports coming in . . ."[21] And Acheson's correspondence from that period demonstrates pessimism about the war he did not share with the President.

Averell Harriman played the hawk for Johnson, so much that he received a scolding from former Kennedy aide Arthur Schlesinger. Harriman brought Schlesinger to his hotel room, took a stiff drink, and told him confidentially that he was *against* the war.[22]

William Bundy wrote in a memoir that he had misgivings about the pro-escalation advice the elder statesmen had given the President, but he did not so advise Johnson.

Referring to Acheson, Lovett, and McCloy, *The Wise Men* asks:

> Even in 1965, they harbored serious doubts about committing U.S. troops to the defense of the government of South Vietnam. Why did they fail to convey those doubts to the President?[23]

That, of course, is the $64,000 question! But Isaacson and Thomas supply no satisfying answer.

In March 1968, in *Science & Mechanics*, a dozen top U.S. military officers made individual statements concerning Vietnam. They summarized how the restrictions on the armed forces had prolonged the war, and asserted that the U.S. could win in a few months if only it would adopt realistic strategy, which they outlined. Such views were considered extremely dangerous in Establishment circles.

That same month, Johnson was scheduled to see the Wise Men again. He expected that, as usual, he would be patted on the back and told to continue the war. But before the conference, the Wise Men received negative briefings about the war from three individuals whom the wily Acheson had been consulting over the previous month.

The next morning, Johnson sat down with the Wise Men, and received the shock of his life. Based on that single set of briefings, they had been wondrously transformed from hawks to doves: the war, they said, was a rotten idea after all. Acheson, seated next to the President, bluntly informed him that thoughts of victory were illusory, and that the time had come for the disengagement process.[24] *The Wise Men* tells us:

> General Maxwell Taylor was appalled and "amazed" at the defection. "The same mouths that said a few months before to the President, 'You're on the right course, but do more,' were now saying that the policy was a failure," recalled Taylor. He could think of no explanation, except that "my Council on Foreign Relations friends were living in the cloud of *The New York Times*."[25]

Johnson hit the roof.

> When the meeting broke up, he grabbed a few of the stragglers and began to rant. "Who the hell brainwashed those friends of yours?" he demanded of George Ball. He stopped General Taylor. "What did those damn briefers say to you?"

This, then, is the picture that now appears to be emerging. For years, the Wise Men had prodded LBJ deeper into Vietnam, until he had committed over a half million combat troops. Now, in effect, they said: "It's all a mistake — sorry about that," and left him holding the bag. It was he, not they, who bore the fury of a rebelling America.

Johnson briefly entertained thoughts of defiantly pushing for victory, but realized he would receive no support from the political infrastructure surrounding him. LBJ's March 1968 meeting with the Wise Men was his last. According to Townsend Hoopes, then Under Secretary of the Air Force, "The President was visibly shocked by the magnitude of the defection."[26] One aide reported that it left him "deeply shaken."[27] Five days later, a broken man, he announced on television: " . . . I shall not seek, and I will not accept, the nomination of my party for another term as your President." A surprised nation was left to conclude that this had been prompted by the good showing Bobby Kennedy and Eugene McCarthy were making in the Democratic primaries.

Ultimately, culpability for the war would be focused on the military. In 1971, Louisiana Congressman John Rarick declared:

> The My Lai massacre, the sentencing of Lt. Calley to life imprisonment, "The Selling of the Pentagon," and the so-called Pentagon papers are leading examples of attempts to shift all the blame to the military in the eyes of the people.
>
> But no one identifies the Council on Foreign Relations — the CFR — a group of some 1400 Americans which includes as members almost every top level decision and policy maker in the Vietnam War.
>
> CBS tells the people it wants them to know what is going on and who is to blame. Why doesn't CBS tell the American people about the CFR and let the people decide whom to blame for the Vietnam fiasco — the planners and top decision makers of a closely knit financial-industrial-intellectual aristocracy or military leaders under civilian control who have had little or no voice in the overall policies and operations and who are forbidden by law to tell the American people their side.
>
> The My Lai incident, "The Selling of the Pentagon," and the Pentagon papers have not scratched the surface in identifying the responsible kingmakers of the new ruling royalty, let alone in exposing the CFR role in Vietnam. Who will tell the people the truth if those who control "the right to know machinery" also control the government?[28]

The war in Vietnam was not created by conservative "hawks." It was created by luminaries of the CFR — whose globalism and tolerance of Communism is a matter of record. As in the world wars, it was these two systems that emerged as the victors. At home, nationalism — the anathema of the CFR — hit an all-time low, as embittered young Americans lost faith in their country. And on the other side of the world, little North Vietnam, like North Korea and Cuba before it, was allowed prestigious triumph against the mighty USA. Furthermore, thanks in part to the war's sapping of the Defense budget, the Soviets, militarily inferior at the war's outset, had reached parity with us by its end.

The Vietnam War is a mystery only if seen through the accumulated myths surrounding it — such as that it resulted from blunder, or from overconfident jingoism. Viewed, however, as an exercise in deliberate mismanagement, it ceases to mystify, for its outcome fulfilled precisely the goals traditional to the CFR.

1968: President Johnson consults with advisors on forthcoming Vietnam peace talks. What's wrong with the picture? Everyone in it, except Johnson, was a member of the CFR. Left to right: Andrew Goodpaster, Averell Harriman, Cyrus Vance, Maxwell Taylor, Walt Rostow, Richard Helms, William Bundy, Nicholas Katzenbach, Dean Rusk, Johnson. (Helms was not a Council member at the time, but later joined.)

David Rockefeller's 1964 trip to Moscow helped pave the way for wartime trade with the Soviet bloc.

The Establishment has frequently exploited the native anti-Communism of the American people to inveigle them into destructive circumstances. In Vietnam, the "rules of engagement," not declassified until 1985, precluded a U.S. victory.

Barry Goldwater's Presidential run worried the Establishment.

Admiral James Stockdale made a shocking revelation about Tonkin Gulf.

Dan Smoot (left), former assistant to J. Edgar Hoover, and Congressman John Rarick (right) were among those who sought to expose the CFR.

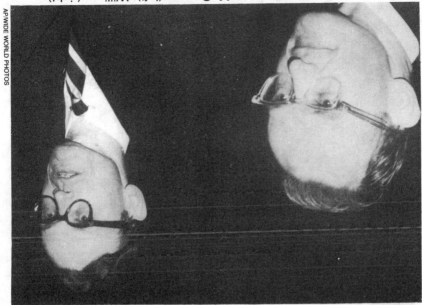

The Bundy brothers — McGeorge (left), William (right)

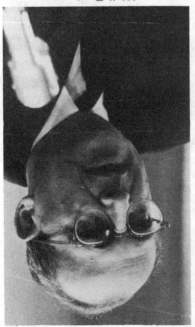

Walt Rostow

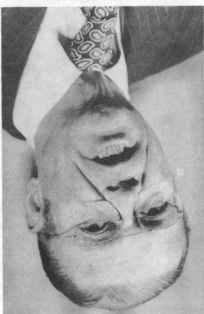

Robert Strange McNamara

Johnson, stunned by the about-face of "the Wise Men,"
prepares speech announcing he will not seek reelection.

Were they meant to lose?

Chapter 9

The Unknown Nixon

In 1968, the American voters were looking for an escape hatch from Vietnam. Richard Nixon won the Presidential election, partly because his Democratic opponent, Hubert Humphrey (CFR), had been Johnson's Vice President, and already bore the war's stigma by association. Liberals wanted an immediate pullout from Vietnam; conservatives wanted a swift, decisive victory. Nixon gave them neither. Instead, four more years of protracted warfare widened America's divisiveness.

Richard Nixon, like Harry Truman and Lyndon Johnson, was not a member of the Establishment by birth and breeding, but his political career became inextricably linked to it. In 1946, Nixon was a small-town lawyer who had never held any elected office, not even town dogcatcher. Yet six years later he was Vice President-elect of the United States. His supersonic success compared to that of his running mate, Dwight Eisenhower.

Nixon's political odyssey began with a race for the House seat of California's 12th District. In the election, he faced Democrat Jerry Voorhis, a ten-year veteran of Congress. Voorhis was an enemy of the banking establishment; he had introduced a bill calling for the dissolution of the Federal Reserve System, and had denounced deficit spending and the international bankers who profit from it in his book *Out of Debt, Out of Danger*.

It was reported that New York financing began to support the Nixon campaign. William Costello, in *The Facts About Nixon* (1960), noted:

The congressman [Voorhis] said the representative of a large New York financial house made a trip to California in October 1945, about the time the Committee of One Hundred was picking Nixon, and called on a number of influential people in Southern California. The emissary "bawled them out" for permitting Voorhis, whom he described as "one of the most dangerous men in Washington," to continue to represent a part of California in the House. As a consequence, Voorhis said, "many of the advertisements which ran in the district newspapers advocating my defeat came to the papers from a large advertising agency in Los Angeles, rather than from any source within the Twelfth District."[1]

Nixon won the Congressional seat. Then in 1950 he was elected to the Senate after a dirty campaign that earned him the nickname "Tricky Dick." Nixon had a hand in exposing Alger Hiss, and although his contribution has been somewhat exaggerated,[2] it gave him an impressive anti-Communist credential that helped the Eisenhower ticket supplant Taft and MacArthur in 1952.

Certainly Nixon was not an "Old Guard" Republican. He was an internationalist with a yen for foreign aid. Congressman Nixon traveled with Christian Herter to Europe as part of the committee that laid the groundwork for the Marshall Plan. In 1947, he brought forward a resolution in the House calling for "a General Conference of the United Nations pursuant to Article 109 for the purpose of making the United Nations capable of enacting, interpreting, and enforcing world law to prevent war."[3] He introduced a similar resolution in 1948.

Nixon served two full terms as Eisenhower's Vice President, rubbing shoulders with CFR members and getting to know the Establishment. In 1960, he was the GOP's candidate for the Presidency, opposing John F. Kennedy.

New York Governor Nelson Rockefeller had also sought the Republican nomination in 1960; he even observed ritual by having an article entitled "Purpose and Policy" published in *Foreign Affairs* that April. Rockefeller was an archetypal Establishment globalist. Speaking at Harvard, he declared that "the nation-state, standing alone, threatens in many ways to seem as anachronistic as the Greek city-state eventually became in ancient times."[4]

Rockefeller could not win the support of enough grass roots party members to secure the nomination. But he did have the power to influence Nixon. Before the Republican National Convention took place in Chicago, the GOP platform committee was working out a conservative program. But as Theodore White said in *The Making of the President, 1960*: "Whatever honor they might have been able to carry from their services on the platform committee had been wiped out. A single night's meeting of the two men in a millionaire's triplex apartment in Babylon-by-the-Hudson, eight hundred and thirty miles away, was about to overrule them . . ."[5] Nixon flew to New York to see Rockefeller at his Fifth Avenue apartment. The result was a new platform to Rockefeller's liking.

Barry Goldwater called this tryst "the Munich of the Republican Party." Edith Kermit Roosevelt commented:

> It was not as a Standard Oil heir, but as an Establishment heir, a man of "world good will," that Nelson Rockefeller forced the Republicans to rewrite their platform. Thus the Republican platform was in effect a carbon copy of the Democratic platform drawn up by Chester Bowles, CFR member and former trustee of the Rockefeller Foundation.[6]

Since the Establishment again had *de facto* control of both parties' candidates, Nixon's defeat that November did not worry them. Ultimately, it didn't bother Nixon either, since he had only to wait for his ship to come in.

In 1961, Nixon joined the Council on Foreign Relations.* In 1962, a conservative, Joe Shell, was bidding to become the Republican nominee for California's governorship. One week after Shell told Nelson Rockefeller he would not support him for President in 1964, he learned that Nixon had entered the gubernatorial race.[7] The former VP defeated Shell in the primary, but lost the election. It was then conventionally regarded that Nixon was washed up in politics.

---

* In 1965 he dropped his CFR membership, which had become an issue in the 1962 gubernatorial race.

But auspiciously, he went to New York and joined the firm of Nelson Rockefeller's personal attorney, John Mitchell (whom Nixon later appointed Attorney General of the U.S.). In New York, he lived in the very apartment at 810 Fifth Avenue where he and Rockefeller had revamped the 1960 platform.[8] The building was owned by Rockefeller, who still lived there, but in a different unit. It would not be going overboard to say that during the years before his '68 Presidential run, Nixon was Rockefeller's neighbor, tenant, and employee. His net worth increased substantially over this period.

In 1968, Nelson Rockefeller made his third consecutive bid for the GOP nomination, logging another article in *Foreign Affairs* ("Policy and the People"). The press characterized him as Nixon's liberal "rival," but they were patently allies. If you can't be President, the next best thing is to have influence over the man who is.

Nixon gave the Establishment his own signals by writing an article for the October 1967 *Foreign Affairs*. Called "Asia After Vietnam," it hinted that the door could be opened to Communist China — a long-time CFR goal that became reality during his Presidency. The article also showed that Nixon was wise to globalist strategy. He wrote of the Asian disposition "to evolve regional approaches to development needs and to the evolution of a new world order."[9] A "new world order" was precisely what Nelson Rockefeller was calling for in his 1968 campaign.

Nixon's CFR Administration

Between 1970 and 1972, the Establishment was rocked by the release of new exposés. These included *The Naked Capitalist* by former FBI official W. Cleon Skousen, and *None Dare Call It Conspiracy* by Gary Allen. The latter, even though it sold over five million copies, was ignored by the mass media. However, some defense of the Council on Foreign Relations began appearing in the press. Anthony Lukas in the *New York Times* and John Franklin Campbell in *New York* magazine wrote feature articles suggesting that the CFR was a has-been collection of foreign-policy fossils, no longer welcome in Washington with the "right-wing" Nixon in office. Campbell even titled his article "The Death Rattle of the American Establishment."

This was far from the truth. Richard Nixon broke all records by giving more than 110 CFR members government appointments. As under Eisenhower, GOP regulars were by and large excluded from the search for administration personnel. Once again, the faces were mostly new, but the ideology was not.

John F. Kennedy's choice for National Security Adviser was McGeorge Bundy, who had been teaching a course at Harvard called "The United States in World Affairs." Nixon's choice for National Security Adviser was the professor who succeeded Bundy in teaching that course: Henry Kissinger.

Kissinger, who advised Bundy during the Kennedy years, was undoubtedly the most powerful figure in the Nixon administration. As Shoup and Minter point out in *Imperial Brain Trust:*

> Diplomatic superstar Henry A. Kissinger was a Council protégé who began his career in foreign affairs as a rapporteur for a Council study group. Kissinger later told Council leader Hamilton Fish Armstrong, who had played a key role in Kissinger's rise to power, "You invented me."[10]

The professor authored many articles for *Foreign Affairs,* including one in January 1969 on how the Vietnam peace talks should be conducted. Not surprisingly, he later became our chief negotiator in Paris.

The Rockefellers' intimacy with Kissinger equaled that of the Council's. J. Robert Moskin notes:

> It was principally because of his long association with the Rockefellers that Henry Kissinger became a force in the Council. The *New York Times* called him "the Council's most influential member," and a Council insider says that "his influence is indirect and enormous — much of it through his Rockefeller connection."[11]

Before joining Nixon's staff, Kissinger had been Nelson Rockefeller's chief advisor on foreign affairs. He dedicated his memoir *White House Years* to Rockefeller, and in the book called him "the single most influential person in my life."[12] How did Nixon happen to select

145

Kissinger? *U.S. News & World Report* commented in 1971: "It was on the advice of Governor Rockefeller, who described Mr. Kissinger as 'the smartest guy available,' that Mr. Nixon chose him for his top adviser on foreign policy."[13]

Nixon twice offered David Rockefeller the Treasury Secretary post.[14] He rejected it. This is not surprising, since it has been said that, for him, even the Presidency would be a demotion.

Nixon named as Commerce Secretary Peter G. Peterson (CFR), who went on to replace David as the Council's chairman in 1985.

Among Nixon's other CFR recruitments: Federal Reserve Board Chairman Arthur Burns; HEW Secretary Elliot Richardson; Housing Secretary James Lynn; foreign policy consultant George Ball; chief economic aide Dr. Paul McCracken; UN Ambassador Charles Yost; NATO Ambassador Harlan Cleveland; Ambassador to the Soviet Union Jacob Beam; and the director of the Arms Control and Disarmament Agency, Gerard Smith. Other Nixon appointees, such as Defense Secretary Melvin Laird, and Treasury secretaries David Kennedy and George Shultz, joined the Council in later years. Nixon's pick for the highly visible Vice Presidency was Spiro Agnew, who, although not a member of the CFR, had been national chairman of the Rockefeller for President Committee in 1968.

Was Nixon a Conservative?

Although liberals detested Richard Nixon, whose rhetoric was often conservative, the record demonstrates that his policies were constructed on the design of the Establishment, not the traditional right.

Nationally syndicated columnist Roscoe Drummond observed in 1969:

> The most significant political fact of the hour is now so evident it can't be seriously disputed:
>
> President Richard M. Nixon is a "secret liberal". . . .
>
> Lyndon Johnson initiated and Congress approved the largest volume of social legislation of any president in history. And Nixon prepares to carry forward every major Johnson measure.

During the eight Eisenhower years 45 new welfare programs were passed. During the five Johnson years some 435 welfare programs were passed and Nixon is not proposing to dismantle them. He is proposing to build on them and his goal is to make sure they achieve their purposes more effectively.[15]

By 1970, syndicated columnist James Reston (CFR) agreed. He wrote:

It is true that Nixon rose to power as an anti-Communist, a hawk on Vietnam, and an opponent of the New Deal, but once he assumed the responsibilities of the presidency, he began moving toward peace in Vietnam, coexistence with the Communist world of Moscow and Peking, and despite all his political reservations, even toward advocacy of the welfare state at home.[16]

By 1971, Reston exclaimed:

The Nixon budget is so complex, so unlike the Nixon of the past, so un-Republican that it defies rational analysis. . . . The Nixon budget is more planned, has more welfare in it, and has a bigger predicted deficit than any other budget in this century.[17]

President Nixon shocked newscaster Howard K. Smith by telling him "I am now a Keynesian in economics." Keynes, of course, was the master advocate of government intervention in the marketplace. Nixon, it is to be recalled, instituted wage and price controls when inflation was a mere four percent. Such measures are pure socialism: a conservative ideologist would not even consider them. Nixon jacked federal spending to unprecedented levels, upped foreign aid, and proposed the Family Assistance Plan (FAP), which would have guaranteed a minimum annual income to every family in America.

Even the very liberal John Kenneth Galbraith was impressed. He wrote in *New York* magazine in 1970:

Certainly the least predicted development under the Nixon administration was this great new thrust to socialism. One encounters people

147

who still aren't aware of it. Others must be rubbing their eyes, for certainly the portents seemed all to the contrary. As an opponent of socialism, Mr. Nixon seemed steadfast . . .[18]

Nixon was no more conservative on foreign policy than domestic. It was his administration that permitted the Soviets to discharge their $11 billion World War II debt at less than ten cents on the dollar, and then receive millions of tons of our grain at subsidized rates. It also opened up forty U.S. ports to their ships, and pushed Congress to grant the USSR most-favored-nation trade status.

Even though the Chinese Communists had been killing literally millions in the Cultural Revolution, Richard Nixon began a new era of friendly relations with them, fulfilling a step long called for by CFR study groups and publications.

The Nixon administration was somewhat less restrictive than its predecessor with the use of force against North Vietnam, but it also concluded an undependable peace settlement. This bizarre agreement allowed Hanoi to keep all of its troops in place in South Vietnam (estimated at 150,000 by Washington, 300,000 by Saigon) while requiring the U.S. to remove all armed forces. President Thieu of South Vietnam refused to sign, calling it a "surrender document,"[19] but acquiesced when the Nixon administration told him it would sign with or without him. The presence of North Vietnam's armies, coupled later with the cutting of supplies to Saigon by Congress, sealed the doom of South Vietnam. Laos and Cambodia fell with it. The promise of peace had helped Nixon get reelected, and the agreement won Kissinger the Nobel Peace Prize. But Southeast Asia's allotment, in the end, was Communism and genocide.

As an epilogue to the Nixon era, it should be noted that Gary Allen, one of the keenest observers of the Establishment, believed that Watergate may have been the final act in Nelson Rockefeller's long quest for the White House. Spiro Agnew, one recalls, was bumped from the Vice Presidency after an old scandal cropped up. Allen suspected that Nixon was told to appoint Rockefeller VP, but that Nixon, perhaps emboldened by his reelection, refused to do so; and that Watergate itself may have been a contrivance to expel the President and his "palace guard" (men like Ehrlichman and Haldeman, who were loyal to Nixon, not Rockefeller). Allen made an impressive case for this in his book *The Rockefeller File*. Say what we will, the scandal left Kissinger and the CFR clique unscathed, and Gerald Ford's choice for Vice President was none other than Nelson Rockefeller.

Nixon chose CFR heavyweight Henry Kissinger (right)
on the advice of Nelson Rockefeller (left), whom Kissinger
called "the single most influential person in my life."

The Rockefeller-Nixon rivalry was largely histrionic.

150

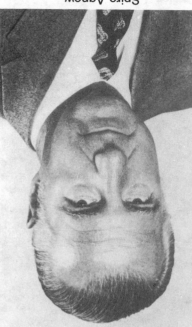

Spiro Agnew

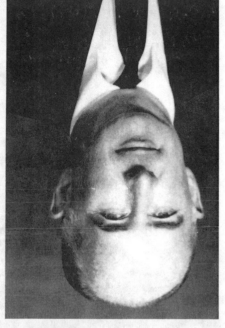

John Mitchell

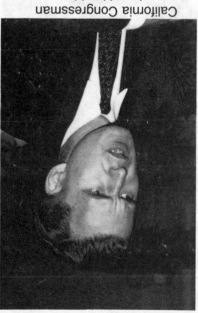

California Congressman
Jerry Voorhis

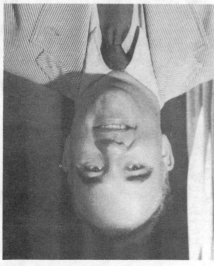

Gary Allen, author of *None Dare
Call It Conspiracy*, may have
pinpointed the real explanation
for the Watergate scandal.

Nixon's actions frequently contradicted his conservative rhetoric and media image. Above, he cavorts with Leonid Brezhnev in 1973.

Meeting Mao in 1972

Vietnamese refugees flee from advancing
Communist forces, March, 1975.

APWIDE WORLD PHOTOS

The peace agreement negotiated by Henry Kissinger
allowed North Vietnam's troops to remain in the South —
virtually guaranteeing its collapse.

Chapter 10

Carter And Trilateralism

The CFR's Little Brother is Born

With *None Dare Call It Conspiracy* putting the heat on the CFR, David Rockefeller moved to form a new internationalist organization — the Trilateral Commission. For some three decades, CFR members had pushed for "Atlantic Union," a bilateral federation of America and Europe. The Trilateral Commission (TC) broadened this objective to include an Asiatic leg.

How did the TC begin? "The Trilateral Commission," wrote Christopher Lydon in the July 1977 *Atlantic*, "was David Rockefeller's brainchild."[1] George Franklin, North American secretary of the Trilateral Commission, stated that it "was entirely David Rockefeller's idea originally."[2] Helping the CFR chairman develop the concept was Zbigniew Brzezinski, who laid the first stone in *Foreign Affairs* in 1970:

> A new and broader approach is needed — creation of a community of the developed nations which can effectively address itself to the larger concerns confronting mankind. In addition to the United States and Western Europe, Japan ought to be included. . . . A council representing the United States, Western Europe and Japan, with regular meetings of the heads of governments as well as some small standing machinery, would be a good start.[3]

That same year, Brzezinski elaborated these thoughts in his book *Between Two Ages*. It showed Brzezinski to be a classic CFR man — a globalist more than lenient toward Communism. He declared that "National sovereignty is no longer a viable concept," and that

154

"Marxism represents a further vital and creative stage in the maturing of man's universal vision. Marxism is simultaneously a victory of the external, active man over the inner, passive man and a victory of reason over belief . . ."[4]

The Trilateral Commission was formally established in 1973 and consisted of leaders in business, banking, government, and mass media from North America, Western Europe, and Japan. David Rockefeller was founding chairman and Brzezinski founding director of the North American branch, most of whose members were also in the CFR.

In the *Wall Street Journal,* David Rockefeller explained that "the Trilateral Commission is, in reality, a group of concerned citizens interested in fostering greater understanding and cooperation among international allies."[5]

But it was not all so innocent according to Jeremiah Novak, who wrote in the *Atlantic* (July 1977):

> The Trilateralists' emphasis on international economics is not entirely disinterested, for the oil crisis forced many developing nations, with doubtful repayment abilities, to borrow excessively. All told, private multinational banks, particularly Rockefeller's Chase Manhattan, have loaned nearly $52 billion to developing countries. An overhauled IMF would provide another source of credit for these nations, and would take the big private banks off the hook. This proposal is the cornerstone of the Trilateral plan.[6]

Senator Barry Goldwater put it less mercifully. In his book *With No Apologies*, he termed the Commission "David Rockefeller's newest international cabal," and said, "It is intended to be the vehicle for multinational consolidation of the commercial and banking interests by seizing control of the political government of the United States."[7]

Zbigniew Brzezinski showed how serious TC ambitions were in the July 1973 *Foreign Affairs,* stating that "without closer American-European-Japanese cooperation the major problems of today cannot be effectively tackled, and . . . *the active promotion of such trilateral*

155

cooperation must now become the central priority of U.S. policy."[8]
(Emphasis in the original.)
The best way to effect this would be for a Trilateralist to soon
become President. One did.

Jimmy Carter Goes to Washington

After Watergate tainted the Republican Party's image, it became
probable that a Democrat would win the 1976 Presidential election.
Candidate James Earl Carter was depicted by the press — and
himself — as the consummate outsider to the Washington Establishment. He was, the story went, a good ol' boy from Georgia, naïve
to the ways of the cigar-puffing, city-slicker politicians. *People* magazine even showed him shoveling peanuts in denims.

Typical of press comment at that time were the words of columnist
Joseph C. Harsch of the *Christian Science Monitor,* who asserted
that Carter

> has that nomination without benefit of any single kingmaker, or of
> any power group or power lobby, or of any single segment of the
> American people. He truly is indebted to no one man and no group
> interest.[9]

But Harsch belonged to the CFR, whose members are loath to
disclose the power of the group, or of its kingmaker, David Rockefeller.

In 1973, Carter dined with the CFR chairman at the latter's Tar-
rytown, New York estate. Present was Zbigniew Brzezinski, who
was helping Rockefeller screen prospects for the Trilateral Commission. Brzezinski later told Peter Pringle of the *London Sunday
Times* that "we were impressed that Carter had opened up trade
offices for the state of Georgia in Brussels and Tokyo. That seemed
to fit perfectly into the concept of the Trilateral."[10] Carter became a
founding member of the Commission — and his destiny became
calculable.

Senator Goldwater wrote:

> David Rockefeller and Zbigniew Brzezinski found Jimmy Carter to
> be their ideal candidate. They helped him win the nomination and

the presidency. To accomplish this purpose, they mobilized the money power of the Wall Street bankers, the intellectual influence of the academic community — which is subservient to the wealth of the great tax-free foundations — and the media controllers represented in the membership of the CFR and the Trilateral.[11]

Seven months before the Democratic nominating convention, the Gallup Poll found less than four percent of Democrats favoring Jimmy Carter for President. But almost overnight — like Willkie and Eisenhower before him — he became *the* candidate. By the convention, his picture had appeared on *Time's* cover three times, and *Newsweek's* twice. *Time's* cover artists were even instructed to make Carter resemble John F. Kennedy as much as possible.[12]

Carter's Elitist Regime

The Trilateral Commission's predominance in the Carter administration has been pointed out by critics as disparate as Ronald Reagan and *Penthouse* magazine. (The latter ran an article entitled "The Making of a President: How David Rockefeller Created Jimmy Carter.") During the campaign, however, only a few conservative sources seemed to spot the connection.

One hint that Carter was more than a peanut-chomping hayseed came in June of 1976, when the *Los Angeles Times* described a "task force" that had helped the candidate prepare his first major foreign policy speech (which began: "The time has come for us to seek a partnership between North America, Western Europe, and Japan"). The Carter advisors enumerated by the *Times* were: Brzezinski, Richard Cooper, Richard Gardner, Henry Owen, Edwin O. Reischauer, Averell Harriman, Anthony Lake, Robert Bowie, Milton Katz, Abram Chayes, George Ball, and Cyrus Vance.[13] There was one problem with the above list. *Every man on it was a member of the CFR.* We alluded earlier to Cooper's *Foreign Affairs* article proposing an international currency, and Gardner's piece calling for "an end run around national sovereignty, eroding it piece by piece."

In a speech in Boston, candidate Carter said: "The people of this country know from bitter experience that we are not going to get . . . changes merely by shifting around the same group of insiders. . . . The insiders have had their chance and they have not delivered."[14] After the election, top Carter aide Hamilton Jordan remarked: "If, after the inauguration, you find a Cy Vance as Secretary of State and Zbigniew Brzezinski as head of National Security, then I would say we failed. And I'd quit. But that's not going to happen."[15] But it did happen, and Jordan did not quit. Carter simply shifted around "the same group of insiders," turning, like his predecessors, to the institutions built by Wall Street and the international banking establishment.

The new President appointed more than seventy men from the CFR, and over twenty members of the much smaller Trilateral Commission. Zbigniew Brzezinski acknowledges in his White House memoirs: "Moreover, all the key foreign policy decision makers of the Carter Administration had previously served in the Trilateral Commission . . ."[16] (Carter is considerably less candid in his own memoirs: he does not even mention the Commission.)

Brzezinski, of course, became National Security Adviser, the same position Kissinger had held. Victor Lasky observed in *Jimmy Carter: The Man and the Myth*: "The Polish-born Brzezinski was to David Rockefeller what the German-born Kissinger was to Nelson Rockefeller."[17]

Secretary of State Cyrus Vance (CFR-Trilateral Commission) was a nephew of John W. Davis (founding president of the Council on Foreign Relations). Vance, who had served in the Kennedy and Johnson administrations, has been called "a product of the inner sanctums of Yale and Wall Street."[18] Robert Moskin commented on the CFR makeup of his departmental staff:

> When Cyrus Vance was called to Washington to be secretary of state in 1977, he took along members of the Council's staff as well as of a study group on nuclear weapons. He explains: "We work with people at the Council, and know they are good."[19]

Vice President Walter Mondale (CFR-TC) had flown his colors in the October 1974 *Foreign Affairs*, where he encapsulated much of the Establishment line in a single sentence: "The economic cooperation that is required will involve us most deeply with our traditional postwar allies, Western Europe and Japan, but it must also embrace a new measure of comity with the developing countries, and include the Soviet Union and other Communist nations in significant areas of international economic life."[20]

Other Carter appointees who were in *both* the CFR and Trilateral Commission: Defense Secretary Harold Brown; Federal Reserve Chairman Paul Volcker; Deputy Secretary of State Warren Christopher; Under Secretary of State Richard Cooper; Assistant Secretary of State Richard Holbrooke; Under Secretary of the Treasury Anthony M. Solomon; Deputy Secretary of Energy John Sawhill; Special Assistant to the President Hedley Donovan; Ambassador at Large Henry Owen; and several others. And of course there were "plain" CFR members like Treasury Secretary W. Michael Blumenthal, HEW Secretary Joseph Califano, SALT negotiator Paul Warnke, and dozens of others. To paraphrase one commentator, by the time Carter got to the White House, virtually the only thing Georgian about him was his accent.

Carter Foreign Policy

Domestically, Jimmy Carter wrought record deficits and double-digit inflation. But it was probably his foreign policy that most singed the nerves of America.

In the July 1980 issue of *Commentary* magazine, Carl Gershman reviewed a number of articles that appeared in *Foreign Affairs* and *Foreign Policy* during the early-to-middle 1970's. (*Foreign Policy*, published by the Carnegie Endowment for International Peace, was founded by Council members as a congenial rival to *Foreign Affairs*.) Gershman saw that these articles proposed a new foreign policy for the United States — one that disdained the "cold war mentality," renounced the use of force against Communism (based on the Vietnam experience), and advocated assisting the type of movements we had previously opposed (i.e., national liberation movements on the left half of the political spectrum). Gershman then disclosed that many of these essays' authors were tapped by the Carter administration for top foreign-policy jobs.[21] This "new foreign-policy establishment," as Gershman called it (really just the same old CFR without the anti-Communist pretense), helped Carter translate its ideas into reality — and a nightmare for the Free World.

Latin America. When the Sandinistas moved to seize power in Nicaragua, Carter took measures that hastened the downfall of President Anastasio Somoza, a West Point graduate and devoted friend of the USA. Somoza, it should be noted, was the duly elected leader of his people. Nicaragua had an election system modeled on that of the United States. There were two major parties, and additional parties could qualify to run their candidates simply by securing enough petitions. The 1974 election that brought Somoza to the presidency was overseen by the OAS, which found no irregularities. Nicaraguans enjoyed full civil liberties, including freedom of the press. American journalists there were permitted to roam at will; nevertheless, most of them portrayed Somoza as a man of consummate evil. This enabled Jimmy Carter to undermine him without significant protest within the United States.

On January 23, 1979, *Valeurs Actuelles,* the French political and economic weekly, reported the following comments by Mexico's President Lopez Portillo:

> When President Carter visited me I told him: "I do not particularly like Somoza or his regime, as you know. But if the Sandinistas unseat him and replace him with a Castro-picked Government it will have a profound effect on Nicaragua's neighbors and certainly touch off a slide to the left in my country." It was as though he did not hear a word of what I had said. He told me: "Oh, Mr. President, you must do something to help me get rid of this Somoza."

Carter forced the IMF and World Bank to halt credit to Nicaragua; embargoed its beef and coffee; and most importantly, prohibited weapons sales to its military, and pressured our allies to do the same (even compelling Israel to recall a ship bound for Nicaragua with munitions). Unknown to most Americans, President Somoza, before his brutal assassination, exposed the Carter conspiracy to depose him in his book *Nicaragua Betrayed.* It contains the transcripts of tape recordings Somoza made of visits to his office by U.S. officials. After the Marxists took power in Managua, the Carter administration pushed through Congress $75 million in aid for them. The new Nicaraguan rulers met the approval of one William M. LeoGrande, who wrote in the Autumn 1979 *Foreign Affairs* that their "program guarantees freedom of the press, speech and association, including the right to organize political parties irrespective of ideology,"[22] which at least proves the magazine is not always prophetic. Incredibly, in his Presidential memoirs, *Keeping Faith*, Jimmy Carter avoids any discussion of the Sandinista overthrow of Somoza, even though it could pass as the most significant foreign policy event of his White House career.

When campaigning in 1976, candidate Carter said in one of his televised debates with Gerald Ford: "I would never give up complete or practical control of the Panama Canal Zone."[23] But that is just what he did, as had been favored in *Foreign Affairs*,[24] even though the Canal Zone is strategically vital, and was no less U.S. territory than Alaska or Hawaii. Americans were goaded into consenting through exploitation of the legacy of no-win warfare: we were told that, unless we surrendered the canal, we would face "another Vietnam."

The Middle East. Iran was an important U.S. ally, not only as an oil source, but as the leading obstacle to Soviet ambitions in the Middle East. The Shah of Iran, who had governed his country since 1941, suddenly, like Somoza, became a mass media archvillain, even though he was probably the most progressive leader in his nation's history. He was attempting to quell uprisings by Islamic fundamentalists and Marxists, but was forced to ease up and make concessions to them when Carter threatened to withhold U.S. support. General Robert Huyser, a Carter emissary, persuaded the Iranian generals not to intervene to save the Shah's government. Khomeini later slaughtered many of those generals. In 1979, Iran collapsed; today it is a world center of terrorism.

When the Soviets invaded Afghanistan later that year, Carter's response was essentially passive; this was not surprising since he had been unwilling to use forceful measures even to release our citizens held hostage by Teheran.

The Far East. As we have noted, the CFR had for many years appealed for U.S. recognition of the Chinese Communists. In the

October 1971 *Foreign Affairs,* Jerome Alan Cohen wrote that "the question is no longer whether to establish diplomatic relations with China, but how to do so. Heaven may be wonderful — the problem is to get there."[25] Jimmy Carter found a way.

The Red Chinese were eager for U.S. credit and technology, but how sincere was their friendship? In 1977, Keng Piao, the Party's Director of the Department for Foreign Liaison, stated in a Peking speech:

> We should carry on indispensable struggle against, as well as making use of, the soft and weak side of the United States . . . . Just wait for the day when the opportune moment comes, we will then openly tell Uncle Sam to pack up and leave.[26]

That same year, Vice-Premier Teng Hsiao-ping explained before the Party's Central Committee:

> In the international united front struggle, the most important strategy is unification as well as struggle. . . . This is Mao Tse-tung's great discovery which has unlimited power. Even though the American imperialists can be said to be the number one nation in scientific and technical matters, she knows absolutely nothing in this area. In the future she will have no way of avoiding defeat by our hands. . . . We belong to the Marxist Camp and can never be so thoughtless that we cannot distinguish friends from enemies. Nixon, Ford, Carter and future "American imperialist leaders" all fall into this category (enemies). . . . What we need mainly is scientific and technical knowledge and equipment.[27]

Carter's right to break our long-standing defense treaty with Taiwan was questionable. Constitutionally, any treaty must be ratified by the Senate. Whether or not Congress must also approve the *abrogation* of a treaty was never specified in the Constitution. In 1978, however, the Senate voted ninety-four to zero that the President should consult that body before trying to change our agreement with Free China. Carter ducked this by waiting for Congress to adjourn for Christmas. On December 15, 1978, his announcement came. He unilaterally terminated the treaty, broke relations with Taiwan, and recognized the Chinese Communists, even though they had killed more people than any other government in history. This challenged the credibility of Carter's stand on "human rights," which he had said was the cornerstone of his foreign policy.

Carter was silent about the Cambodian genocide, which does not rate a single mention in his memoirs.* And he sought to remove our troops from South Korea, which could have brought renewed Communist invasion.

Africa. Carter maintained a trade embargo against Rhodesia, and refused even to meet with Prime Minister Ian Smith when he came to America to plead for his country. Rhodesia became Zimbabwe, the dominion of Marxist Robert Mugabe. And in other African regions, the Soviets and Cubans stepped in with little if any U.S. opposition.

To his many injuries to freedom-loving peoples, Carter added a slap in the face: he handed over the Crown of St. Stephen (Hungary's symbol of national independence and faith, which had been smuggled out of that country before the Communists took over) to the Red regime in Budapest.

Like the Grim Reaper wielding a scythe, Jimmy Carter left behind a bloody trail of betrayed allies. Communism had been strengthened in every corner of the globe. One is hard pressed to find major Carter foreign policy decisions that served the interests of the American people or the Free World. It would appear, however, that he very satisfactorily executed the Trilateral-CFR game plan.

---

* The closest he comes is to note that Leonid Brezhnev said the Cambodians were grateful to the Vietnamese for ousting "the abhorrent regime of Pol Pot."[28]

1977 meeting of the Trilateral Commission. Barry Goldwater called the organization a "vehicle for multinational consolidation of the commercial and banking interests by seizing control of the political government of the United States."

Jimmy Carter tapped fellow Trilateralists Zbigniew Brzezinski (center) and Cyrus Vance (right) for National Security Adviser and Secretary of State, despite assurances from Hamilton Jordan that it would never happen.

In his book *Nicaragua Betrayed*, Anastasio Somoza revealed the part Carter played in bringing the Sandinistas to power.

The Shah of Iran

The President welcomes Ortega at the White House.

Carter was selective in the application of his human rights policy.

With Teng Hsiao-ping

Chapter 11

A Second Look At Ronald Reagan

Reagan and the Establishment

After Mao Tse-tung took power in 1949 with help from the State Department, the cry in America was "Who lost China?" In the Autumn 1979 *Foreign Affairs*, editor William P. Bundy wrote a piece called "Who Lost Patagonia? Foreign Policy in the 1980 Campaign." Bundy patently feared that Jimmy Carter's foreign intrigues would revive deep scrutiny of the U.S. government and its Establishment connection. His article contended that our allies were falling apart on their own; that it was happenstance that this occured "on Jimmy Carter's watch"; and that there should be no "reckless charges," like those raised about postwar China.

Many Americans, however, had different ideas. Even those unfamiliar with the Establishment and its *modus operandi* sensed something very wrong with Jimmy Carter's foreign policy. Though the major media kept mum, smaller publications joined with conservatives in stripping the Trilateralist of his farmboy mask.

Even campaigner Ronald Reagan hopped on the bandwagon, addressing Trilateral monopolization of the Carter regime. (See, for example, the February 8, 1980 *New York Times*.) This helped Reagan win the backing of Main Street conservatives and primary victories over George Bush, who was known as the Establishment's Republican in 1980. David Rockefeller, Edwin Rockefeller, Helen Rockefeller, Laurence Rockefeller, Mary Rockefeller, and Godfrey Rockefeller all gave the maximum contribution allowable under law to Bush, a true Establishment scion. His father, along with Robert Lovett, had been a partner in Brown Brothers, Harriman — Averell Harriman's international banking firm. George Bush was a Skull

167

and Bonesman, a director of the Council on Foreign Relations, and a member of the Trilateral Commission. He shrewdly resigned from the latter two as he initiated his campaign.

Ronald Reagan thus began by playing the Goldwater of 1980. But soon he proved that his Hollywood training was not for naught. Carey McWilliams noted in the *Los Angeles Times* in July of that year:

> It is my belief that the Establishment — that elusive but very real force in American life — has of recent weeks opted decisively for Ronald Reagan.[1]

In the August 1980 *Playboy*, Robert Scheer reported:

> Prior to the New Hampshire primary, David Rockefeller convened a secret meeting of like-minded Republicans aimed at developing a strategy for stopping Reagan by supporting Bush and, failing that, getting Gerald Ford into the race. Reagan heard about the meeting and was, according to one aide, "really hurt." This aide reports that Reagan turned to him and demanded, "What have they got against me? I support big oil, I support big business, why don't they trust me?" . . .
>
> In any event, when Reagan scored his resounding triumph in New Hampshire in February, the overtures to the East began to work. New York establishment lawyer Bill Casey [CFR], who became campaign director the day of the New Hampshire victory, began building bridges and promising that a more moderate Reagan would emerge after the Republican Convention.[2]

Indeed, one did. Reagan picked Bush for his running mate, and, after the election, put together a transition team that included twenty-eight CFR men, among them the eternal John J. McCloy. As President, he appointed more than eighty individuals to his administration who were members of the Council, the Trilateral Commission, or both.

For his Chief of Staff (later Treasury Secretary), Reagan designated James Baker, who had been Bush's campaign manager.

For Treasury Secretary (later chief of staff) he chose Donald Regan, a Harvard-Wall Street-CFR man.

His original Secretary of State was Alexander Haig, a former assistant to Cyrus Vance and Henry Kissinger. When Haig joined Kissinger's staff in 1969, he was a colonel; by 1972 he had become a four-star general, in a leapfrogging career reminiscent of Marshall and Eisenhower. Later he became supreme commander of NATO and was, of course, a member of the Council on Foreign Relations.

Succeeding Haig at State in 1982 was George Pratt Shultz, a director of the CFR and a member of the Pratt family of the Standard Oil fortune (it was Mrs. Harold Pratt who donated Pratt House to the Council). His appointment seemed pleasing to back-to-back authors in *Foreign Affairs*,[3] to which the Secretary contributed the lead article for the spring 1985 issue. Known as an advocate of accommodation with the USSR, it was he who, years earlier, had signed the accords resulting in the Kama River truck factory being built for the Soviets by the West.

When Shultz picked retired banker John C. Whitehead for Deputy Secretary of State, the *New York Times* commented: "Mr. Whitehead brings to the job no apparent expertise in international diplomacy .... In describing his attributes for the job, Mr. Shultz said that Mr. Whitehead was a member of the Council on Foreign Relations and was regularly invited to dinners given by Henry A. Kissinger, the former secretary of state."[4]

As Secretary of Defense, the President named Caspar Weinberger, who had been a Nixon administrator and belonged to the Trilateral Commission. He was replaced in 1987 by Frank Carlucci of the CFR.

In 1985, Winston Lord, president of the Council on Foreign Relations and a former Kissinger aide, became Reagan's ambassador to the People's Republic of China.

When Lord left Pratt House to assume his new responsibilities, the Council needed a new president. One of the three final candidates under consideration was Robert McFarlane, who had been Ronald Reagan's National Security Adviser.

Reagan chose Malcolm Baldrige (CFR) as Commerce Secretary, William Brock (CFR) as Labor Secretary, Alan Greenspan (CFR-TC) as Federal Reserve Board Chairman, and on the list goes.

Reagan Policy

Ronald Reagan has been billed as a thoroughgoing conservative. But history bears witness that, like Eisenhower's and Nixon's, his conservatism rarely goes beyond his speeches.

Campaigning in 1980, Reagan said he intended to balance the budget by 1983. Jimmy Carter's annual federal deficits ranged from $40.2 billion to $78.9 billion. Under Mr. Reagan, the red ink came to a record $127.9 billion in fiscal 1982, then skyrocketed to $208.9 billion in 1983. The subsequent deficits, in billions of dollars, were as follows:

    1984 — 185.3
    1985 — 212.3
    1986 — 220.7
    1987 — 173.2 (estimated)

Reagan's annual deficits have actually exceeded the annual *budgets* of Lyndon B. Johnson, who had a Vietnam War to pay for as well as the Great Society. He has chalked up more government debt than all the Presidents before him combined. It is true that Congress shares in the responsibility for this, but the blame cannot simply be offloaded on them; the President's own budget proposals have contained estimated deficits in the $100-200 billion range since fiscal 1983.

Reagan is touted as an enemy of taxation and big government. Yet during his first term, although he did cut tax rates, he also pushed through the largest single tax increase in our nation's history, as well as boosts in the gasoline and Social Security taxes. And big government got bigger: the civilian work force in the executive branch grew by nearly 100,000 between 1981 and 1986.

In 1983, Walter Heller, former economic advisor to Presidents Kennedy and Johnson, was prompted to write a column in the *Wall Street Journal* entitled "Mr. Reagan Is a Keynesian Now." In 1984, economist Richard Parker echoed this conclusion in the *Los Angeles Times*, noting: "While he proclaims Reaganomics' success, Reagan also owes Americans a shocking confession: He's become a born-again Keynesian." That same year, economist Lester Thurow observed in *Newsweek* that "President Reagan has become the ultimate Keynesian." He continued:

> Not only is the Reagan Administration rehabilitating exactly the economic policies it pledged to bury when entering office, it is applying them more vigorously than any Keynesian would have dared. Imagine what conservatives would be saying if a liberal Keynesian Democratic president had dared to run a $200 billion deficit.[5]

Supposedly a proponent of military strength, candidate Reagan criticized Jimmy Carter for abiding by the Salt II Treaty, which the Senate had refused to ratify. He called it "fatally flawed" and said he would spurn it. Yet as President he complied with Salt II until late 1986, *even after the treaty would have expired had it ever been ratified, and despite numerous Soviet violations.* In 1986, he ordered two Poseidon ballistic missile submarines dismantled to ensure we would stay within Salt II limits.

The President agreed to no increase in defense spending for 1986, whereas White House hopeful Walter Mondale had advocated increases of at least three percent annually. Thus Reagan's defense budget that year was actually smaller than the one proposed by his liberal Democratic rival. In *The New American* in 1986, William F. Jasper summed other holes in the President's warrior reputation:

> The Reagan administration has also cut back construction of new Trident submarines; refused deployment of Minuteman III missiles despite its authorization by Congress; reduced MX missile planned deployment; continued deactivation of B-52 strategic bombers; cancelled production of air-launched cruise missile B and Trident I submarine-launched ballistic missiles; cut back production of the B-1 bomber; and failed to reconstruct our dismantled anti-ballistic missile (ABM) system. In short, Mr. Reagan's policies have been disastrous for America's defense capabilities.[6]

Today, while the prospect of SDI is becoming increasingly remote, few Americans seem to realize that the nuclear deterrent of the United States still consists principally of: antiquated B-52 bombers,

171

designed under Truman and constructed under Eisenhower and Kennedy; ICBM's from the Kennedy-Johnson-Nixon years (after sitting in their silos for two decades, no one really knows how well they would work); and Poseidon submarines built before 1967. Ronald Reagan has reinforced these with some new B-1 bombers, MX missiles, and Trident submarines, but in very limited quantities — considerably less than the rates of attrition would call for. In contrast, the Soviets have never stopped expanding and modernizing all segments of their nuclear forces. Reagan's most significant strategic advance was probably the placement of medium-range missiles in Europe — and these he agreed to withdraw completely when he signed the INF treaty in late 1987! Contrary to the popular impression, the Reagan administration has left America on the brink of decisive nuclear inferiority.

Most people consider the President a determined anti-Communist; this was an image he established early on with his well-publicized description of the Soviet Union as an "evil empire." But here again, his actions have fallen short of his words.

• When Communist Poland defaulted on its interest payments to American banks in 1982, Ronald Reagan didn't pressure Warsaw — instead, he bailed out the banks by having the U.S. taxpayers pick up the tab.

• The Reagan administration channeled money into El Salvador to help José Napoleón Duarte win his 1984 election over the anti-Communist Roberto d'Aubuisson.[7] Duarte is a socialist; he has seized the nation's banks and large farms; in fact, when he previously ran for president in 1972, his running mate was Guillermo Ungo — current leader of El Salvador's Marxist guerrillas.

• When Jimmy Carter broke relations with Taiwan, Ronald Reagan called it an "outright betrayal of a close friend and ally."[8] As President, however, he did not attempt to restore relations with Free China. Furthermore, in August 1982 he issued a joint communiqué with Peking stating that the U.S. "does not seek to carry out a long-term policy of arms sales to Taiwan." Under Reagan, trade with Red China has greatly multiplied; in 1986, the administration pressed through Congress the sale of $550 million in advanced avionics

A SECOND LOOK AT RONALD REAGAN

equipment, giving some of the mainland's fighters an all-weather capacity Taiwan's air force lacks.

• In Angola, Jonas Savimbi's UNITA freedom fighters are trying to unseat the pro-Soviet ruling regime, which is kept in power by nearly 40,000 Cuban troops. Much publicity has been accorded the $15 million in military assistance given Savimbi by Reagan — but overlooked is the more than $200 million in credits granted Angola's Marxist government by the Export-Import Bank. Tens of millions in aid have also been sent to Communist Mozambique, even though it is using Soviet weapons to suppress a liberation movement by the pro-Western RENAMO (Mozambique National Resistance).

• When the Philippine crisis reached its climax in 1986, Ronald Reagan joined hands with the international left, withdrawing support from President Marcos. *Foreign Affairs,* which had previously served as a forum for Benigno Aquino, anticipated the situation in its winter 1984/85 issue:

> If Marcos cannot or will not accept the reforms necessary to ensure stability, then we must be willing to call his bluff, and look even further down the line, toward the inevitable emergence of a new Philippine leadership.[9]

The article stated that the fate of the Philippines must remain an internal affair, but added: "U.S. leverage should not be underestimated; U.S. efforts to shape the setting for the inevitable Philippine transition can almost certainly have some benefit."

Ferdinand Marcos was no saint, but he may look like one compared to the Communists, if and when they wrest the islands from Corazon Aquino.

• In response to the Afghanistan invasion, Jimmy Carter embargoed grain to the Soviet Union. But Mr. Reagan approved sale of our wheat to Moscow again — at heavily subsidized rates. On December 27, 1986, the President warned that Soviet leaders "must be made to understand that they will continue to pay a higher and higher price until they accept the necessity for a political solution involving the prompt withdrawal of their forces from Afghanistan and self-determination for the Afghan people."[10] The very next day,

173

however, administration officials said they were ending most controls on the export of oil and gas equipment and technology to the USSR. Reagan did allow Afghanistan's brave freedom fighters, the Mujahideen, some weapons, but he pledged to cut these off during his negotiations with Mikhail Gorbachev in December 1987! The curtailment had in fact been brewing as much as two years earlier. At that time, according to William Safire in the *New York Times*:

> [T]hree State Department functionaries cooked up a plan to accommodate Soviet demands about withdrawal from Afghanistan. The key concession: permit the Russians to continue arms shipments to its puppet Government while the US cut off aid to the *Mujahedeen* ...
>
> The secret letter assured Moscow that upon the day its troop withdrawal began, "foreign interference" would stop — meaning that the C.I.A.-channeled aid to the [Afghan rebels] would be terminated ....
>
> It is known to insiders as "the Day One deal": American aid to the Afghan resistance, but not Soviet aid to the puppet Kabul regime, would stop on Day One of the yearlong Soviet troop pullout.[11]

After exposure led to public protest, the President began to disavow the policy. But a UPI story dated March 21, 1988 carried this incredible report:

> The United States and Soviet Union, seeking to ensure an orderly Soviet troop withdrawal from Afghanistan, are sharing data on radical Islamic guerrilla factions viewed as a threat to a settlement, according to administration officials. ...
>
> Such maneuvering may mean curbing U.S. support for the Islamic rebel factions the administration has so relied on during the 8½-year-old guerrilla war against Soviet occupation forces, they said. ...
>
> A CIA source, speaking of the rebels, confirmed a shift in the US position, [and] said, "We want to see some groups fed to other groups" — intelligence terminology for neutralizing undesirable elements. ...
>
> Asked about US-Soviet discussions about the mujahideen, a State Department spokesman declined comment on grounds it is an intelligence matter.[12]

Conservatives have been pleased with some facets of Ronald Reagan's performance, such as his judicial appointments and the Grenada rescue mission. There is, of course, the controversial "Contra aid" he has sought. But this, despite energetic Congressional opposition, is far less than the Nicaraguan freedom fighters would need to defeat the Sandinistas, whose army takes to the field with heavy tanks and helicopter gunships from the Soviet Union. At best, they are being allowed to fight a "no-win" war of containment. Furthermore, the administration has backed ex-Sandinistas and other former opponents of Somoza (such as Eden Pastora and Adolfo Calero) as heads of the Contras, giving the whole operation the smell of a sellout. Even Pastora, known as "Commander Zero," has been a guest at Pratt House. (As this book went to press, the Contras had been forced into a cease-fire on Sandinista terms, with a *de facto* surrender in the works.)

The Reagan record shows that, all things considered, his policies are the same ones that have steered our nation for over fifty years. That the Establishment has tolerated him for two terms tends to suggest that it may be more comfortable with a conservative-image Republican as President. This allows its program to advance relatively unhindered, and puts Washington watchdogs to sleep.

In 1971, Lyndon Baines Johnson said of President Nixon: "Can't you see the uproar if I had been responsible for Taiwan getting kicked out of the United Nations? Or if I had imposed sweeping national controls on prices and wages? Nixon has gotten by with it. If I had tried to do it, or Truman, or Humphrey, or any Democrat, we would have been clobbered."[13] Walter Mondale must have similar thoughts about Ronald Reagan.

In an article in *Foreign Affairs* in 1981, former Kissinger aide William G. Hyland wrote foreseeingly: "Just as Nixon had the anti-Communist credentials to develop an opening to Peking, so Reagan has the credentials to initiate a new relationship with the U.S.S.R."[14] That, presumably, applied to the rest of the Establishment agenda as well. We presume Mr. Hyland is familiar with the Establishment agenda. In 1984, he replaced William Bundy as editor of *Foreign Affairs*.

175

George Bush and George Shultz headed a long list of personnel that President Reagan drew from the Eastern Establishment.

Donald Regan

Alexander Halg

The President's performance in office
did not match his conservative rhetoric.

With Red China's Zhao Ziyang

Chapter 12

The Media Blackout

Establishment Control of the Media

All of the American history we have just finished reviewing is factual. Yet it is far from the traditional version. So the question naturally arises: Why do the media avoid the various circumstances shown in this account, or at best downplay them? Why don't investigative news shows like *Sixty Minutes*, perceived as gutsy and no-holds-barred, tackle the Pearl Harbor cover-up, American financing of questionable projects behind the Iron Curtain, or the Trilateralist-CFR hold on our government? Surely such material would have sufficient audience appeal.

The answer is almost self-evident. The mass media are subject to the same "power behind the throne" as Washington. For the Establishment to induce public cooperation with its program, it has always been expedient to manipulate the information industry that is so responsible for what people think about current events. A prime mover in this process was J. P. Morgan — the original force behind the CFR.

In 1917, Congressman Oscar Callaway inserted the following statement in the *Congressional Record:*

> In March, 1915, the J. P. Morgan interests, the steel, shipbuilding, and powder interests, and their subsidiary organizations, got together 12 men high up in the newspaper world and employed them to select the most influential newspapers in the United States and sufficient number of them to control generally the policy of the daily press of the United States.
>
> These 12 men worked the problem out by selecting 179 newspapers, and then began, by an elimination process, to retain only those nec-

178

essary for the purpose of controlling the general policy of the daily press throughout the country. They found it was only necessary to purchase the control of 25 of the greatest papers. The 25 papers were agreed upon; emissaries were sent to purchase the policy, national and international, of these papers; an agreement was reached; the policy of the papers was bought, to be paid for by the month; an editor was furnished for each paper to properly supervise and edit information regarding the questions of preparedness, militarism, financial policies, and other things of national and international nature considered vital to the interests of the purchasers. . . .

This policy also included the suppression of everything in opposition to the wishes of the interests served.[1]

The press, thus controlled, was very successful in persuading Americans to support our entry into World War I. However, in subsequent years, a number of books appeared that challenged the justification of our involvement, the merits of the Allied cause, and the wisdom of Colonel House and his colleagues in devising the Versailles Treaty. These books included Harry Elmer Barnes' *Genesis of the World War* (1926), Sidney Fay's *Origins of the World War* (1928), and many others.

After World War II, however, the Establishment moved to preclude such investigation. The eminent historian Charles Beard, former president of the American Historical Association, stated in a *Saturday Evening Post* editorial in 1947:

The Rockefeller Foundation and Council on Foreign Relations . . . intend to prevent, if they can, a repetition of what they call in the vernacular "the debunking journalistic campaign following World War I." Translated into precise English, this means that the foundation and the council do not want journalists or any other persons to examine too closely and criticize too freely the official propaganda and official statements relative to "our basic aims and activities" during World War II. In short, they hope that, among other things, the policies and measures of Franklin D. Roosevelt will escape in coming years the critical analysis, evaluation and exposition that befell the policies and measures of President Woodrow Wilson and the Entente Allies after World War I.[2]

Dr. Beard noted that the Rockefeller Foundation had granted $139,000 to the CFR, which in turn hired Harvard professor William Langer to author a three-volume chronicle of the war.

Historians whose writings concurred with the "authorized" versions of events, such as Langer, Samuel Morison, Herbert Feis, Henry Steele Commager, and Arthur Schlesinger, Jr., were generally guaranteed exclusive interviews, access to government documents and statesmen's diaries, sure publication, and glowing appraisals in the front of the *New York Times Book Review*. Most of these men had served in the administrations they wrote about.

On the other hand, historians who dared question foreign policy under Roosevelt and Truman, such as Beard, Harry Elmer Barnes, Charles Tansill, John T. Flynn, and William Henry Chamberlin, suddenly found themselves blacklisted by the publishing world that had previously welcomed their works. Beard succeeded in issuing two volumes critical of the Roosevelt administration only because he had a devoted friend at Yale University Press. Before his death in 1948, he was smeared in the media as senile.

In 1953, Barnes described how the censorship process worked:

> The methods followed by the various groups interested in blacking out the truth about world affairs since 1932 are numerous and ingenious, but, aside from subterranean persecution of individuals, they fall mainly into the following patterns or categories: (1) excluding scholars suspected of revisionist views from access to public documents which are freely opened to "court historians" and other apologists for the foreign policy of President Roosevelt; (2) intimidating publishers of books and periodicals, so that even those who might wish to publish books and articles setting forth the revisionist point of view do not dare to do so; (3) ignoring or obscuring published material which embodies revisionist facts and arguments; and (4) smearing revisionist authors and their books. . . .
>
> As a matter of fact, only two small publishing houses in the United States — the Henry Regnery Company and the Devin-Adair Company

— have shown any consistent willingness to publish books which frankly aim to tell the truth with respect to the causes and issues of the second World War. Leading members of two of the largest publishing houses in the country have told me that, whatever their personal wishes in the circumstances, they would not feel it ethical to endanger their business and the property rights of their stockholders by publishing critical books relative to American foreign policy since 1933. And there is good reason for this hesitancy. The book clubs and the main sales outlets for books are controlled by powerful pressure groups which are opposed to truth on such matters. These outlets not only refuse to market critical books in this field but also threaten to boycott other books by those publishers who defy their blackout ultimatum.[3]

The historical suppression described by Dr. Barnes thirty-five years ago still operates today. It could be pointed out — quite rightfully, of course — that in more recent years American policy and policy makers have occasionally been savaged (as with Vietnam, Watergate, and the Iran-Contra affair). However, such episodes did not bruise the Council on Foreign Relations or its allies; instead they stigmatized those people whom the Establishment disliked, and those very policies it had always opposed (nationalism and anti-Communism).

What we have operating in America is an Establishment media. As erstwhile *New York Times* editor John Swinton once said: "There is no such thing as an independent press in America, if we except that of little country towns."

The *Times* itself was bought in 1896 by Alfred Ochs, with backing from J. P. Morgan, Rothschild agent August Belmont, and Jacob Schiff of Kuhn, Loeb. It was subsequently passed on to Ochs' son-in-law Arthur Hays Sulzberger (CFR), then to Orville E. Dryfoos (CFR), and finally to the present publisher, Arthur Ochs Sulzberger (CFR). The *Times* has had a number of CFR members in its stable of reporters, including Herbert L. Matthews, Harrison Salisbury, and Lester Markel. Currently, executive editor Max Frankel, editorial page editor Jack Rosenthal, deputy editorial page editor Leslie

Gelb, and assistant managing editors James L. Greenfield, Warren Hoge, and John M. Lee are all in the Council.

The *Times'* friendly rival, the *Washington Post*, was bought by Eugene Meyer in 1933. Meyer, a partner of Bernard Baruch and Federal Reserve Board governor, had joined the CFR in 1929. Meyer began his reign at the *Post* by firing its editor for refusing to support U.S. recognition of the Soviet Union.[4]

Today the *Post* is run by Meyer's daughter, Katharine Graham (CFR). Managing editor Leonard Downie, Jr., editorial page editor Meg Greenfield, and deputy editorial page editor Stephen S. Rosenfeld are all Council members.

The Washington Post Company owns *Newsweek,* which is a descendant of the weekly magazine *Today*, founded by Averell Harriman, among others, to support the New Deal and business interests. *Newsweek's* editor-in-chief Richard M. Smith and editor Maynard Parker both belong to the CFR, as have a number of its contributors. Both *Newsweek* and the *Post* have donated money to the Council.

Time magazine maintains the same kind of rivalry with *Newsweek* as the *New York Times* does with the *Post*: they compete for readers, not in viewpoint. *Time* was founded by Henry Luce (CFR-IPR-Atlantic Union), who rose as a publisher with loans from such individuals as Dwight Morrow and Thomas Lamont (both Morgan partners and CFR members), Harvey Firestone (CFR), and E. Roland Harriman (CFR).

Time's longtime editor-in-chief was Hedley Donovan (Trilateral Commission member, CFR Director, trustee of the Ford Foundation and Carnegie Endowment for International Peace, and eventually Special Assistant to President Jimmy Carter). The current editor-in-chief, Henry Grunwald, is in the CFR, along with managing editor Henry Muller. Time, Inc., which also publishes *People, Life, Fortune, Money,* and *Sports Illustrated*, has several Council members on its board of directors.

The CFR also has interlocks with the major TV networks. William S. Paley, chairman of the board at CBS for many years, belonged to the Council on Foreign Relations, as does the chairman today, Thomas H. Wyman, and eleven of the fourteen board members listed for 1987. CBS news anchor Dan Rather is in the CFR. CBS helped finance the Trilateral Commission, and the CBS Foundation has contributed funds to the Council.

NBC is a subsidiary of RCA, which was formerly headed by David Sarnoff (CFR). Sarnoff had financial backing from Kuhn, Loeb and other Rothschild-linked banking firms. He was succeeded by his son Robert, who married Felicia Schiff Warburg, daughter of Paul Warburg and great granddaughter of Jacob Schiff. RCA's chairman of the board now, Thornton Bradshaw, is a CFR man, as are several other board members. The Council has had a number of NBC newsmen on its roster over the years, including Marvin Kalb, John Chancellor, Garick Utley, and Irving R. Levine.

There are CFR figures on ABC's board, and in its news department, including Ted Koppel and David Brinkley.

The Council on Foreign Relations also has links to the *Wall Street Journal*, the *Los Angeles Times*, the Associated Press wire service, PBS, and other major news sources. The Council's annual report for 1987 notes that 262 of its members are "journalists, correspondents, and communications executives."

What does this mean? Membership in the CFR is not by itself an indictment. However, when large numbers of Council men are clustered at the helm of a media outlet, then its editorial policy, news slant, and personnel selection are almost guaranteed to reflect the globalist, pro-socialist thinking that typifies the Council.

Media Bias

Recently, a number of studies have revealed strong prejudice in the mass media. Beyond doubt, the leader in the movement to expose and combat this bias has been Reed Irvine's Washington-based organization, Accuracy in Media (AIM).

In 1981, professors Robert Lichter (George Washington University) and Stanley Rothman (Smith College) published tabulated results of interviews they had conducted with the media elite: journalists from the *New York Times, Washington Post, Wall Street Journal, Time, Newsweek, U.S. News & World Report,* ABC, CBS, NBC, and PBS. The survey showed the media far to the left of the public at large. Of those casting ballots for major party candidates in the 1964 election, ninety-four percent had voted for Lyndon Johnson, and only six percent for Barry Goldwater. Even in Richard Nixon's 1972 landslide, eighty-one percent voted for George McGovern. The leftward stance of the media was also shown by their answers to questions on social and political issues. For example, ninety percent took the pro-choice position on abortion, and fifty-seven percent agreed with the Marxist thesis that the U.S. causes poverty in the Third World by exploiting it.[5]

The Lichter-Rothman survey was corroborated in 1985 by a *Los Angeles Times* poll of 3000 editors and reporters from over 600 newspapers. After comparing the results to those of readers, the *Times* was forced to conclude that "members of the press are predominantly liberal, considerably more liberal than the general public."[6]

But do journalists allow their attitudes to influence their reporting? Research shows that they do.

One area where this shows up is national defense. News commentators are fond of reciting how many warheads the U.S. has, but they almost never mention that most of our ICBM's, ballistic missile submarines, and strategic bombers are some twenty years old and nearing obsolescence. A study by the Institute of American Strategy determined that, on the subject of national defense, CBS News gave over sixty percent of its coverage to proponents of reducing our defenses, and only 3.5 percent to advocates of greater strength — a ratio higher than 17-1.[7] One can imagine the impact of such imbalance on public opinion.

Equally pronounced is the media's selectivity in covering foreign affairs. Although we often hear about human rights abuses by anti-Communist governments, Marxist violations are commonly ignored.

An illustration is the genocide in Cambodia, where at least a third of the population died under the Khmer Rouge. First, the American press contributed to the holocaust by demanding withdrawal of U.S. support from the government of the Republic of Cambodia. Norodom Sihanouk helped set the pace in the October 1970 *Foreign Affairs*, writing that "I can only hope for the total victory of the revolution," which, he said, "cannot but save my homeland and serve the deepest interests of the mass of the 'little' Khmer people."[8] Sihanouk also made the bizarre prediction that U.S.-Cambodian relations would "once again become good" as soon as Washington stopped helping the government combat the Communists.

The U.S. media echoed Sihanouk's viewpoint. On April 13, 1975 — just four days before the fall of Phnom Penh — the *New York Times* ran this headline: "Indochina Without Americans: For Most a Better Life."

By the end of 1976, more than a million Cambodians had died under the Communists' reign of terror. Yet during that year, the *New York Times* carried only four stories on human rights problems in Cambodia; by contrast, it published sixty-six on abuses in Chile. The *Washington Post* had just nine human rights stories on Cambodia; fifty-eight about Chile. And on the network evening news in 1976, NBC never referred to the problem in Cambodia; ABC mentioned it once, and CBS twice.[9]

A similar blackout has occurred more recently with Afghanistan, where the Soviets have slaughtered more than one million people and turned millions more into refugees. Reed Irvine notes that, on a single evening in December 1986, network news devoted more time to the "Irangate" controversy (fifty-seven minutes) than it had to the war in Afghanistan during all of 1985 (fifty-two minutes).[10] Human rights stories still get attention — but only if in selected countries. AIM surveyed the *New York Times* and *Washington Post* from May to July, 1986, and found that the two papers ran a total of 415 stories on South Africa during that stretch.[11]

Abdul Shams, former economic advisor to Afghanistan's late President Hafizullah Amin, had this to say about U.S. media coverage of his homeland, in a 1985 interview with *The Review of the News*:

> The major American news media have ignored what is happening in Afghanistan and they have also ignored Afghans like me who try to tell what is happening. But the smaller newspapers and radio and TV stations have been very cooperative. . . .
>
> Every day, hundreds or thousands of my people are killed and the networks and major news media say nothing. But if one person is killed in South Africa, immediately the media start screaming . . . .
>
> I have talked to many, many people here in the United States, many of them refugees from Communist countries themselves and they can-

not believe the things they see in the major news media. They say that the American news media are on the other side. Much of the time I am forced to believe that they are correct.[12]

Disproportionate news reporting gives Americans a distorted world view — and because it may affect what they tell their representatives in Congress, it also affects world events.

President Anastasio Somoza made revelations about our media's methods and impact in his book *Nicaragua Betrayed:*

> On Sunday afternoon, *Sixty Minutes* is the most watched network show in the United States . . . . I have watched the show and I am familiar with the format. Generally speaking, the show is not complete unless someone is nailed to the cross. Also, the program will invariably sneak in a touch of propaganda. You can be sure this propaganda is slanted to the Left.
>
> When I was advised that *Sixty Minutes* wanted to interview me, I certainly had misgivings . . . .
>
> However, I wanted so much for the American people to understand the realities of our situation in Nicaragua and to know what the administration in Washington was doing to us, that I agreed to do the program. All arrangements were made and Dan Rather was sent down to do the program. That interview I shall always remember.
>
> Rather tried every conceivable journalistic trick to trip me up on questions. He knew in advance the answers he wanted and come "hell or high water" he was going to find the question to fit his preconceived answer. Well, he never succeeded. From watching the show, one would never know that Dan Rather spent two and one-half hours grilling me. It's difficult to believe, but Rather condensed that entire time to seven minutes. . . .
>
> I didn't realize what the power of film editing really meant. With that power, Rather cast me in any role he chose. Everything good I said about Nicaragua was deleted. Any reference to Carter's effort to destroy the government of Nicaragua was deleted. Every reference to the Communist activity and Cuba's participation was deleted.
>
> His insistence that there was torture in my government probably disturbed me the most. We would go over the subject and then we

would come back to it again. He just wasn't getting the answers he wanted. Finally he said: "May we visit the security offices of the Nicaraguan government?" He had heard that this was a torture chamber and he believed it. I replied: "Yes, Mr. Rather, you may visit those offices and you may take your camera." Then I added: "You go right now. Take that car and go immediately so that you can't say I rigged it." Well, he did go, and he saw where the people worked and talked to many of them. When the show came on the air, he made no mention of the fact that he had personally visited our security offices and was free to film, talk to people, or do anything he wanted to do. He knew in advance how he wanted to portray me and his predetermined plan was followed.

When Rather left my office, I was convinced he would take me apart. I was right. The show was a disaster. Rather depicted a situation that didn't exist in Nicaragua. That show did irreparable harm to the government of Nicaragua and to me. Such massive disinformation also does harm to the American people.[13]

President Somoza's comments are a good example of "the other side of the story" that the American viewer is not allowed to see. Doubtless other recipients of *Sixty Minutes* interviews could give similar accounts.

Media personnel with sound ethics will report news factually and reserve their opinions for editorials. In reality, however, opinion usually mingles with the news. It is ironic that many journalists, while insisting there be no press censorship, themselves censor stories. They demand, as during the Iran-Contra hearings, that "all the facts" be told, yet do not themselves tell all the facts.

The leftist bias of the media strongly confirms that the Establishment is not conservative. If the Establishment, with its colossal wealth and links to press management, wanted news reporting with a conservative orientation, or simply with balance, we would get it. We do not.

Historian Charles Beard, appearing with his wife
before the Senate Foreign Relations Committee in 1941

Historian Harry Elmer Barnes

Reed Irvine of Accuracy in Media

The major mass media can be counted on
to sell the Establishment line.

Hedley Donovan of *Time* and Dan Rather of CBS —
two of many media giants who have belonged to the Council.

Bones of victims of the Communist genocide in Cambodia, unearthed from a mass grave near Phnom Penh. During 1976, the *New York Times* ran sixty-six human rights stories about Chile, but only four about Cambodia.

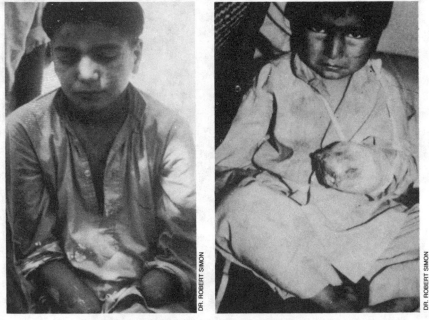

Coverage of Soviet atrocities in Afghanistan was also avoided by most of the media.

Chapter 13

The CFR Today

This book's detractors will say it has exaggerated the power and influence of the CFR. Admiral Chester Ward, a former Council member whom we referred to in chapter one, made a point of clarification germane to this:

> CFR, *as such*, does not write the platforms of both political parties or select their respective presidential candidates, or control U.S. defense and foreign policies. But CFR members, as individuals, acting in concert with other individual CFR members, do.[1]

It is true, of course, that the Council is not an oath-bound brotherhood that dictates its members' words and deeds. A number of individuals are apparently invited into the CFR simply because they have a distinguished name or other enhancing qualities, and they may join without endorsing or even knowing the Council's habitual viewpoint. For this reason, no one should be censured merely for belonging to the CFR. However, the membership's great majority, and by all means its core of leaders, have been chronically pro-socialist and pro-globalist.

It is also true that, while the Council maintains an extraordinarily low profile, it is not a secret society. Dr. Carroll Quigley called it "a front group," Arthur Schlesinger, Jr. a "front organization," and it is helpful to understand it in these terms. It is not *the* Establishment, but a surface component of it. Nor is it a theater of illegitimate activities; it publishes an annual report in which it makes a good account of its finances, and generally it maintains the trappings of a public-spirited institution. Behind all of this, however, is a movement to effect a new world order. Because this movement has persisted for seven unrelenting decades, has been lavishly funded, and has been forwarded by the conscious, deliberate actions of CFR members in government, many have called it a conspiracy. History speaks loudly enough to vindicate the use of this term. Some speculate that there is, within the Council, a cadre which is the heartbeat of its globalism.

So if indeed we have committed the sin of overestimating the role of the Council on Foreign Relations, let us then certainly acknowledge that other sources have grossly *underestimated* it.

What about the Council today? What does the future hold for it — and vice versa? A number of changes are in evidence.

We noted earlier the Council's eventual switch from a bilateral objective (Atlantic Union) to a trilateral one. Another path to world government that more or less fell into disuse was direct widening of UN authority. Richard Gardner's April 1974 *Foreign Affairs* article, "The Hard Road to World Order," charted a new course. Gardner explained that "the 'house of world order' will have to be built from the bottom up rather than the top down." In other words, since greater UN power had been successfully resisted by the public, another approach was needed: strengthening the various ingredients of world government, bit and piece. Gardner laid out ten commandments as a guide to action. And in succceding years, the phrase "new world order" and its variations — which had long been inscribed on the pages of *Foreign Affairs* — began to dwindle in appearance. There was an emphasis shift toward Gardner's plan: articles commending the Law of the Sea Treaty, international currency reform, international trade measures, and so forth.

Recently, however, even this trend has faded. Today, *Foreign Affairs* shows few traces of globalism, and for the first time has begun looking like its professed identity: a more or less balanced journal of world affairs, rather than a handmaiden for the international bankers.

It would be tempting to ascribe this transition to the arrival of new editor William G. Hyland in 1984. However, *Foreign Affairs'* improved look appears to be part of an overall process of image reconstruction by the CFR.

The Council has long been accused of being elitist. In 1961, Edith Kermit Roosevelt remarked that it had "a membership of at least ninety percent Establishment figures."[2] This is no longer the case. The CFR has been making an overt drive to recruit members from outside the banking/law stereotype and from beyond the Northeastern seaboard (its membership's natural habitat). In keeping with this, the leadership has passed from old-line Establishment figures to men with unfamiliar, plebeian-sounding names. When David Rockefeller retired as chairman in 1985, he was succeeded by Peter Peterson, the son of Greek immigrants. Winston Lord, who vacated the presidency that same year, was a Pillsbury heir whose forebears had been regularly inducted into Skull and Bones since the mid-nineteenth century. Lord's replacement was Peter Tarnoff, grandson of Russian immigrants. Despite the cosmetology, Moskin's 1987 *Town & Country* article quotes one CFR officer as saying: "We are still an elitist organization," and a Council "veteran" who admits: "The great irony is that it is now operating more as a club than years ago. It is the biggest exclusive club in America. It is an almost Jamesian form of corruption. People of culture get to meet people from Wall Street and become consultants."[3]

Additionally, John Rees, publisher of *Information Digest,* noted in 1984 that "the American Right has been so successful at exposing the power and Leftward bias of the C.F.R. that a conscious effort has been made to add token Conservatives and moderates to the membership list for protective coloring . . ."[4] A few individuals broadly recognized as anti-Communists, such as Arnaud de Borchgrave and Norman Podhoretz, are now on the Council's roster.

While these various modifications could be regarded as genuine reforms, they may constitute an effort to "refute," retroactively, the blistering charges traditionally made against the Council — that it is an elitist front for the international banking community, globalist and pro-Communist in outlook.

Even the Council's annual report has been spruced up. Once a dry recitation of names, by-laws, and activities, it now appears in a handsome, enlarged edition, filled with photos of Council members chatting with world dignitaries over cocktails.

More image renovation has taken place at the bookstore. The trend-setter here may have been David Halberstam's *The Best and the Brightest* which, while giving only passing attention to the CFR as an organization, was an episodic profile of Establishment notables during the Kennedy-Johnson era. Halberstam scratched out the required minimum of criticisms of these men (that McGeorge Bundy was arrogant, that Robert McNamara was too statistics-minded, etc.), but this was overshadowed by his reverence for their intellects, as his title suggests. For example, he referred to Bundy as "the brightest light in that glittering constellation around the President," with a "cool, lucid mind, the honed-down intelligence of the mathematician, the insight of the political-science scholar at Harvard."[5] Halberstam told us, or quoted others who told us, that with McNamara "the mind was first-rate, the intellectual discipline awesome," that for William Bundy "brains were not his problem," that Kennedy was "exceptionally cerebral," and so forth, which is not to deny their intelligence, but only to note the book's preoccupation with it. Halberstam did make some uncompromising denunciations, but only of those people associated with anti-Communism or the conservative tradition. He called Vietnam commander General Paul Harkins "a man of compelling mediocrity" who "was ignorant of the past, and ignorant of the special kind of war he was fighting,"[6] referred to "the wild irrationality, the deviousness, the maliciousness and venality of the South Vietnamese,"[7] and revealed his disdain for what he called "God-fearing, Russian-fearing citizens," and Christian missionaries who went to China because "it was, by and large, more exciting than Peoria." Halberstam, it is duly observed, is a member of the Council on Foreign Relations.

The year 1984 saw publication of Robert Shulzinger's *The Wise Men of Foreign Affairs: The History of the Council on Foreign Relations.* Here again, the title exalts the professed intellectual powers of the Establishment, although the text grants that this has been overrated. Shulzinger's preface carefully points out that his book is a balanced account, neither tribute nor diatribe. Like Halberstam, however, he rarely faults Council members for anything more substantive than pomposity. One of his biggest criticisms is that "Council officials and friends have often exaggerated the body's importance."[8] This is just the sort of "criticism" Council members must savor! For in the interest of minimizing public scrutiny, they have always *downplayed* their importance, which is the net effect of Shulzinger's book. Again like Halberstam, he shoots more than blanks, but his real bullets are reserved for the Establishment's enemies. He can wait only until the second sentence of his book to bring up The John Birch Society, the CFR's most persistent and erudite critic. The first sentence quotes a condemnation of the CFR Shulzinger says he saw "scrawled on a bathroom wall," and he apparently hopes readers will then associate such tactics with The John Birch Society. Perhaps, instead, they find it a comment on where he does his research. Shulzinger was an International Affairs Fellow under the Council's sponsorship in 1982.

Then there is Isaacson and Thomas's monumental *The Wise Men* (1986), where again the title congratulates intellect. As we have noted, all six of the "wise men" were in the CFR — as are the authors themselves. Of the five endorsements on the book's jacket, four were written by Council members. The book is a prime example of the Establishment scratching the Establishment's back. Although biographical in focus, it intermittently mentions the CFR. And while it does yield significant revelations about American policy making, it is manifestly written as a glorification of its six subjects. It tells us of John McCloy's "discreet counsel, his rocklike wisdom, his reassuring steadiness";[9] and of how Robert Lovett "seemed devoid of personal ambition or ulterior motives. His discreet and selfless style of operating came to be idealized by others as the benchmark for a certain breed of public servant."[10] *The Wise Men* portrays its biographees as a rather conservative lot who, after World War II, aroused Americans from Coke-guzzling complacency to the dangers of the Soviet Union. But in reality, as we have seen, CFR conservatism is usually quite selective, turning on only when it serves the interests of Wall Street or globalism. As with Halberstam and Shulzinger, the book betrays an unmistakable antipathy toward the Establishment's main enemy: those people identified as devoutly anti-Communist — a word Isaacson and Thomas seem to think comes with the suffix "hysteria." McCloy, Acheson, Lovett, and the rest are portrayed as demigods, steering America through the treacherous rapids of foreign policy as they deftly humor egocentric generals and backwoods congressmen whose folly would land us on the shoals.

Why all this CFR-Establishment image-building? If we follow a human analogy, people give the most attention to their looks right before a date, a job interview, a speech, or a photograph session — that is, right before undergoing scrutiny.

Some answers may lie in the CFR's 1986 annual report. Chairman Peter G. Peterson noted that an endowment drive called "the Campaign for the Council" had raised over fifteen million dollars, which he said "greatly strengthens the base from which we may contemplate future steps." Peterson continued:

> To prepare the way for the possibility of such steps, David Rockefeller, with the approval of the Board of Directors, last spring established a special Committee on the Council's National Role .... it seemed an opportune time to reassess how, if at all, our functions, programs, and policies might be altered to reflect the possibility of a new national role.[11]

What this new role might be the report didn't specify, but it did note:

> A major goal has been the development of a Washington program of activities similar to those that take place at the Harold Pratt House.[12]

In 1987, Council president Peter Tarnoff stated:

> Because of the importance of Washington as the center of American foreign policy making and the presence there of 27 percent of our stated membership, we have decided to increase the size of our operations in the nation's capital. ... Over the next three years, we also intend to allow the stated membership in Washington to rise from the present level of 464 to 600. ...[13]

Will a switch of focus from New York to Washington be part of the Council's "new national role?" And if so, why?

Aging CFR member George Kennan, the originator of "containment," may have supplied a clue in an interview with Walter Cronkite televised by CBS on March 31, 1987. Cronkite introduced Kennan as "one of our genuine wise men." These were their final remarks, perhaps intended to stick the most in viewer consciousness.

> Cronkite (narrating): To help the United States establish a sound foreign policy, and stay within its principles, Kennan believes we should have a council of wise men drawn from all areas of national life.
>
> Kennan: I think it ought to be a permanent body; it ought to be advisory both to the President and to the Congress . . . and they should have, for the government, for the executive branch, and for the legislative branch, some of the prestige and authority of opinions of the Supreme Court . . . In our legal system, we deal on the basis of precedent. If a court has said something, we take it into account. I would like to see that prestige given to such a body.

Such ambitions are nothing new to the Council. Back in 1924, Count Hugo Lerchenfeld wrote in *Foreign Affairs:*

> Could not a body of highly deserving and competent men, such as are found in every nation as representatives of its highest moral forces — a kind of Areopagus — meet to give decisions on highly important contested matters? Could not a council be formed whose high judgement and impartiality would be taken for granted, and which would guide public opinion all over the world?[14]

What Kennan is suggesting today is that foreign policy, like judicial matters, be settled by an unelected elite. But to found such a body would require a restructuring of our government so radical that it could probably not be achieved except by a constitutional convention. Lo and behold, a convention is now being called for.

Winston Lord

David Rockefeller

Peter G. Peterson

Kennan now suggests a foreign
policy "council of wise men"
akin to the Supreme Court.

Chapter 14

On The Threshold Of
A New World Order?

The Threat to the Constitution

During the constitutional bicentennial, some have celebrated the Constitution; others have urged a new one. As the *Christian Science Monitor* noted in 1984:

> Amid the planning for festivals and finery, pomp and ceremony, there's a deeper meaning we must be careful not to miss. The bicentennial gives an opportunity for a rededication to the principles of the Constitution and the Bill of Rights, and for some careful thought about *the wisdom of constitutional revision.*[1] (Emphasis added.)

Warren Burger resigned as Chief Justice of the Supreme Court to work on the official Commission on the Bicentennial of the United States Constitution. This implies the project has more than trifling significance. The Burger Court was long accused of misconstruing the Constitution to advance a political agenda. But what better way to accomplish this than to change the Constitution itself? Justice Burger has insisted that the Commission's meetings be held in secret — an odd stipulation if its only purpose is celebration.

Burger is also Honorary Chairman of Project '87, a bicentennial organization that, according to its literature, "is dedicated to commemorating the Bicentennial of the United States Constitution by promoting public understanding and *appraisal* of this unique document."[2] (Emphasis added.) Co-chairman of Project '87 is James

MacGregor Burns, an advocate of constitutional revision. Burns wrote in his 1984 book *The Power To Lead*:

> Let us face reality. The framers [of the Constitution] have simply been too shrewd for us. They have outwitted us. They designed separated institutions that cannot be unified by mechanical linkages, frail bridges, tinkering. If we are to "turn the founders upside down" — to put together what they put asunder — we must directly confront the constitutional structure they erected.[3]

Burns serves on the board of yet another bicentennial group — the Committee on the Constitutional System (CCS). As of January 1987, the CCS had forty-eight board directors, more than a third of them members of the Council on Foreign Relations. Co-chairing the CCS is Douglas Dillon who, with David Rockefeller, also co-chaired the aforementioned Campaign for the Council that raised fifteen million dollars so that the CFR could contemplate "a new national role."

The CCS is proposing drastic changes in the Constitution. These were outlined in the 1985 book *Reforming American Government: The Bicentennial Papers of the Committee on the Constitutional System*. Ensuing are some of them.

• One proposal would have us emulate the European parliamentary system; American voters would be unable to cast ballots for individual candidates, restricted instead to choosing a party slate across the board. This would eliminate independent candidates (which would suit the Establishment very well).

• The Congress would be expanded. The party whose nominee became President would designate one-sixth of all representatives in the House and one-third of all senators. This would diminish the elective power of the voters and the balance between the executive and legislative spheres.

• The requirement for Senate ratification of treaties would be lowered.

• The CCS has also advocated extending representatives' terms from two to four years and senators' from six to eight, and allowing congressmen to serve in the executive branch while still holding their seats in Congress.

Not surprisingly, these proposals have perceptible ancestry in a *Foreign Affairs* article. It was written in 1980 by Lloyd N. Cutler (CFR), Counsel to President Carter, after the Senate refused to ratify the dubious Salt II Treaty. He finished his article by noting that, while a constitutional convention could achieve the changes he contemplated, a "more practicable first step would be the appointment of a bipartisan presidential commission . . ." Cutler went on to become co-chairman of the CCS.

The aggregate measures sought by the group are ostensibly designed to facilitate the policy-making process. But they reduce the say of the American voters and play havoc with our system of checks and balances, thus increasing the potential for an eventual dictatorship.

CCS members are not just mulling over modifications, but the possibility of a whole new Constitution. In *Reforming American Government* we read:

> The change will require major surgery. One cannot stop short of bold and decisive departures. And yet a guiding principle should be to *write the new Constitution* in a way that permits considerable leeway.[4] (Emphasis added.)

The idea of a "modern" Constitution is not itself new — in fact, one has already been written! It was published in 1970 by the Center for the Study of Democratic Institutions, which was established by Ford Foundation financing. This constitution was primarily drafted by Rexford Guy Tugwell, an old member of FDR's "brain trust." Among the extreme changes its articles called for were the conversion of the Senate from an elected body to one entirely appointed by the President, its members (some of whom would come from private groups) to serve for a lifetime; transfer of states' powers to the federal government; nationalization of the communications industry; and conditional removal of the right to trial by jury.[5]

There hasn't been a constitutional convention since the original one in 1787. But if you think we are far from having another, think again. Such a proceeding transpires if two-thirds of the state legislatures call for it. As of early 1988, thirty-two of the required thirty-four states had done so. They gave their approval because a constitutional convention has been publicized as the means to require a balanced federal budget — a context conveniently created by wild deficit spending under Ronald Reagan. Few of the state legislators were aware of the radical agenda for constitutional change that has been formulated. Once such a convention begins, there is no telling where it might go. Whether or not it could be limited to balancing the budget is considered debatable, since there is little precedent to go on.

Of course, the only way to justify the severe constitutional mutations intended by groups like the CCS would be the existence of a national crisis. This has not been overlooked. The report of the first New England Regional Meeting of the CCS said that co-chairman Douglas Dillon "thinks needed changes can be made only after a period of great crisis." Project '87 co-chairman James MacGregor Burns stated in *Reforming American Government*:

> I doubt that Americans under normal conditions could agree on the package of radical and "alien" constitutional changes that would be required. They would do so, I think, only during and following a stupendous national crisis and political failure.[6]

In a lengthy cover article in the October 1987 *Atlantic*, CFR chairman Peter G. Peterson forecast an economic crunch — if not crash — for the near future.

We have seen that the international bankers have historically been quite adept at instigating disasters in order to compel redirection of American policy. As is rather well known, western banks in recent years have loaned out hundreds of billions of dollars to Third World and Communist nations. For many of these countries, repayment appears impossible. The banks keep rescheduling installments, but some analysts anticipate that eventually the debtors will simply renege, officially and permanently, in a united front. This would probably collapse the U.S. banking system and economy — unless extreme measures were introduced.

Should this crisis, by some coincidence, erupt in the midst of a constitutional convention to balance the budget, then our entire way of life might be altered. Richard Cooper's dream of an international currency, along with dozens of other Orwellian changes propounded by *Foreign Affairs* and the bicentennial groups, might then appear. And perhaps George Kennan's "council of wise men" (i.e., members of the CFR) would be instituted as a Supreme Court of foreign policy on the pretext that it offers the best brains available. Could this be the ultimate meaning behind the CFR's "new national role" and its plans for a quasi-Pratt House in Washington? It may also explain why the Council is giving itself an extensive face lift. For if it is to become a division of our government (as it succeeded in doing on a small scale during World War II), it would probably first be subject to investigative hearings and screenings — thus the necessity to erase all outward appearances that might tend to corroborate the elitism, globalism, and pro-Communism long imputed to it.

Admittedly, this is speculation. But history is not speculation, and history contains enough specimens of Establishment scheming to warrant our vigilance. This is especially true in light of the very real constitutional reform movement.

The Constitution guarantees our liberties — our freedom of speech, press, assembly, and religion; our right to choose our leaders and our right to fair trials. Half of mankind lacks these liberties; our desire to keep them also justifies our vigilance.

If the Establishment has its way, when will the constitutional convention take place? In *Between Two Ages* — published the same year as Tugwell's "new constitution" — Zbigniew Brzezinski forecast:

> The approaching two-hundredth anniversary of the Declaration of Independence could justify the call for a national constitutional convention to re-examine the nation's formal institutional framework. Either 1976 or 1989 — the two-hundredth anniversary of the Constitution — could serve as a suitable target date for culminating a national dialogue on the relevance of existing arrangements, the workings of the representative process, and the desirability of imitating the various European regionalization reforms and of streamlining the administrative

structure. More important still, either date would provide a suitable occasion for redefining the meaning of modern democracy . . .[7]

The year 1976 has come and gone, but was not neglected by the globalists. To mark the occasion, the World Affairs Council of Philadelphia issued a "Declaration of INTERdependence." It proclaimed: "Two centuries ago our forefathers brought forth a new nation; now we must join with others to bring forth a new world order."

Nineteen seventy-six witnessed no constitutional convention, but proponents still hope that Brzezinski's other year, 1989, will. It is somewhat curious that he labeled this the 200th anniversary of the Constitution, since — although it became effective in 1789 — it was written and signed in 1787, and ratified by the required number of states in 1788. Perhaps it is more to the point that 1989 is the 200th anniversary of the French Revolution, which many theorists see as the historical genesis of the collectivist movement. It is also the 100th anniversary of the Socialist International.

Years ending in "nine" have been good ones for globalists and Communists — bad ones for the rest of us. Marked by 1989 will be the seventieth anniversary of the League of Nations (and the Paris meetings at which the CFR and RIIA were founded); the sixtieth of the stock market crash; the fiftieth of World War II; the fortieth of the fall of China; the thirtieth of Castro's assumption of power in Cuba, giving the Soviets their first base in the Western Hemisphere; the twentieth of the beginning of our pullout from Vietnam; and the tenth of Jimmy Carter's banner year, 1979 — when Iran and Nicaragua fell, the Soviets invaded Afghanistan, Salt II was signed, and we formally commenced relations with Red China.

Aside, then, from other portents now in place, it may not be entirely facetious to say that sentiment alone could prompt a major Establishment move in 1989.

Wall Street's Biggest Merger

If the changes envisioned by constitutional reformers come to pass, what will be our nation's destiny? A U.S. financial cave-in would probably draw the whole planet into its vortex, as did the Great Depression. In the long run, a new world order under one government would be offered as a global panacea. This would incorporate Free World countries with Communist states.

From Romania to Vietnam, CFR men acting as U.S. diplomats have tried to force coalition governments on nations struggling against Communism. Such coalitions have inevitably resulted in Communism, because the Communists have always violated and exploited the agreements made, and usurped all power. Indeed, as Louis Budenz, a high-ranking American Communist and editor of the *Daily Worker*, was to acknowledge after renouncing the Party: "The coalition government was a device used by the Communists always to slaughter those whom they brought into the coalition."[8] What the globalists are ultimately seeking is a *macrocosmic* coalition government.

For decades, the Council on Foreign Relations has advocated regional alliances against the Soviet Union, but with the footnote that, in the end, the USSR should be brought into "the community of nations." This would be preceded by a fusion of Eastern and Western Europe, a favorite *Foreign Affairs* theme.

We alluded earlier to the abortive Reece Committee, whose investigations discovered that the Establishment foundations were funding the promotion of world government and socialism. In the fall of 1953, Norman Dodd, Director of Research for the Reece Committee, was invited to the headquarters of the Ford Foundation by its president, H. Rowan Gaither (CFR). According to Dodd, Gaither told him: "Mr. Dodd, all of us here at the policy-making level have had experience, either in O.S.S. or the European Economic Administration, with directives from the White House. We operate under those directives here. Would you like to know what those directives are?" Dodd replied that he would. Gaither said: "The substance of them is that we shall use our grant-making power so to alter our life in the United States that we can be comfortably merged with the Soviet Union."[9]

Dodd, stunned, asked if he would repeat that before the House committee for the enlightenment of the American people.

Gaither answered: "This we would not think of doing."

This helps account for the compatibility of the CFR's globalism with its pro-Communism. There can be no one-world government without a U.S.-USSR merger.

Recent events foretoken such a merger. As we observed near the outset of this book, a Council delegation visited with Gorbachev and other Russian leaders in February 1987. *This was at the Soviets' invitation*, which is a gauge of the respect Pratt House commands at the Kremlin. *Facts on File* reports that the CFR contingent "declined to openly talk about the details of the discussion."[10]

Gorbachev in the meantime has staged a campaign of paltry reforms known as *glasnost*. Millions today languish in Soviet gulags, but when Gorbachev releases one or two prominent dissidents, the U.S. press receives it like the Emancipation Proclamation, while continuing to disregard the dictator's butchering of Afghanistan. The American people are being deluged with media hype which proclaims the supposed new openness of the USSR. Paid propagandists of the Soviet government, such as Vladimir Posner, are presented to TV viewers as "journalists," as if, like U.S. correspondents, they had the freedom to criticize their country's rulers.

Today we are told that anyone against accommodation with the Soviet Union is a warmonger, and that striking the right bargain with Moscow will lead to a new age of world peace. We have been reminded repeatedly that "After all, the Russians are people just like us" — which is assuredly true. But the Soviet *lifestyle* is glaringly *unlike* ours. Economic hardships in the USSR — where one must stand in line all night to buy a container of milk — are but the least of the system's demerits. It is a totalitarian state, void of civil liberties. So great is the prohibition against freedom of speech and press that it is against the law even to own a mimeograph machine. Barbed wire and machine guns guard against would-be emigrants. According to Solzhenitsyn, more than sixty million human beings have perished in Soviet slave labor camps. Is this the kind of society Americans want to be coupled with? Unequivocally, it is not. We prefer to keep sleeping without wondering if a knock on the door will mean the secret police have come to abduct us into a nightmare from which there will be no awakening. Yet the globalists long for a Soviet merger.

History Has a Pattern

According to some, history is basically a jumble of events: blunders, coincidences, and happenstances that have brought us to where we are today. This outlook does nothing to elucidate our past. However, seen in the context of globalist influence and maneuvering, history — especially twentieth century American history — begins to make sense, as if snapping into place upon a calculated blueprint.

With little exception, American policy has conformed to this blueprint ever since the New Deal. A good illustration is our China policy, which has brought us toward rapprochement with the Chinese Communists as swiftly as the American people could be persuaded to allow it. Every President since FDR has had a part in this continuum.

• Roosevelt: ceded Manchurian ports to Stalin during World War II, and agreed to equip the Soviets' expedition into China, where they armed Mao Tse-tung's revolutionaries.

• Truman: through his proxy, George Marshall, permitted the fall of China by truce negotiations, a weapons embargo against the Nationalists, and the obstruction of Congressionally mandated military aid.

• Eisenhower: forced Taiwan to relinquish the Tachen Islands to Peking, and interceded to prevent Chiang Kai-shek from invading the mainland in 1955.

• Kennedy: also prevented Chiang from invading the mainland, in 1962 — when it was in turmoil and ripe for overthrow.

• Johnson: terminated economic aid to Taiwan.

• Nixon: visited China, breaking the ice with the Communists.

• Ford: presided over the withdrawal of most of the U.S. troops from Taiwan, and visited the mainland.

• Carter: broke relations with Taiwan; recognized Peking.

• Reagan: proliferated trade with Red China, and promised reduced arms sales to Taiwan.

Step by step, our China policy, like our broad foreign policy, has followed an essentially unwavering course. It matters little which party occupies the White House. Anyone can see that when the "conservative" Richard Nixon went to Peking, he was paving the way for the "liberal" Jimmy Carter to recognize it.

Our history has a pattern. Thomas Jefferson once said: "Single acts of tyranny may be ascribed to the accidental opinion of a day; but a series of oppressions, begun at a distinguished period, and pursued unalterably through every change of ministers, too plainly prove a deliberate systematical plan of reducing us to slavery."

Jefferson's words could well be applied to the American historical process in this century. If that process continues unimpeded, we can anticipate a national crisis, a constitutional convention, and a new world order binding the Free World to the countries of the Iron and Bamboo Curtains.

Zbigniew Brzezinski

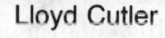

AP/WIDE WORLD PHOTOS

Lloyd Cutler

Warren Burger

H. Rowan Gaither:
". . . that we can be comfortably
merged with the Soviet Union."

Chapter 15

Solutions And Hope

How can we prevent materialization of the developments projected in the last chapter? First, we still dwell in a free country, with free speech and the power to vote. And we can exercise these rights to demand and enforce change.

For more than fifty years, American policy has been formulated mostly by one group. As the titles of the recent books we cited in Chapter Thirteen hint, the main qualification claimed for these people is intelligence. FDR had a "brain trust." In a memorandum, Assistant Secretary of State George Messersmith said the use of the CFR's War and Peace Studies Project during World War II was justified because the Council could "call upon the best brains in international relations."[1] In his prospectus for the Trilateral Commission, David Rockefeller stated it was his intention to bring the "best brains in the world" together. George Bush and other Establishment candidates for President have pleaded their fitness for office by saying that, if elected, they would call the nation's top minds to Washington.

But there is a problem in this. The word "genius," it is to be remembered, is often paired with the word "evil." Intellect alone does not make a statesman. There is another requisite ingredient: character. What good are brains in public officials if they aren't used to serve the interests of the electorate? So far, the "best brains" have brought us staggering debt and taxation, the Vietnam War, the collapse of allies around the world, and much other detriment. It would take a crackerjack of a résumé writer to launder their record.

Only one American in 100,000 belongs to the Council on Foreign Relations. Why should this clique continue to set policy? Why should others be denied an opportunity? This is our nation. And we have a right to leaders who represent *us*, not international banking or world government.

We Americans can make a difference. We can speak out, alerting our friends and neighbors to the danger facing our republic. And we can elect congressmen who will fight the Establishment — this means congressmen who will:

• Support the Constitution and oppose a constitutional convention.

• Support a strong U.S. defense and oppose any treaty that moves us toward alignment with the Soviet Union.

• Support effectual aid to foreign peoples battling Communist aggression, and oppose trade and credits for Marxist regimes.

• Oppose the strengthening of the UN and other international agencies of dubious merit.

• Support reductions in federal spending, taxation, and bureaucracy.

Where we cannot elect representatives devoted to such a platform, we can still urge them to vote this way on individual legislative issues.

And we can seek a President who will jettison the CFR.* Of course, all White House candidates claim to have no strings attached. Woodrow Wilson ran as the anti-Money Trust candidate, FDR as the anti-Wall Street candidate, Jimmy Carter as the anti-"insider" candidate, and Ronald Reagan as the anti-Trilateral Commission candidate. As Chief Executives, however, all of these men were guided by the very forces they allegedly opposed. So the voters have to choose with exquisite wisdom.

It is also time to call for a Congressional investigation of both the Council on Foreign Relations and the Trilateral Commission, as the American Legion did in 1980.

---

* One candidate in the 1988 campaign explicitly pledged to do so if elected. Pat Robertson stated on November 16, 1987: "I intend to eliminate the influence of the Council on Foreign Relations and the Trilateral Commission from the State Department and the Treasury Department. I intend to appoint as Secretary of State someone who puts the long range interests of the United States first, rather than trying to sacrifice our interests in order to achieve global accommodation with the Soviet Union." On the other hand, of eight foreign policy advisors listed for Michael Dukakis in *Time* magazine for May 2, 1988, seven were members of the CFR.

Furthermore, Americans must be vigilant toward events overseas. In instance after instance where the Establishment has joined forces with the international left to destabilize a country, a certain pattern has emerged that it behooves us to be aware of.

(1) Insurgent Communists, equipped by the Soviet Union or one of its surrogates, begin a campaign of terror in the nation.

(2) To protect the population, the government cracks down on the revolutionary terrorists. Some are killed, others imprisoned.

(3) The American press now begins to denounce the government for "oppressing dissenters," "violating human rights," and "jailing political prisoners." The country's leader is targeted as a "tyrant" and "neo-Nazi." There are rumors of torture by his security forces. In the meantime, the Communists are described not as Communists, but as "democratic reformers."

(4) The United States — via CFR diplomats — intervenes. It demands that the government make concessions to the rebels, including the release of those captured, and form a coalition government with them. If the government refuses, the U.S. embargoes trade and weapons. If it gives in, the terrorists carry on with impunity. Either way, the nation is doomed.

(5) Under the irresistible pressure of both the USSR and the U.S., the government now collapses, and the Marxists assume power. There is no longer any pretense about whether or not they are Communists. They convert the country into a police state, executing opponents, seizing the press, suppressing religion, and prohibiting free speech as "counter-revolutionary." But the American mass media are no longer concerned about human rights there — they are too busy taking aim at someone new.

The above scenario, with minor variations, has been used successfully to topple China, Cuba, South Vietnam, Cambodia, Iran, Nicaragua, and Rhodesia. It is in the late stages in the Philippines, only with Corazon Aquino serving as an unwitting Kerensky intermediate to Communist takeover. It is currently being applied to Chile, South Africa, and South Korea. It will not stop with them — later it will be Honduras, Guatemala, Taiwan, Singapore, and assorted other lands. The scenario has been rerun more times than an old *Star Trek* episode, and one asks when the American people will finally realize that what they are witnessing is not a unique situation but part of a continuum.

We must learn to recognize the pattern. It does not matter whether the nation at risk is being accused of "tyranny" as in Nicaragua, "racism" as in Rhodesia, or "corruption" as in the Philippines. The specific charge, whether true or not, matters little to men of the Establishment; their object is to destabilize the country — and, for the American people to accept that, a suitable excuse has to be furnished. We must instruct our congressmen to oppose further subversion of our allies. And the next time a journalist complains that, in South Korea, freedom of the press has been restricted, ask him to explain why he doesn't mention that, in North Korea, it has been *annihilated*.

The task of stopping the rush toward a Communist-style "new world order" seems formidable. It would be easier, of course, if there was an organization designed to stop it. There is. Perhaps the best way to introduce this group is to examine one of the most recent entries in the Establishment's anthology of "coincidences."

The Ultimate Coincidence

On September 1, 1983, the Korean Air Lines Flight 007, en route from Alaska to Seoul, was obliterated by air-to-air missiles from a Soviet interceptor. All 269 passengers and crew, including 61 Americans, were lost. Soviet fighters had trailed the plane for over two hours. Nearly all observers agreed that it could not have been shot down without top clearance from Moscow. The question was: Why did the Soviets do it? Why did they risk the inevitable backlash of world opinion to eliminate a harmless civilian airliner? There had to be something or someone on board important enough to make the consequences worth it. There was — someone all but ignored by the mass media: Dr. Lawrence Patton McDonald, member of Congress.

McDonald was the most dedicated anti-Communist on Capitol Hill. *The Review Of The News* noted: "From the time he took his oath of office in 1975 until the moment of his death, Congressman McDonald had systematically carried out a campaign against the Soviet Communists of a sort which no other U.S. elected official had ever done on his own."[2] Author Jeffrey St. John, in his book about the KAL 007 tragedy, *Day of the Cobra*, observed: "Congressman Lawrence McDonald had spent his entire career warning against the use of terrorism as an instrument of Soviet policy, particularly the use of the threat of nuclear war by the Kremlin as a weapon to paralyze the United States and its Western allies' will to resist."[3] McDonald was Washington's most outspoken critic of trade and technology transfer to the USSR. He was the president and founder of the Western Goals Foundation, which produced books and videotapes on Soviet-generated terror and espionage. He had recently written a series of articles about Yuri Andropov and the KGB. Voting appraisals gave him the most conservative rating in Congress during his five terms in office. And most significantly, Lawrence McDonald was chairman of The John Birch Society — the world's largest and most sophisticated anti-Communist organization. He was condemned in *Pravda*, *Izvestia*, and on Radio Moscow. Dr. Lawrence McDonald was, arguably, the Kremlin's number one enemy.

The odds against such a man "just happening" to be on the flight the Soviets destroyed were astronomical. Yet the news media neglected the obvious potential significance. After the incident, a host of "experts" were called in who assured the public that there was no specific reason for the attack — instead, they explained, it was due to the generalized phenomenon of Soviet "paranoia concerning their airspace." The following statement by Secretary of State George Shultz was typical:

> The answer to the broader question of motivation seems to lie in the character of the Soviet Union. There is a massive concern for security, a massive paranoia, and I think this act was an expression of that excessive concern over security.[4]

It should be noted that as chairman of The John Birch Society (JBS), McDonald was not only an archenemy of the Soviet Union, but of the American Establishment — of which the JBS is the most vocal critic. For years, the Society has been intellectually at crossed swords with the CFR. Congressman McDonald even wrote the foreword to Gary Allen's *The Rockefeller File*, in which he spoke out against "the drive of the Rockefellers and their allies to create a one-world government, combining super-capitalism and Communism under the same tent . . ."

When Lawrence McDonald established the Western Goals Foundation, its stated purpose was "to rebuild and strengthen the political, economic, and social structure of the United States and Western Civilization so as to make any merger with totalitarians impossible." Such a merger now looms closer than ever before. When the CFR delegation paid a visit to Gorbachev and his minions in February 1987, one could only reflect on how timely McDonald's removal was for the globalist vision.

Lawrence McDonald is dead, but his cause survives — and so does the organization he left behind.

The John Birch Society

Spokesmen for the Establishment are not only fond of lauding its collective IQ, but of twitting its "right-wing" critics as ignorant riffraff. You could not prove this by Robert Welch (1899-1985), who founded The John Birch Society in 1958. At age two, he learned to read; at seven he read all nine volumes of Ridpath's *History of the World*; at twelve he was a freshman at the University of North Carolina. America entered World War I, and Welch, a college degree already under his belt, enrolled at the U.S. Naval Academy at age seventeen. After two years he ranked fourth in a class of nearly one thousand. When the war ended, so did his motivation, and he resigned. He attended Harvard Law School from 1919 to 1921, but withdrew to start what would be an extremely successful business career. He was on the board of directors of the National Association of Manufacturers for seven years, traveled extensively, authored several books, and ran for lieutenant governor in Massachusetts. In 1958, aroused by the growth of Communism and the Eisenhower administration's hollow conservatism, Welch brought together several prominent Americans to found an anti-Communist society.

It was named after John Birch, a young Christian missionary serving in China when World War II broke out. Birch came to the assistance of General Claire Chennault's Flying Tigers, who were helping the Chinese resist the Japanese invasion. He volunteered for service in the U.S. Army, rose to the rank of captain, and was

215

highly decorated by both the American and Chinese governments. But, a few days after the war's end, the Chinese Communists murdered him. His death was regarded as perhaps the first casualty in the final postwar struggle between the Free World and Communism. The John Birch Society soon had tens of thousands of enthusiastic members, organized into individual chapters throughout the country. These chapters became the vanguard of the American movement against Communism, big government, world government, and the proverbial Establishment itself. "Education," said Robert Welch, "is our total strategy." That strategy came to life in scores of books — both new ones and reprints of old classics; a monthly journal, *American Opinion* (whose modern successor is called *The New American*); filmstrips; tabulations of Congressional voting records; a national lecture circuit for distinguished speakers; and even summer camps for youth. All these activities continue today.

The response from the Communists and the Establishment was predictable. The tactic used had a prototype in a directive issued by the Communist Party to its U.S. members in 1943. It read:

> When certain obstructionists become too irritating, label them, after suitable build-ups, as Fascist or Nazi or anti-Semitic, and use the prestige of anti-Fascist and tolerance organizations to discredit them. In the public mind constantly associate those who oppose us with those names which already have a bad smell.[5]

A certain element has always used Hitler's war against the Soviet Union as proof that Communism is the natural antithesis of Nazism. In point of fact, the two systems are cousins — both are forms of totalitarianism (total government). What The John Birch Society and other ideologically conservative groups espouse is *limited* government, which fits on the opposite end of the spectrum from both Communism and Naziism. Nevertheless, a rather successful misrepresentation has been carried out.

The Communist and Establishment press operated in sync. In 1961, *People's World*, the West Coast Communist newspaper, described the Society as a secret fascist outfit. *Pravda*, which carried as many as six attacks on the JBS in one issue, called Robert Welch an "American Fuhrer," "brandishing the bludgeon of the Hitlerite storm trooper." Not to be outdone, *Time* magazine (March 10, 1961) reported that many considered Birchers "barely a goosestep away from the formation of goon squads." Robert Welch had said that "truth is our only weapon." But CBS News claimed the Society was purchasing guns — a story that turned out to be complete fabrication. JBS spokesman G. Edward Griffin notes that part of the campaign against the Society included "dirty tricks" such as calling people in the night and saying: "This is The John Birch Society. Get out of town, ya dirty Commie!"

The stereotype assigned Birchers was that of people looking under their beds for Communists. They were, it was reported, anti-Semitic as well as paranoid about the Russians. The author of this book, who is partly of Russian-Jewish lineage, finds these charges ridiculous. To be sure, there is anti-Semitism in the world, but anyone who tries to find one shred of it in any Birch Society publication will come away empty-handed. As to paranoia about Soviet Communism, one has only to think of the millions that system has made into corpses and ask: What did these people die from — paranoia?

Although the stereotype was established with fair success, the media assault, on the whole, backfired. All the publicity helped the Society grow. The approach in more recent years has been to give it "the silent treatment."

As Robert Welch reached the twilight of his life, he handed over the reins of leadership to Lawrence McDonald. Dr. McDonald, a surgeon as well as a Congressman, was young, handsome, articulate, and a born activist. But he died at Soviet hands with 268 others on September 1, 1983. In December of that year, Welch made his final public appearance at ceremonies marking the Society's twenty-fifth anniversary. He suffered a crippling stroke a few days later, and died on January 6, 1985.

The John Birch Society continues to spearhead the fight against world government. To be sure, it is the underdog in this conflict. Unlike the Establishment, the JBS does not have billions in foundation assets it can tap to make its case. But perhaps that's just why it will win — its members are motivated by something greater than money.

If you think you would like to learn more about The John Birch Society, contact the organization at its headquarters (Post Office Box 8040, Appleton, Wisconsin 54913). Its staff would be delighted to hear from you!

What Is It All About?

America now confronts a distinct choice. In a few short years, we could be part of a totalitarian "new world order," or we could remain a free and independent nation. Our forefathers fought and died so that we might have that freedom and independence — something to think about before giving them away. Patriotism was long regarded as virtue. But now it is often slighted. Patriotism, we are told, is nationalism, and nationalism, we are told, is fascism, the stuff of Adolph Hitler. (Oddly enough, the people who advance this view frequently call Communist rebels in the Third World "nationalists" — in which case they consider the term unobjectionable. It is a sin, apparently, only for the rest of us.)

But Hitler's nationalism was largely a fanatic devotion to race. In America, we are a compound of all races. For us, patriotism is not just allegiance to a people, it is allegiance to the *principles* our country was built on.

Of course, the idea of a new world order may sound inviting, and it certainly will if the mass media promote it during an economic crisis, a rash of terrorism, or the imminence of war. Even today, globalists — whose numbers are by no means confined to the walls of Pratt House — talk of a "New Age" in which all men will live in peace and harmony. There is a serious flaw, however, in their thesis.

America's founders devised an arrangement of governmental checks and balances. The executive, legislative, and judicial branches all served to restrain each other's power. The House counterbalanced the Senate, and the states counterbalanced Washington itself, whose authority was further limited by the Bill of Rights. Why was all this so? Because the founders knew that unrestricted power leads to tyranny. "Government," declared George Washington, "is not reason, it is not eloquence — it is force. Like fire, it is a dangerous servant and a fearful master." James Madison said: "The accumulation of all power — legislative, executive, and judiciary — in the same hands . . . may justly be pronounced the very definition of tyranny."

There is a saying: "Power tends to corrupt and absolute power corrupts absolutely." An everyday example would be an abusive boss. Upon those beneath him, he inflicts wrath he would never dare show his own superiors — because around his subordinates, he has power; there is no risk to a bad temper, nothing to act as a restraint. In other words, in the absence of restraints, man's worst side tends to come out. History has repeatedly illustrated this. In 1919, Boston's police went on strike, and mob violence reigned in the city. Hundreds of stores were looted, with many "ordinary citizens" partaking in the crime. With the restraints gone, the worst in people emerged.

The authors of the Constitution understood this phenomenon, and understood that political power, being the greatest power on earth, is extremely dangerous unless confined. This is why the globalist plan must be stopped. If all power is vested in a single international authority, what force except God Himself could save us from the abuses certain to follow?

Why is it that America has never experienced genocide or police-state terror like other parts of the world? Because the decentralization of power decreed by the Constitution makes them impossible. For two centuries, refugees have come to the United States to escape oppression overseas. But what if America is absorbed by a world government that turns despotic? There will be no new country for anyone to flee to.

Actually, the nations of the world themselves act as a sort of check-and-balance system against each other. If a dictator oppresses his people too greatly, they may seek foreign assistance. Even the Soviets are afraid to persecute *too* extensively lest they forfeit Western trade and credits. If, however, our world pluralism is junked for a world government, we are apt to see atrocities far worse than any the world has known.

What could possess anyone to believe that erasing national boundaries will erase evil from mankind? Yet that, in effect, is what many globalists proclaim.

Of course, some say there is no such thing as evil — that it's all relative, a matter of a man's opinion. But there is evil: the bones of

Dachau and Cambodia cry it out. And this evil has been with man for a long time.

There is, as anyone can see, a perennial conflict throughout the world. It has been called the struggle between left and right, between the Iron Curtain and the Free World, and between atheistic Communism and Christianity. Actually, this clash of global forces is simply a macrocosm of the battle going on inside every man. Here it has been termed the conflict between material and spiritual values, between desire and conscience, and between Satan and God. But whatever we call it, the conflict is there. This is why we have the paradox of capitalists allied with Communists. Contrary to Marxist doctrine, life is not a class struggle but a spiritual one. People can choose one side or the other, whether they are rich or poor, or their name is Carnegie or Castro.

In essence, history itself is the story of this conflict. Those who view history as a series of accidents, it is interesting to note, also usually believe that the universe itself *began* as an accident — a "big bang" — and that man resulted from random molecular collisions.

There are, however, those of us who accept the causality of God. Many centuries ago, the Hebrew Old Testament (as in the book of Daniel) and the Christian New Testament (as in the book of Revelation) prophesied that ultimately a beautiful kingdom will prevail over all creation under Messiah or Christ. But they also warned of an evil, one-world government: the kingdom of the Antichrist, which would signify terror and tribulation for the earth. We might do well to ask if that kingdom is now taking shape, as nation after nation falls to Communism, with its totalitarianism, genocide, and persecution of Jews, Christians, and all other dissenters.

Many notables of the American Establishment have given themselves over to one side in this conflict, and it is not the side the ancient scriptures recommend. Whether or not they are conspirators, whether they are conscious or not of the ultimate consequences of their actions, their powerful influence has helped move the world toward apocalyptic events. This book has been written not as a condemnation of them — for who among us is without culpability? — but as a warning to avert catastrophe.

Ancient Israel was founded as a land of God. It thrived and knew great power. But eventually it became engrossed with its material abundance, forgot the laws of God, grew weak, and was conquered, its people scattered abroad. Similarly, America was founded as a land of God, a Christian land. It became the freest and strongest nation on earth. But, like Biblical Israel, it too is losing sight of its religious roots, floundering in materialism. Will the United States also be conquered?

We Americans must make a choice — liberty or new world order. If we wait too long, a national crisis may sweep us into the wrong decision irrevocably. Perhaps with the help of The John Birch Society, we can thwart the ends of globalism. One thing is for sure: the job will be a lot easier if we turn our hearts toward God and ask for his assistance. If not, all the signs say, night's curtain will surely fall.

Robert Welch

Lawrence P. McDonald

Dr. McDonald's wife, Kathryn, and son, Trygvvi, at
Washington memorlal service for the slain congressman

Footnotes

Abbreviations: CFR — Council on Foreign Relations; *FA — Foreign Affairs.*

Chapter One. A Primer on the CFR

1. Curtis B. Dall, *FDR: My Exploited Father-In-Law* (Washington, D.C.: Action Associates, 1970), p. 67.
2. Don Bell, "Who Are Our Rulers?," *American Mercury*, September 1960, p. 136.
3. *F.D.R.: His Personal Letters* (New York: Duell, Sloan and Pearce, 1950), p. 373.
4. Phoebe and Kent Courtney, *America's Unelected Rulers: The Council on Foreign Relations* (New Orleans: Conservative Society of America, 1962), pp. 1-2.
5. Edith Kermit Roosevelt, "Elite Clique Holds Power in U.S.," *Indianapolis News*, December 23, 1961, p. 6.
6. Arthur Schlesinger, Jr., *A Thousand Days* (Boston: Houghton Mifflin, 1965), p. 128.
7. David Halberstam, *The Best and the Brightest* (New York: Random House, 1972), p. 6.
8. *Newsweek*, September 6, 1971, p. 74.
9. Richard Rovere, "The American Establishment," *Esquire*, May 1962, p. 107.
10. J. Anthony Lukas, "The Council on Foreign Relations: Is It a Club? Seminar? Presidium? Invisible Government?," *New York Times Magazine*, November 21, 1971, p. 129.
11. Advertisement in *Foreign Affairs*, Summer 1986.
12. Theodore White, *The Making of the President, 1964* (New York: Atheneum, 1965), p. 67.
13. *Christian Science Monitor*, September 1, 1961, p. 9.
14. Joseph Kraft, "School For Statesmen," *Harper's*, July 1958, p. 64.

15. John Franklin Campbell, "The Death Rattle of the American Establishment," *New York*, September 20, 1971, p. 48.

16. Lukas, pp. 125-26.

17. CFR, *Annual Report, 1985-86*, p. 27.

18. CFR, *Annual Report, 1986-87*, p. 5.

19. J. Robert Moskin, "Advise and Dissent," *Town & Country*, March 1987, p. 154.

20. Kraft, p. 64.

21. Phyllis Schlafly and Chester Ward, *Kissinger on the Couch* (New Rochelle, New York: Arlington House, 1975), p. 151.

22. CFR, *Annual Report, 1986-87*, p. 5.

23. Moskin, p. 208.

24. Richard J. Barnet, *Roots of War* (New York: Atheneum, 1972), p. 49.

25. Kraft, p. 66.

26. Schlafly and Ward, pp. 144-50.

27. Charles W. Eliot, "The Next American Contribution to Civilization," *FA*, September 15, 1922, p. 59.

28. Philip Kerr, "From Empire to Commonwealth," *FA*, December 1922, pp. 97-98.

29. *American Public Opinion and Postwar Security Commitments* (New York: CFR, 1944), quoted in Alan Stang, *The Actor* (Belmont, Mass.: Western Islands, 1968), p. 35.

30. Richard N. Gardner, "The Hard Road to World Order," *FA*, April 1974, p. 558.

31. Kurt Waldheim, "The United Nations: The Tarnished Image," *FA*, Fall 1984, p. 93.

32. Max Eastman, "The Character and Fate of Leon Trotsky," *FA*, January 1941, p. 332.

33. Leonard Silk and Mark Silk, *The American Establishment* (New York: Basic Books, 1980), pp. 192-93.

34. CFR, *Annual Report, 1985-86*, p. 17.

35. Roosevelt, p. 6.

36. *Congressional Record*, December 15, 1987, Vol. 133, p. S18146.

Chapter 2. Background to the Beginning

1. Gary Allen, with Larry Abraham, *None Dare Call It Conspiracy* (Rossmoor, Calif.: Concord Press, 1972), p. 41.

2. Carroll Quigley, *Tragedy and Hope* (New York: Macmillan, 1966), pp. 326-27.

3. Ibid., p. 324.

4. Gustavus Myers, *History of the Great American Fortunes* (New York: The Modern Library, 1936), p. 556.

5. Bob Adelmann, "The Federal Reserve System," *The New American*, October 27, 1986, p. 31.

6. Frederick Lewis Allen, "Morgan The Great," *Life*, April 25, 1949, p. 126.

7. *Congressional Record*, December 22, 1913, Vol. 51, p. 1446.

8. Frank Vanderlip, "Farm Boy to Financier," *Saturday Evening Post*, February 9, 1935, pp. 25, 70.

9. *Congressional Record*, December 22, 1913, Vol. 51, pp. 1446-47.

10. A. Ralph Epperson, *The Unseen Hand* (Tucson, Arizona: Publius Press, 1985), p. 182.

11. *Congressional Record*, December 22, 1913, Vol. 51, p. 1446.

12. Woodrow Wilson, *The New Freedom* (New York: Doubleday, Page, 1914), pp. 13-14.

13. Dall, p. 137.

14. Ferdinand Lundberg, *America's 60 Families* (New York: Vanguard, 1938), pp. 110-11.

15. Charles Seymour, ed., *The Intimate Papers of Colonel House* (Boston: Houghton Mifflin, 1926), Vol. 1, p. 114.

16. Arthur D. Howden Smith, *Mr. House of Texas* (New York: Funk & Wagnalls, 1940), p. 70.

17. Ibid., p. 23.

18. George Sylvester Viereck, *The Strangest Friendship in History* (New York: Liveright, 1932), p. 28.

19. Dall, p. 71. Concerning the Rockefellers, see William Hoffman, *David: Report on a Rockefeller* (New York: Lyle Stuart, 1971), p. 51.

20. William P. Hoar, *Architects of Conspiracy* (Belmont, Mass.: Western Islands, 1984), p. 92.

21. Colin Simpson, *The Lusitania* (Boston: Little, Brown, 1972), p. 157.

22. Ibid., pp. 264-65.

23. Ibid., p. 131.

24. Ibid., p. 147.

25. Ibid., p. 131.

225

26. Viereck, pp. 106-15.

27. Seymour, Vol. 4, p. 38.

Chapter 3.   The Council's Birth and Early Links to Totalitarianism

1. Laurence H. Shoup and William Minter, *Imperial Brain Trust: The Council on Foreign Relations and U.S. Foreign Policy* (New York: Monthly Review Press, 1977), p. 16.

2. Eliot, p. 65.

3. Robert D. Shulzinger, *The Wise Men of Foreign Affairs: The History of the Council on Foreign Relations* (New York: Columbia University Press, 1984), p. 6.

4. Campbell, p. 47.

5. Quigley, p. 952.

6. Ibid.

7. Edward Mandell House, *Philip Dru: Administrator* (New York: B. W. Huebsch, 1912), p. 276.

8. Antony C. Sutton, *Wall Street and the Bolshevik Revolution* (New Rochelle, New York: Arlington House, 1974), p. 25.

9. Ibid., p. 46.

10. Ibid., pp. 71-81.

11. Ibid., p. 83.

12. Ibid., p. 156.

13. Ibid., p. 147.

14. Paul D. Cravath, "The Pros and Cons of Soviet Recognition," *FA*, January 1931, pp. 266-76.

15. *Human Events*, November 10, 1962, p. 853.

16. Walter Isaacson and Evan Thomas, *The Wise Men* (New York: Simon and Schuster, 1986), pp. 100-101.

17. *New York Times*, November 17, 1919, p. 1.

18. Allen, *None Dare*, pp. 99-100.

19. Frederick C. Howe, *Confessions of a Monopolist*, (Chicago: Public Publishing Co., 1906), p. v.

20. Ibid., p. 157.

21. Hoar, p. 89.

22. Quigley, p. 308.

23. *New York American*, June 24, 1924, quoted in Bell, p. 136.

24. Antony C. Sutton, *Wall Street and the Rise of Hitler* (Seal Beach, Calif.: '76 Press, 1976), p. 35.

25. *New York Times*, October 21, 1945, Section 1, p. 12.

26. Joseph Borkin, *The Crime and Punishment of I. G. Farben* (New York: The Free Press, 1978), pp. 122-23.

27. Sutton, *Wall Street and Hitler*, p. 109.

28. Ibid., p. 35.

Chapter 4.   The CFR and FDR

1. Antony C. Sutton, *Wall Street and FDR* (New Rochelle, New York: Arlington House, 1975), p. 18.

2. John T. Flynn, *The Roosevelt Myth* (New York: Devin-Adair, 1948), pp. 268-70.

3. Dall, p. 185.

4. Charles A. Lindbergh, Sr., *The Economic Pinch* (reprinted by Omni Publications, Hawthorne, Calif., 1968), p. 95, quoted in Allen, *None Dare*, p. 53.

5. Louis T. McFadden, *On The Federal Reserve Corporation*, remarks in Congress, 1934 (Boston: Forum Publication Co.), p. 89, quoted in Allen, *None Dare*, p. 55.

6. Dall, p. 49.

7. Quoted in Allen, *None Dare*, pp. 54-55.

8. Allen, *None Dare*, p. 63.

9. John Kenneth Galbraith, *The Great Crash, 1929* (Boston: Houghton Mifflin, 1955), p. 105.

10. Hoar, p. 190.

11. Hugh S. Johnson, *The Blue Eagle from Egg to Earth* (New York: Doubleday, Doran, 1935), p. 141.

12. Flynn, p. 24.

13. Ibid., p. 27.

14. Sutton, *Wall Street and FDR*, p. 134.

15. Ibid., pp. 138, 141.

16. Herbert Hoover, *The Memoirs of Herbert Hoover: The Great Depression 1929-1941* (New York: Macmillan, 1952), p. 420.

17. *Congressional Record*, June 19, 1940, Vol. 86, p. 8641.

Chapter 5.   A Global War with Global Ends

1. Shoup and Minter, p. 119.

2. Ibid., p. 160.

3. Samuel I. Rosenman, comp., *The Public Papers and Addresses of Franklin D. Roosevelt* (New York: Macmillan, 1941), p. 517.

4. John Toland, *Infamy: Pearl Harbor and Its Aftermath* (New York: Doubleday, 1982), pp. 115-18.

5. Winston Churchill, *The Grand Alliance* (Boston: Houghton Mifflin, 1950), p. 23.

6. William Stevenson, *A Man Called Intrepid* (New York: Harcourt Brace Jovanovich, 1976), p. 157.

7. Ibid.

8. Shulzinger, p. 271.

9. Geoffrey Crowther, "Anglo-American Pitfalls," *FA*, October 1941, p. 1.

10. Shoup and Minter, p. 123.

11. Toland, pp. 275-76.

12. Robert A. Theobald, *The Final Secret of Pearl Harbor* (Old Greenwich, Conn.: Devin-Adair, 1954), p. 76.

13. Shoup and Minter, pp. 131-35.

14. Toland, p. 316.

15. Shulzinger, pp. 116-17.

16. Antony C. Sutton, *National Suicide: Military Aid to the Soviet Union* (New Rochelle, New York: Arlington House, 1973), pp. 82-84.

17. Hoar, p. 303.

18. *The Review Of The News*, May 31, 1972, p. 60.

19. Shoup and Minter, pp. 169-71.

20. A. K. Chesterton, *The New Unhappy Lords* (London: Candour, 1969), p. 156.

21. Gary Allen, "Stop the Bank Gang," *American Opinion*, February 1979, p. 12.

22. Ibid.

23. Ibid., p. 102.

24. Joseph Collins and Frances Moore Lappe, "World Bank: Does It Bind Poor to Poverty?," *Los Angeles Times*, September 24, 1978, Part IX, p. 3.

25. Shirley Hobbs Scheibla, "Down a Rathole?," *Barron's*, September 25, 1978, p. 9.

26. *Congressional Record*, December 15, 1987, Vol. 133, p. S18148.

Chapter 6. The Truman Era

1. Isaacson and Thomas, p. 19.
2. Shoup and Minter, p. 35.
3. Isaacson and Thomas, p. 410.
4. Tyler Cowen, "The Great Twentieth-Century Foreign-Aid Hoax," *Reason*, April 1986, p. 40.
5. Isaacson and Thomas, p. 289.
6. Ibid., p. 365.
7. Ibid., p. 398.
8. Ibid., p. 397.
9. Charles L. Mee, Jr., *The Marshall Plan* (New York: Simon and Schuster, 1984), p. 234.
10. Eduard Beneš, "After Locarno: The Problem of Security Today," *FA*, January 1926, p. 210.
11. Oswaldo Aranha, "Regional Systems and the Future of U.N.," *FA*, April 1948, p. 420.
12. Courtney and Courtney, p. 51.
13. Roberto Ducci, "The World Order in the Sixties," *FA*, April 1964, pp. 389-90.
14. Courtney and Courtney, p. 23.
15. Freda Utley, *The China Story* (Chicago: Henry Regnery, 1951), pp. 44-45.
16. James MacGregor Burns, *John Kennedy: A Political Profile* (New York: Harcourt, Brace & World, 1961), p. 80.
17. A. J. Grajdanzev, "Korea in the Postwar World," *FA*, April 1944, p. 482.
18. *American Public Opinion and Postwar Security Commitments*, p. 10, quoted in Stang. pp. 35-36.
19. *American Foreign Policy, 1950-55: Basic Documents* (Washington, D.C.: U.S. Government Printing Office, 1957), Vol. II, p. 2468.
20. Charles A. Willoughby and John Chamberlain, *MacArthur, 1941-1951* (New York: McGraw-Hill, 1954), p. 402.
21. Douglas MacArthur, *Reminiscences* (New York: McGraw-Hill, 1964), p. 375.
22. Mark W. Clark, *From the Danube to the Yalu* (New York: Harper & Bros., 1954), p. 315.

23. Isaacson and Thomas, p. 698.

24. Adlai Stevenson, "Korea in Perspective," *FA*, April 1952, p. 360.

Chapter 7.   Between Limited Wars

1. Robert Welch, *The Politician* (Belmont, Mass.: Belmont Publishing, 1963), pp. 7-8.

2. Stephen E. Ambrose, *Eisenhower* (New York: Simon and Schuster, 1983), Vol. 1, p. 437.

3. Ibid.

4. Kraft, p. 66.

5. Ambrose, Vol. 1, pp. 459-60.

6. See, for example, Julius Epstein, *Operation Keelhaul* (Old Greenwich, Conn.: Devin-Adair, 1973), and Nicholas Bethell, *The Last Secret* (New York: Basic Books, 1974).

7. Gary Allen, *Richard Nixon: The Man Behind the Mask* (Belmont, Mass.: Western Islands, 1971), p. 115.

8. Ibid., p. 116.

9. *Human Events*, December 2, 1959.

10. Stang, p. 164.

11. January 1963 issue.

12. Allen, *Richard Nixon*, p. 183.

13. Ambrose, Vol. 2 (1984), p. 155.

14. René A. Wormser, *Foundations: Their Power and Influence* (New York: Devin-Adair, 1958), pp. 304-5.

15. Report, Special House Committee to Investigate Tax-Exempt Foundations, 1954, pp. 176-77, quoted in John Stormer, *None Dare Call It Treason* (Florissant, Missouri: Liberty Bell Press, 1964), p. 210.

16. Wormser, p. 349.

17. Lukas, p. 123.

18. Ambrose, Vol. 2, p. 57.

19. *Congressional Record*, August 31, 1960, Vol. 106, p. 18785.

20. Michel Sturdza, *Betrayal by Rulers* (Belmont, Mass.: Western Islands, 1976), pp. 218.

21. *New York Times*, February 24, 1957, p. 34.

22. *New York Times*, September 26, 1979, p. A24.

23. Earl E. T. Smith, *The Fourth Floor* (New York: Random House, 1962), pp. 169-74.

24. Schlesinger, p. 128.
25. Ibid.
26. Lukas, p. 126.
27. Halberstam, p. 60.
28. Mario Lazo, *Dagger in the Heart: American Policy Failures in Cuba* (New York: Twin Circle, 1968), p. 271.
29. Ibid., p. 289.
30. Ibid., p. 298.
31. Ibid., p. 372.
32. Isaacson and Thomas, p. 630.

Chapter 8.   The Establishment's War in Vietnam
1. Shulzinger, p. 45.
2. *New York Times*, March 2, 1966, p. 40.
3. James E. King, Jr., "Nuclear Plenty and Limited War," *FA*, January 1957, p. 256.
4. *Science & Mechanics*, March 1968, pp. 90-91.
5. Zbigniew Brzezinski, "Peaceful Engagement in Eastern Europe," *FA*, July 1961, p. 645.
6. April 1968 issue.
7. Allen, *None Dare*, p. 102.
8. See articles by Wallis W. Wood, "Vietnam: While Brave Men Die," *American Opinion*, June 1967; "It's Treason!: Aid and Comfort to the Vietcong," *American Opinion*, May 1968.
9. James Kunen, *The Strawberry Statement: Notes of a College Revolutionary* (New York: Random House, 1969), p. 112.
10. Walt Rostow, *The United States in the World Arena* (New York: Harper & Brothers, 1960), p. 549.
11. M. Stanton Evans, *The Politics of Surrender* (New York: Devin-Adair, 1966), p. 340.
12. Isaacson and Thomas, p. 710.
13. Frank L. Kluckhohn, *Lyndon's Legacy: A Candid Look at the President's Policymakers* (New York: Devin-Adair, 1964), p. 112.
14. Moskin, p. 157.
15. Felix Wittmer, "Freedom's Case Against Dean Acheson," *American Mercury*, April 1952, p. 11.
16. Ibid., p. 7.

17. Ibid.

18. Isaacson and Thomas, p. 716.

19. Ibid., p. 652.

20. Ibid., p. 653.

21. Halberstam, p. 403.

22. Isaacson and Thomas, p. 660.

23. Ibid., p. 653.

24. Townsend Hoopes, *The Limits of Intervention* (New York: David McKay, 1969), p. 216.

25. Isaacson and Thomas, pp. 700-701.

26. Hoopes, p. 217.

27. Lloyd C. Gardner, ed., *American Foreign Policy: Present to Past* (New York: The Free Press, 1974), p. 30.

28. "You've A Right To Know," circular of Congressman John R. Rarick, July 15, 1971.

Chapter 9.   The Unknown Nixon

1. William Costello, *The Facts About Nixon* (New York: Viking, 1960), p. 51.

2. See Allen, *Richard Nixon*, pp. 140-42.

3. Newsletter of Congressman John G. Schmitz, October 18, 1972. See also *Congressional Record*, July 9, 1947, Vol. 93, p. 8567.

4. Barry Goldwater, *With No Apologies* (New York: William Morrow, 1979), p. 279.

5. Theodore White, *The Making of the President, 1960* (New York: Atheneum, 1961), p. 199.

6. Roosevelt, p. 6.

7. Allen, *Richard Nixon*, p. 217.

8. Ibid., p. 223.

9. Richard Nixon, "Asia After Vietnam," *FA*, October 1967, p. 113.

10. Shoup and Minter, p. 5.

11. Moskin, p. 156.

12. Henry Kissinger, *White House Years* (Boston: Little, Brown, 1979), p. 4.

13. *U.S. News & World Report*, November 1, 1971, p. 26.

14. Silk and Silk, p. 207.

15. Roscoe and Geoffrey Drummond, "President Proves Himself To Be A Liberal-In-Action," *Indianapolis News*, January 22, 1969, p. 17.

16. *Washington Star*, January 21, 1970, quoted in Allen, *Richard Nixon*, p. 14.

17. *New York Times*, January 31, 1971, p. E13.

18. John Kenneth Galbraith, "Richard Nixon and the Great Socialist Revival," *New York*, September 21, 1970, p. 25.

19. Richard Nixon, *No More Vietnams* (New York: Arbor House, 1985), p. 167.

Chapter 10.   Carter and Trilateralism

1. Christopher Lydon, "Jimmy Carter Revealed: He's a Rockefeller Republican," *Atlantic Monthly*, July 1977, p. 52.

2. Gary Allen, "They're Catching On," *American Opinion*, November 1977, p. 4.

3. Zbigniew Brzezinski, "America and Europe," *FA*, October 1970, p. 29.

4. Zbigniew Brzezinski, *Between Two Ages* (New York: Viking, 1970), p. 72.

5. David Rockefeller, "Foolish Attacks on False Issues," *Wall Street Journal*, April 30, 1980, p. 26.

6. Jeremiah Novak, "The Trilateral Connection: Meet the President's Tutors in Foreign Policy," *Atlantic Monthly*, July 1977, p. 59.

7. Goldwater, p. 280.

8. Zbigniew Brzezinski, "U.S. Foreign Policy: The Search For Focus," *FA*, July 1973, p. 723.

9. Gary Allen, *Jimmy Carter, Jimmy Carter* (Seal Beach, Calif.: '76 Press, 1976), p. 69.

10. Victor Lasky, *Jimmy Carter: The Man and the Myth*, (New York: Richard Marek, 1979), p. 160.

11. Goldwater, p. 286.

12. Allen, *Jimmy Carter*, p. 139.

13. *Los Angeles Times*, June 24, 1976, Part I, p. 12.

14. Robert C. Turner, *I'll Never Lie to You: Jimmy Carter in his Own Words* (New York: Ballantine Books, 1976), p. 48.

15. Lasky, p. 161; Isaacson and Thomas, p. 726.

16. Zbigniew Brzezinski, *Power and Principle: Memoirs of the National Security Adviser, 1977-1981* (New York: Farrar, Straus, Giroux, 1983), p. 289.

17. Lasky, p. 160.

18. Isaacson and Thomas, p. 726.

19. Moskin, p. 210.

20. Walter Mondale, "Beyond Détente: Toward International Economic Security," *FA*, October 1974, p. 7.

21. Carl Gershman, "The Rise & Fall of the New Foreign-Policy Establishment," *Commentary*, July 1980, p. 20.

22. William M. LeoGrande, "The Revolution in Nicaragua: Another Cuba?," *FA*, Autumn 1979, p. 44.

23. *The Review Of The News*, December 28, 1977, p. 59.

24. See, for example, Martin B. Travis and James T. Watkins, "Control of the Panama Canal: An Obsolete Shibboleth," *FA*, July 1959, or Stephen S. Rosenfeld, "The Panama Negotiations — A Close-Run Thing," *FA*, October 1975.

25. Jerome Alan Cohen, "Recognizing China," *FA*, October 1971, p. 30.

26. David Nelson Rowe, *U.S. China Policy Today* (Washington, D.C.: University Professors for Academic Order, 1979), pp. 27-28.

27. David Nelson Rowe, *The Carter China Policy: Results and Prospects* (1980), p. 16.

28. Jimmy Carter, *Keeping Faith: Memoirs of a President* (New York: Bantam, 1982), p. 256.

Chapter 11.   A Second Look at Ronald Reagan

1. Carey McWilliams,. "Establishment Picks Reagan to Run — and Rule," *Los Angeles Times*, July 2, 1980, Part II, p. 7.

2. Robert Scheer, "The Reagan Question," *Playboy*, August 1980, pp. 240, 242.

3. Stephen S. Rosenfeld, "Testing the Hard Line," and Andrew Knight, "Ronald Reagan's Watershed Year?," *FA, America and the World 1982*.

4. *New York Times*, April 19, 1985, p. A6.

5. *Newsweek*, January 23, 1984, p. 49.

6. William F. Jasper, "Ronald Reagan," *The New American*, July 28, 1986, p. 32.

7. *Wall Street Journal*, May 10, 1984, p. 2.

8. Rowe, *The Carter China Policy*, p. 10.

9. Robert A. Manning, "The Philippines in Crisis," *FA*, Winter 1984/85, p. 410.

10. *The New American*, January 19, 1987, p. 3.
11. William Safire, "Derailing 'Day One,'" *New York Times*, March 24, 1988, p. A35.
12. *Boston Globe*, March 21, 1988, p. 9.
13. *Washington Star*, December 1, 1971, quoted in Allen, *None Dare*, p. 125.
14. William G. Hyland, "U.S.-Soviet Relations: The Long Road Back," *FA, America and the World 1981*, p. 548.

Chapter 12.   The Media Blackout
1. *Congressional Record*, February 9, 1917, Volume 54, pp. 2947-48.
2. Charles Beard, "Who's to Write the History of the War?," *Saturday Evening Post*, October 4, 1947, p. 172.
3. Harry Elmer Barnes, ed., *Perpetual War for Perpetual Peace* (Caldwell, Idaho: Caxton, 1953), pp. 15-16, 18.
4. Gary Allen, "Control of the Media," *American Opinion*, May 1983, p. 96.
5. S. Robert Lichter, Stanley Rothman, and Linda S. Lichter, *The Media Elite* (Bethesda, Maryland: Adler & Adler, 1986), pp. 29-30.
6. Reed Irvine, "How the Media Cheat," *Conservative Digest*, September 1986, p. 66.
7. Ernest W. Lefever, *TV and National Defense* (Boston, Va.: Institute for American Strategy Press, 1974), p. 193.
8. Norodom Sihanouk, "The Future of Cambodia," *FA*, October 1970, p. 10.
9. Interview with Reed Irvine, *The Review Of The News*, January 24, 1979, p. 35.
10. *AIM Report*, December-B, 1986.
11. *AIM Report*, October-A, 1986.
12. *The Review Of The News*, July 31, 1985, pp. 37, 39.
13. Anastasio Somoza, with Jack Cox, *Nicaragua Betrayed* (Belmont, Mass.: Western Islands, 1980), pp. 205-7.

Chapter 13.   The CFR Today
1. Schlafly and Ward, p. 150.
2. Roosevelt, p. 6.
3. Moskin, p. 210.

4. John Rees, "The Council is Watching," *American Opinion*, January 1984, p. 23.
5. Halberstam, p. 44.
6. Ibid., pp. 183, 185.
7. Ibid., p. 482.
8. Shulzinger, p. xi.
9. Isaacson and Thomas, p. 336.
10. Ibid., p. 337.
11. CFR, *Annual Report, 1985-86*, p. 10.
12. Ibid., p. 86.
13. CFR, *Annual Report, 1986-87*, p. 13.
14. Count Hugo Lerchenfeld, "Dawn," *FA*, September 1924, p. 122.

Chapter 14.   On the Threshold of a New World Order?

1. *Christian Science Monitor*, April 26, 1984, p. 27.
2. *This Constitution* (a quarterly published by Project '87), Winter 1985, rear cover.
3. James MacGregor Burns, *The Power to Lead* (New York: Simon and Schuster, 1984), p. 189.
4. Donald L. Robinson, ed., *Reforming American Government: The Bicentennial Papers of the Committee on the Constitutional System* (Boulder, Colorado: Westview Press, 1985), p. 149.
5. See Robert L. Preston, *The Plot to Replace the Constitution* (Salt Lake City: Hawkes Publishing, 1972).
6. Robinson, p. 162.
7. Brzezinski, *Between Two Ages*, p. 258.
8. Utley, p. 213.
9. Alan Stang, "Foundations Pay the Way," *American Opinion*, January 1977, p. 41.
10. *Facts on File*, 1987, p. 123.

Chapter 15.   Solutions and Hope

1. Shulzinger, p. 61.
2. *The Review Of The News*, September 14, 1983, p. 31.
3. Jeffrey St. John, *Day of the Cobra* (Nashville: Thomas Nelson, 1984), p. 73.
4. Ibid., p. 208.

5. "Propaganda and the Alert Citizen," *Soviet Total War; Historic Mission of Violence and Deceit*, Vol. 1, published by the House Committee on Un-American Activities, September 23, 1956, p. 347, quoted in G. Edward Griffin, *This is the John Birch Society* (Thousand Oaks, Calif.: American Media, 1972), p. 51.

INDEX

ABC, 183, 185
Accuracy in Media (AIM), 183, 185
Acheson, Dean, 81, 83, 90, 93, 94,
  106, 110, 114, 129-33, 195
Actor, The, 104
Adams, Sherman, 107
Admiral Kimmel's Story, 75
Aeroflot, 13
Afghanistan, 173-74, 185-86, 190
Agnew, Spiro, 146, 148, 151
Agricultural Adjustment
  Administration (AAA), 58,
  60
Aldrich, Nelson, 22-23, 25, 33
Allen, Frederick Lewis, 21
Allen, Gary, 19, 144, 148-49, 151,
  214
Ambrose, Stephen, 101, 105, 106
Amerasia, 88
America Is in Danger, 113
American I. G., 48
American League to Aid and
  Cooperate with Russia, 41
American Legion, 126, 211
American Mercury, 126
American Opinion, 216
*American Public Opinion and
  Postwar Security
  Commitments*, 11
American-Russian Chamber of
  Commerce, 43
America's Retreat From Victory,
  107
*America's Unelected Rulers: The
  Council on Foreign
  Relations*, 126
Amin, Hafizullah, 185
Anderson, Dillon, 116
Anderson, Robert, 104
Andropov, Yuri, 214
Angola, 173
Aquino, Benigno, 173
Aquino, Corazon, 173, 212
Armstrong, Hamilton Fish, 64, 75,

79, 84, 129, 145
Associated Press, 183
Atlantic, 154, 155, 202
Atlantic Council, 85
Atlantic Union, 85, 95-96, 104, 154

Baker, James, 168
Baker, Ray Stannard, 31
Baldrige, Malcolm, 169
Ball, George, 111, 133, 146, 157
Baltic States, 69, 70
Bank of the United States, 20-21
Bao Dai, 120
Barnes, Harry Elmer, 75, 179, 180-
  81, 188
Barnet, Richard, 9
Barr, Robert, 41
Barron's, 74
Baruch, Bernard, 21, 27, 29, 32,
  57, 59, 62, 63, 102, 116, 182
Batista, Fulgencio, 108-109
Bay of Pigs invasion, 112-13, 119,
  125
Beam, Jacob, 146
Beard, Charles, 179-80, 188
Belmont, August, 181
Beneš, Eduard, 84
Best and the Brightest, The, 6, 110,
  194
Betrayal by Rulers, 108
Betrayers, The, 128
Between Two Ages, 154, 203
Birch, John, 215-16
Bissell, Richard, 112
Blumenthal, W. Michael, 159
Bohlen, Charles, 81, 83, 106
Bowie, Robert, 157
Bowles, Chester, 143
Bowman, Isaiah, 71, 78
Bradshaw, Thornton, 183
Bretton Woods Conference, 72-74
Brezhnev, Leonid, 152, 163, 166
Bricker Amendment, 105
Brinkley, David, 183

239

Ford Foundation, 5, 129, 201, 205
Foreign Affairs, 6, 8-14, 16, 17, 37,
 41, 42, 46, 54, 58, 60, 64, 65,
 66, 72, 73, 75, 83-86, 87, 92-
 93, 102, 103-105, 110, 111,
 121, 123, 129, 142, 144, 145,
 154, 155, 157, 158, 159, 161,
 167, 169, 173, 175, 184, 192,
 197, 201, 203, 205
Foreign Policy, 159
Formosa, *see* China, Republic of
Forrestal, Henry, 98
Forrestal, James, 98
Fortune, 182
foundations, 5, 26, 88, 105-106,
 157, 205
*Foundations: Their Power and
 Influence*, 106
Fowler, Henry, 111
Fox, Victor J., 126
Frankel, Max, 181
Frankey, William, 17
Frankfurter, Felix, 3, 130
Franklin, George, 154
From Major Jordan's Diaries, 70

Gaither, H. Rowan, 205, 209
Galbraith, John Kenneth, 6, 57,
 111, 147
Gardner, Richard N., 11, 17, 157,
 192
Gay, Edwin F., 51
Gelb, Leslie, 181-82
Genesis of the World War, 179
Germany, reparations and rise of
 Nazis in, 46-48
Gershman, Carl, 159
Gillette, Guy, 67, 75
Gilpatric, Roswell, 111
glasnost, 206
globalism, 218-221
 of the CFR, 10-12, 14-15, 37, 71-
 72, 84-86, 106, 192, 205-
 206

see also world government
Goldwater, Barry, 126, 131, 138,
 143, 155, 156, 164, 184
Goodnow, Frank, 41
Goodpaster, Andrew, 136
Gorbachev, Mikhail, 13, 174, 177,
 206, 215
Gould, Jay, 45
Graham, Katharine, 182
Grand Alliance, The, 65
Gray, Gordon, 104
Great Crash, 1929, The, 57
Great Depression, 23, 57-58
Greenfield, James L., 182
Greenfield, Meg, 182
Greenspan, Alan, 169
Grew, Joseph, 67
Grey, Edward, 30
Griffin, G. Edward, 217
Groton School, 5, 53, 130
Grunwald, Henry, 182

Hagedorn, Hermann, 40
Haig, Alexander, 169, 176
Halberstam, David, 6, 7, 93, 110,
 125, 132, 194, 195
Haldeman, Robert, 148
"Hard Road to World Order, The,"
 11, 192
Harding, Warren, 53
Harkins, Paul, 194
Harper's, 7, 9, 102
Harper's Weekly, 27
Harriman, Averell, 41-42, 52, 81,
 83, 111, 129, 131, 132, 136,
 157, 167, 182
Harriman, E. Roland, 182
Harriman, Henry I., 60
Harsch, Joseph C., 156
Hartley, Fred, 115
Hays, Wayne, 106
Heller, Walter, 170
Helms, Jesse, 14, 18, 74
Helms, Richard, 136

Salt II Treaty, 171, 201
Sandinistas, 160-61, 175
Sarnoff, David, 183
Sarnoff, Robert, 183
Saturday Evening Post, 22, 179
Savimbi, Jonas, 173
Sawhill, John, 159
Scheer, Robert, 168
Schiff, Jacob, 21, 22, 27, 34, 39-40,
    50, 181, 183
Schiff, John, 39
Schiff, Mortimer, 40
Schlafly, Phyllis, 9, 128
Schlesinger, Arthur, Jr., 6, 109-10,
    111, 113, 132, 180, 191
Science & Mechanics, 132
Scott, John, 69
SDS, 117
SEATO, 86, 121
Senate Committee on the
    Judiciary, 88
Service, John Stewart, 130
Seymour, Charles, 28, 31
Shah of Iran, 161, 165
Shams, Abdul, 185-86
Sheehy, Maurice, 98
Shell, Joe, 143
Sherwood, Robert, 65
Short, Walter C., 68, 76
Shoup, Laurence, 82, 145
Shultz, George, 146, 169, 176, 214
Shulzinger, Robert D., 37, 120,
    194-95
Sihanouk, Norodom, 184
Simpson, Colin, 31
Simpson, Cornell, 98
Sixty Minutes, 178, 186-87
Skousen, W. Cleon, 144
Skull and Bones, 5, 167-68, 193
Smith, Arthur D. Howden, 28
Smith, Earl E. T., 109, 118
Smith, Gerard, 146
Smith, Howard K., 147
Smith, Ian, 163

Smith, Richard M., 182
Smoot, Dan, 126, 138
socialism, 43-45, 74, 147-48
Solomon, Anthony M., 159
Solzhenitsyn, Aleksandr, 14, 206
Somoza, Anastasio, 160-61, 165,
    186-87
Sorenson, Ted, 112, 123
"Sources of Soviet Conduct, The,"
    83-84
South Africa, 185
Soviet Union, 13-14, 38-43, 69-71,
    84, 86-87, 89, 90-91, 108-
    109, 113-14, 123-24, 130,
    135, 147, 174, 175, 205-206,
    212, 213-14
Soviet-American Friendship
    Society, 130
Spofford, Charles M., 82
Sports Illustrated, 182
Stalin, Joseph, 52, 69-71, 77, 84,
    86, 87, 130, 207
Standard Oil of New Jersey, 43,
    48, 59
Standard Oil of New York, 43
State Department, U.S., 5, 64, 88,
    107, 109, 111, 130, 167, 174
Stettinus, Edward, 60
Stevenson, Adlai, 103, 112
Stevenson, William, 65
Stimson, Henry, 8, 60, 66-67, 75
stock market crash of 1929, 55-57
Stockdale, James, 121, 138
*Strangest Friendship in History,
    The*, 28
Straus, Oscar, 41
Strauss, Lewis, 104, 116
*Strawberry Statement: Notes of a
    College Revolutionary, The*,
    126
Streit, Clarence, 66
Strong, Benjamin, 24
*Study No. 7, Basic Aims of U.S.
    Foreign Policy*, 11

251

Acknowledgements

I convey my gratitude to Charles Mann for undertaking the publication of this book, and for the energy he devoted to it; to John McManus and F. R. Duplantier for their editorial advice; and to Gerald Mazzarella for his encouragement and faith in my work. I also thank Don Eckelkamp, Joan Manzi, Lance Wilder, Dorothy Smith, and all others whose hard work and professionalism contributed to the production of *The Shadows of Power*.

About The Author

As a student at Colby College and Boston University during the latter years of the Vietnam War, James Perloff included himself in the new generation that had gone radical left — an outlook he voiced as a school columnist and cartoonist. However, when he probed America's power structure deeply, he was shocked to learn that he and his fellow students had moved in the precise direction intended by the Establishment — that unofficial ruling entity they thought they had been rebelling against. Several years of research persuaded him that the American Establishment was a far more clever organism than anyone had ever dreamed, and culminated with his writing *The Shadows of Power*. Mr. Perloff is a contributing editor to *The New American*, the biweekly journal of news and opinion.

Publisher's Appendix

Our listing of the names of those who hold membership in the Council on Foreign Relations is not meant to imply that all members are fully cognizant of the history of the organization or in agreement with its purposes as described in this book.

— Editor, Western Islands

Officers and Directors, 1987–1988

OFFICERS

Peter G. Peterson
Chairman of the Board

Peter Tarnoff
President

Warren Christopher
Vice Chairman

John Temple Swing
Executive Vice President

Lewis T. Preston
Treasurer

Alton Frye
Vice President, Washington

William H. Gleysteen, Jr.
Vice President, Studies

John A. Millington
*Vice President, Planning
and Development*

Margaret Osmer-McQuade
Vice President, Meetings

DIRECTORS

Graham T. Allison, Jr.
Harold Brown
James E. Burke
Richard B. Cheney
Warren Christopher
Robert F. Erburu
Richard L. Gelb
Alan Greenspan

Karen Elliott House
Stanley Hoffmann
B. R. Inman
Jeane J. Kirkpatrick
Juanita Kreps
Charles McC. Mathias, Jr.
Donald F. McHenry
Ruben F. Mettler
Peter G. Peterson
Lewis T. Preston
William D. Rogers
Robert A. Scalapino
Brent Scowcroft
Stephen Stamas
Peter Tarnoff, *ex officio*
Glenn E. Watts
Clifton R. Wharton, Jr.

**HONORARY OFFICERS
AND DIRECTORS EMERITI**

Arthur H. Dean*
Douglas Dillon
George S. Franklin
Caryl P. Haskins
Joseph E. Johnson
Grayson Kirk
John J. McCloy
Honorary Chairman
James A. Perkins
Philip D. Reed
David Rockefeller
Honorary Chairman
Charles M. Spofford
Cyrus R. Vance

*Died November 1987

Membership Roster   June 30, 1988

A
Aaron, David L.
Abboud, A. Robert
Abegglen, James C.
Abel, Elie
Abely, Joseph F., Jr.
Abizaid, John P.
Abram, Morris B.
Abramowitz, Morton I.
Abrams, Elliott
Abshire, David M.
Aburdene, Odeh
Ackerman, Peter
Adam, Ray C.
Adams, Robert McCormick
Adams, Ruth Salzman
Adelman, Kenneth L.
Aggarwal, Vinod K.
Agnew, Harold M.
Agronsky, Martin
Aguirre, Horacio
Aho, C. Michael
Aidinoff, M. Bernard
Ajami, Fouad
Akers, John F.
Akins, James E.
Albright, Archie E.
Albright, Madeleine
Alderman, Michael H.
Aldrich, George H.
Aleinikoff, T. Alexander
Alexander, Robert J.
Allan, F. Aley
Allard, Nicholas W.
Allbritton, Joe L.
Allen, John R..

Allen, Lew, Jr.
Allison, Graham T., Jr.
Allison, Richard C.
Alpern, Alan N.
Altman, Emily
Altman, Roger C.
Altschul, Arthur G.
Andersen, Harold W.
Anderson, John B.
Anderson, Lisa
Anderson, Marcus A.
Anderson, Paul F.
Anderson, Robert
Anderson, Robert O.
Andreae, Charles N., III
Andreas, Dwayne O.
Angermueller, Hans H.
Angulo, Manuel R.
Anschuetz, Norbert L.
Ansour, M. Michael
Anthoine, Robert
Anthony, John Duke
Apter, David E.
Araskog, Rand V.
Arboleya, Carlos J.
Arledge, Roone
Armacost, Michael H.
Armstrong, Anne
Armstrong, C. Michael
Armstrong, DeWitt C., III
Armstrong, John A.
Armstrong, Willis C.
Arnhold, Henry H.
Arnold, Millard W.
Art, Robert J.
Arthurs, Alberta

Artzt, Edwin L.
Asencio, Diego C.
Asher, Robert E.
Aspin, Les
Assousa, George E.
Atherton, Alfred L., Jr.
Attwood, William
Atwood, J. Brian
Auspitz, Josiah Lee
Ayers, H. Brandt

B
Babbitt, Bruce
Bachman, David Mark
Bacot, J. Carter
Bader, William B.
Bailey, Charles W.
Baird, Charles F.
Baker, Howard H., Jr.
Baker, James E.
Baker, Pauline H.
Balaran, Paul
Baldwin, David A.
Baldwin, Robert E.
Baldwin, Robert H. B.
Bales, Carter F.
Ball, David George
Ball, George W.
Bandow, Doug
Banta, Kenneth W.
Barber, Charles F.
Barber, James A., Jr.
Barber, Perry O., Jr.
Barger, Teresa C.
Barghoorn, Frederick C.
Barker, Robert R.

Barlow, William E.
Barnathan, Joyce
Barnds, William J.
Barnes, Harry G., Jr.
Barnes, Michael D.
Barnet, Richard J.
Barnett, A. Doak
Barnett, Frank R.
Barnett, Marguerite R.
Barnett, Robert W.
Baroody, William J., Jr.
Barr, Thomas D.
Barron, Thomas A.
Bartholomew, Reginald
Bartlett, Joseph W.
Bartlett, Richard Allen
Bartlett, Thomas A.
Bartley, Robert L.
Barzelay, Michael
Baskin, Bo
Bassow, Whitman
Batkin, Alan R.
Bator, Francis M.
Battle, Lucius D.
Bauman, Robert P.
Baumann, Carol Edler
Beam, Jacob D.
Bean, Atherton
Beasley, William Howard, III
Beattie, Richard I.
Beckler, David Z.
Beecher, William
Beeman, Richard E.
Begley, Louis
Behrman, Jack N.
Beim, David O.

*Includes individuals to whom invitations were extended by the Board at its June 1988 meeting and who had accepted by the time this Report went to press.

255

256

Coolidge, Nicholas J.
Coolidge, T. J., Jr.
Coombs, Philip H.
Coon, Jane Abell
Cooney, Joan Ganz
Cooper, Charles A.
Cooper, Chester L.
Cooper, Richard N.
Corrigan, E. Gerald
Corrigan, Kevin
Cott, Suzanne
Cotter, William
Cousins, Norman
Cowan, L. Gray
Cowles, John, Jr.
Cox, Pamela M. J.
Cox, Robert G.
Coyne, Thomas A.
Crane, Winthrop Murray
Crawford, Anne W.
Crawford, John F.
Creel, Dana S.
Cremin, Lawrence A.
Crittenden, Ann
Crocker, Chester A.
Crook, William H.
Cross, June V.
Cross, Sam Y.
Crovitz, Gordon
Crow, Trammell
Crowe, William J., Jr.
Crystal, Lester M.
Culver, John C.
Cumming, Christine
Cummings, Robert L., Jr.
Cummiskey, Frank J.
Cuomo, Mario M.
Curran, Timothy J.
Curtis, Gerald L.
Cutler, Lloyd N.
Cutler, Walter L.
Cutter, W. Bowman
Cyr, Arthur

D

Dale, William B.
Dalley, George A.
Dallin, Alexander
Dallmeyer, Dorinda
Dalton, James E.
Dam, Kenneth W.
Danforth, William H.
Daniel, D. Ronald
Danner, Mark
Darman, Richard G.
Davant, James W.
Davidson, Daniel I.
Davidson, Ralph K.
Davidson, Ralph P.
Davis, Dorothy M.
Davis, Jacquelyn K.
Davis, Jerome
Davis, John A.
Davis, Kathryn W.
Davis, Lynn E.
Davis, Nathaniel
Davis, Shelby Cullom
Davis, Vincent

Davison, Daniel P.
Davison, W. Phillips
Dawkins, Peter M.
Dawson, Horace G., Jr.
Dawson, Horace G., III
Day, Arthur R.
Deagle, Edwin A., Jr.
Dean, Jonathan
Dean, Robert W.
Dean, Thompson
Debevoise, Eli Whitney
Debevoise, Eli Whitney, II
De Borchgrave, Arnaud
Debs, Barbara Knowles
Debs, Richard A.
DeCrane, Alfred C., Jr.
Decter, Midge
De Cubas, Jose
Dees, Bowen C.
De Habsburgo Dobkin,
   Inmaculada
De Hoyos, Debora
De Janosi, Peter E.
De Menil, George
De Menil, Lois Pattison
Deming, Frederick L.
Denison, Robert J.
Dennard, Cleveland L.
Dennison, Charles S.
Denny, Brewster C.
Denton, E. Hazel
DePalma, Samuel
Derian, Patricia Murphy
De Rosso, Alphonse
Destler, I. M.
Deutch, John M.
Deutch, Michael J.
DeVecchi, Robert P.
Devine, C. Robert
Devine, Thomas J.
De Vries, Rimmer
DeWind, Adrian W.
DeYoung, Karen
Dickey, Christopher S.
Dickson, R. Russell, Jr.
Diebold, John
Diebold, William, Jr.
Dietel, William M.
Dillon, Douglas
Dilworth, J. Richardson
Dine, Thomas A.
Dobriansky, Paula
Dodd, Christopher J.
Doetsch, Douglas A.
Doherty, William C., Jr.
Dominguez, Jorge I.
Donahue, Donald J.
Donahue, Thomas R.
Donaldson, William H.
Donnell, Ellsworth
Donnelly, H. C.
Donovan, Hedley
Doty, Paul M.
Douglas, Paul W.
Douglass, Robert R.
Downie, Leonard, Jr.
Draper, William H., III
Drayton, William, Jr.

Dreier, John C.
Drell, Sidney D.
Drew, Elizabeth
Dreyfuss, Joel
Drumwright, J. R.
Dubow, Arthur M.
DuBrul, Stephen M., Jr.
Duffey, Joseph
Duffy, James H.
Duke, Angier Biddle
Dulany, Peggy
Duncan, Charles W., Jr.
Duncan, John C.
Duncan, Richard L.
Dunn, Kempton
Durham, G. Robert
Dutton, Frederick G.

E

Eagleburger, Lawrence S.
Earle, Gordon
Earle, Ralph, II
Easum, Donald B.
Eaton, Leonard J., Jr.
Eberle, William D.
Eberstadt, Nicholas N.
Ecton, Donna R.
Edelman, Albert I.
Edelman, Eric S.
Edelman, Gerald M.
Edelman, Marian Wright
Edelstein, Julius C. C.
Edson, Gary R.
Edwards, Howard L.
Edwards, Robert H.
Ehrlich, Thomas
Eichenberg, Richard C.
Eilts, Hermann Frederick
Einaudi, Luigi R.
Einaudi, Mario
Einhorn, Jessica P.
Eisendrath, Charles R.
Eliot, Theodore L., Jr.
El Koury, Jaime A.
Elliott, A. Randle
Elliott, Byron K.
Elliott, Osborn
Ellis, James R.
Ellis, Patricia
Ellis, Richard H.
Ellison, Keith P.
Ellsberg, Daniel
Ellsworth, Robert F.
Embree, Ainslie T.
Emerson, Alice F.
Enders, Thomas Ostrom
English, Robert D.
Enthoven, Alain
Epstein, David B.
Epstein, Jason
Erb, Guy F.
Erb, Richard D.
Erbsen, Claude E.
Erburu, Robert F.
Ercklentz, Alexander T.
Estabrook, Robert H.
Esty, Daniel C.

Etzioni, Amitai
Evans, John C.
Evans, John K.
Evans, Rowland, Jr.
Ewing, William, Jr.
Exter, John

F

Fabian, Larry L.
Fairbanks, Douglas
Falco, Mathea
Falk, Pamela S.
Falk, Richard A.
Fallows, James
Fanning, Katherine W.
Farer, Tom J.
Farmer, Thomas L.
Fascell, Dante B.
Feiner, Ava S.
Feldman, Mark B.
Feldstein, Martin S.
Fenster, Steven R.
Ferguson, Glenn W.
Ferguson, James L.
Ferguson, Tim W.
Ferrari, Frank E.
Ferraro, Geraldine A.
Ferre, Maurice A.
Fessenden, Hart
Fierce, Milfred C.
Fifield, Russell H.
Finberg, Barbara D.
Finger, Seymour Max
Finkelstein, Lawrence S.
Finley, Murray H.
Finn, James
Finney, Paul B.
Firestone, James A.
Firmage, Edwin B.
Fisher, Pieter A.
Fisher, Richard W.
Fisher, Roger
Fishlow, Albert
Fitz, Lauri J.
FitzGerald, Frances
Fitzgibbons, Harold E.
Flanagan, Stephan J.
Flanigan, Peter M.
Fogleman, Ronald R.
Foley, S. R., Jr.
Foley, Thomas S.
Foote, Edward T., II
Ford, Gerald R.
Forrestal, Michael V.
Forrestal, Robert P.
Forrester, Anne
Fowler, Henry H.
Fox, Donald T.
Fox, John D.
Fox, Joseph C.
Fox, William T. R.
Franck, Thomas M.
Francke, Albert, III
Frank, Charles R., Jr.
Frank, Isaiah
Frank, Richard A.
Frankel, Andrew V.
Frankel, Francine R.

257

Frankel, Marvin E.
Frankel, Max
Franklin, George S.
Frederick, Pauline
Frederick, Robert R.
Fredericks, Wayne
Freeman, Harry L.
Freeman, Orville L.
Frelinghuysen, Peter H. B.
Fremont-Smith, Marion R.
Freund, Gerald
Frey, Donald N.
Freytag, Richard A.
Fribourg, Michel
Fribourg, Paul
Fried, Edward R.
Friedberg, Aaron L.
Frieden, Jeffrey A.
Friedman, Benjamin M.
Friedman, Irving S.
Friedman, Stephen
Friedman, Stephen J.
Friedman, Thomas L.
Fromkin, David
Fromm, Joseph
Fromuth, Peter
Frost, Ellen L.
Frost, F. Daniel
Frye, Alton
Frye, William R.
Fuerbringer, Otto
Funari, John
Funkhouser, E. N., Jr.
Furlaud, Richard M.
Futter, Ellen V.

G

Gabriel, Charles A.
Gaddis, John Lewis
Gaffney, A. Devon
Galbraith, Evan G.
Gallatin, James P.
Galvin, John R.
Galvis, Carlos
Ganoe, Charles S.
Garber, Larry
Gard, Robert G., Jr.
Gardner, James A.
Gardner, Richard N.
Garment, Leonard
Garment, Suzanne
Garrels, Anne
Garretson, Albert H.
Garrison, Lloyd K.
Garrison, Mark
Gart, Murray J.
Garten, Jeffrey E.
Garthoff, Raymond L.
Garvin, Clifton C., Jr.
Garwin, Richard L.
Gates, Philomene A.
Gates, Robert M.
Gati, Charles
Gati, Toby Trister
Geertz, Clifford
Geiger, Theodore
Gejdenson, Sam
Gelb, Leslie H.

Gelb, Richard L.
Gell-Mann, Murray
Gellman, Barton David
George, Alexander L.
Georgescu, Peter A.
Gerber, Louis
Gergen, David R.
Gerstner, Louis V., Jr.
Getler, Michael
Geyelin, Henry R.
Geyelin, Philip L.
Gibney, Frank B.
Giffen, James H.
Gigot, Paul A.
Gil, Peter P.
Gilbert, H. N.
Gilbert, Jackson B.
Gilbert, Jarobin, Jr.
Gilbert, S. Parker
Gilmore, Kenneth O.
Gilpatric, Roswell L.
Gilpin, Kenneth N., III
Gilpin, Robert R., Jr.
Ginsburg, David
Ginsburg, Ruth Bader
Ginsburgh, Robert N.
Glaser, Charles L.
Glazer, Nathan
Gleysteen, William H., Jr.
Globerman, Norma
Godchaux, Frank A., III
Godwin, I. Lamond
Goekjian, Samuel V.
Goheen, Robert F.
Goizueta, Roberto C.
Goldberg, Arthur J.
Goldberg, Samuel
Goldberger, Marvin L.
Golden, James R.
Golden, William T.
Goldin, Harrison J.
Goldman, Charles N.
Goldman, Guido
Goldman, Marshall I.
Goldman, Merle
Goldmark, Peter C., Jr.
Goldschmidt, Neil
Goldstein, Elizabeth A.
Goldstein, Jeffrey A.
Gomory, Ralph E.
Gompert, David C.
Gong, Gerrit W.
Goodby, James E.
Goodman, George J. W.
Goodman, Herbert I.
Goodman, Roy M.
Goodman,
   Sherri L. Wasserman
Goodpaster, Andrew J.
Goodsell, James Nelson
Gordon, Albert H.
Gordon, Lincoln
Gorman, Joseph T.
Gorman, Paul F.
Gornick, Alan L.
Gotbaum, Victor
Gottlieb, Gidon A. G.
Gottlieb, Thomas M.

Gottsegen, Peter M.
Gould, Peter G.
Gousseland, Pierre
Grace, J. Peter
Graff, Henry F.
Graff, Robert D.
Graham, Bob
Graham, Katharine
Graham, Thomas, Jr.
Graham, William R.
Grant, James P.
Grant, Stephen A.
Granville, Maurice F.
Graubard, Stephen R.
Gray, Hanna Holborn
Green, Bill
Green, Carl J.
Greenberg, Maurice R.
Greenberg, Sanford D.
Greene, James C.
Greene, James R.
Greene, Joseph N., Jr.
Greene, Margaret L.
Greenfield, James L.
Greenfield, Meg
Greenough, William C.
Greenspan, Alan
Greenwald, Joseph A.
Greenway, H. D. S.
Greenwood, Ted
Gregorian, Vartan
Grenier, Richard
Griffith, Thomas
Griffith, William E.
Grose, Peter
Gross, Ernest A.
Gross, Patrick W.
Grossman, Gene M.
Grove, Brandon H., Jr.
Groves, Ray J.
Grune, George V.
Grunwald, Henry A.
Gullion, Edmund A.
Gulliver, Adelaide Cromwell
Gutfreund, John H.
Guthman, Edwin O.
Gwertzman, Bernard M.
Gwin, Catherine

H

Haas, Peter E.
Haas, Robert D.
Habib, Philip C.
Haggard, Stephan
Haig, Alexander M., Jr.
Halaby, Najeeb E.
Haley, John C.
Hallingby, Paul, Jr.
Halperin, Morton H.
Halpern, Sue M.
Halsted, Thomas A.
Hamburg, David A.
Hamburg, Margaret Ann
Hamilton, Ann O.
Hamilton, Charles V.
Hamilton, Edward K.
Hamilton, Michael P.
Hammer, Armand

Hancock, Judith L.
Hansen, Carol Rae
Hansen, Roger D.
Hanson, Robert A.
Hanson, Thor
Harari, Maurice
Harding, Harry
Hardt, John P.
Hargrove, John Lawrence
Harman, Sidney
Harpel, James W.
Harper, Conrad K.
Harper, Paul C., Jr.
Harper, Zenola
Harriman, Pamela C.
Harris, Irving B.
Harris, Joseph E.
Harris, Scott Blake
Harrison, Selig S.
Harsch, Joseph C.
Hart, Augustin S.
Hart, Douglas M.
Hart, Parker T.
Hartley, Fred L.
Hartman, Arthur A.
Hartman, J. Lise
Hartnack, Carl E.
Haskell, John H. F., Jr.
Haskins, Caryl P.
Hatfield, Robert S.
Hauge, John R.
Hauser, Rita E.
Hauser, William L.
Hauspurg, Arthur A.
Haviland, H. Field, Jr.
Hawkins, Ashton
Hayes, Margaret Daly
Hayes, Samuel P.
Haynes, Fred
Haynes, Ulric, Jr.
Hayward, Thomas B.
Hazard, John N.
Healy, Harold H., Jr.
Heard, Alexander
Heck, Charles B.
Heckscher, August
Hedstrom, Mitchell W.
Heginbotham, Stanley J.
Hehir, J. Bryan
Heifetz, Elaine F.
Heimann, John G.
Heintzen, Harry L.
Helander, Robert C.
Heldring, Frederick
Hellman, F. Warren
Hellmann, Donald C.
Helmboldt, Niles E.
Helms, Richard
Henderson, Lawrence J., Jr.
Henkin, Alice H.
Henkin, Louis
Hennessy, John M.
Herling, John
Hermann, Charles F.
Herskovits, Jean
Herter, Christian A., Jr.
Herter, Frederick P.
Hertzberg, Arthur

258

Herzfeld, Charles M.
Herzstein, Robert E.
Hesburgh, Theodore M.
Hess, John B.
Hessler, Curtis A.
Hester, James M.
Hewitt, William A.
Hewlett, Sylvia Ann
Heyns, Roger W.
Higgins, Robert F.
Highet, Keith
Hight, B. Boyd
Hillenbrand, Martin J.
Hilsman, Roger
Hinerfeld, Ruth J.
Hines, Gerald D.
Hinshaw, Randall
Hinton, Deane R.
Hirschman, Albert O.
Hoagland, Jim
Hoch, Frank W.
Hodgson, James D.
Hoeber, Amoretta M.
Hoehn, William E., Jr.
Hoenlein, Malcolm
Hoepli, Nancy L.
Hoffman, Michael L.
Hoffmann, Stanley
Hoge, James
Hoge, Warren
Hoguet, George R.
Hoguet, Robert L.
Hohenberg, John
Holbrooke, Richard C.
Holcomb, M. Staser
Holderman, James B.
Holland, Robert C.
Hollick, Ann L.
Holmes, H. Allen
Holst, Willem
Holt, Pat M.
Hooks, Benjamin L.
Hoopes, Townsend W.
Hoover, Herbert W., Jr.
Horelick, Arnold L.
Hormats, Robert D.
Horn, Garfield H.
Horn, Karen N.
Horn, Sally K.
Horner, Matina S.
Horowitz, Irving Louis
Horton, Alan W.
Horton, Elliott
Horton, Frank B., III
Hosmer, Bradley C.
Hottelet, Richard C.
Houghton, Amory, Jr.
Houghton, Arthur A., Jr.
Houghton, James R.
House, Karen Elliott
Hovey, Graham
Hovey, J. Allan, Jr.
Howard, John B.
Howard, John R.
Hoyt, Mont P.
Huber, Richard L.
Hudson, Manley O., Jr.
Huebner, Lee W.

Hufbauer, Gary C.
Huffington, Roy M.
Hufstedler, Shirley
Hugel, Charles E.
Huggins, Nathan I.
Hughes, John
Hughes, Thomas L.
Huglin, Henry C.
Huizenga, John W.
Hummel, Arthur W., Jr.
Hunsberger, Warren S.
Hunter, Robert E.
Hunter-Gault, Charlayne
Huntington, Samuel P.
Hurewitz, J. C.
Hurlock, James B.
Huyck, Philip M.
Hyde, Henry B.
Hyland, William G.

I

Ignatius, David
Iklé, Fred C.
Ilchman, Alice S.
Inderfurth, Karl F.
Ingersoll, Robert S.
Inman, B. R.
Intriligator, Michael D.
Ireland, R. L., III
Irish, Leon E.
Irwin, John N., II
Irwin, John N., III
Isaacson, Walter
Iselin, John Jay
Isenberg, Steven L.
Isham, Christopher
Issawi, Charles
Istel, Yves-Andre
Izlar, William H., Jr.

J

Jabber, Paul
Jablonski, Wanda
Jackson, Elmore
Jackson, Eugene D.
Jackson, Henry F.
Jackson, John H.
Jackson, William E.
Jacob, John E.
Jacobs, Eli S.
Jacobs, Nehama
Jacobs, Norman
Jacobson, Harold K.
Jacobson, Jerome
Jacoby, Tamar
Jahrling, Robert V. W.
Jamieson, J. K.
Janklow, Morton L.
Janow, Merit E.
Jansen, Marius B.
Jastrow, Robert
Jenson, John W.
Jervis, Robert L.
Jessup, Alpheus W.
Jessup, Philip C., Jr.
Johnson, Chalmers
Johnson, Howard W.

Johnson, Joseph E.
Johnson, Paul G.
Johnson, Richard A.
Johnson, Robbin S.
Johnson, Robert H.
Johnson, Thomas S.
Johnson, W. Thomas
Johnson, Willard R.
Johnston, Philip
Jones, David C.
Jones, Peter T.
Jones, Sidney R.
Jones, Thomas V.
Jordan, Amos A.
Jordan, Vernon E., Jr.
Jorden, William J.
Joseph, Geri M.
Joseph, James A.
Josephson, William
Joyce, John T.
Junz, Helen B.
Juster, Kenneth I.

K

Kagan, Robert W.
Kahan, Jerome H.
Kahin, George McT.
Kahn, Harry
Kahn, Tom
Kaiser, Philip M.
Kaiser, Robert G.
Kalb, Marvin
Kalicki, Jan
Kamarck, Andrew M.
Kaminer, Peter H.
Kampelman, Max M.
Kamsky, Virginia A.
Kann, Peter R.
Kanter, Arnold
Kaplan, Gilbert E.
Kaplan, Harold J.
Kaplan, Helene L.
Kaplan, Mark N.
Karalekas, Anne
Karis, Thomas G.
Karnow, Stanley
Karns, Margaret P.
Kass, Stephen L.
Kassinger, Theodore W.
Kassof, Allen H.
Katz, Abraham
Katz, Milton
Katz, Ronald S.
Katzenbach, Nicholas deB.
Katzenstein, Peter J.
Kaufman, Henry
Kaufmann, William W.
Kaysen, Carl
Kearns, David T.
Keatley, Anne
Keene, Lonnie S.
Keeny, Spurgeon M., Jr.
Kelleher, Catherine M.
Kellen, Stephen M.
Keller, George M.
Kelley, P. X.
Kelly, George Armstrong
Kelly, John H.

Kelman, Herbert C.
Kemp, Geoffrey
Kempe, Frederick
Kempner, Maximilian W.
Kendall, Donald M.
Kenen, Peter B.
Keniston, Kenneth
Kennan, Christopher J.
Kennan, Elizabeth T.
Kennan, George F.
Kennedy, David M.
Kennedy, Donald
Kennedy, Randall L.
Kenney, F. Donald
Keohane, Nannerl O.
Keohane, Robert O.
Keppel, Francis
Kern, Harry F.
Kester, John G.
Ketelsen, James L.
Keydel, John F.
Khalilzad, Zalmay
Khuri, Nicola N.
Kiermaier, John
Kieschnick, W. F.
Kilson, Martin
Kimmitt, Robert M.
King, Henry L.
King, John A., Jr.
Kintner, William R.
Kipper, Judith
Kirby, Michael A.
Kirk, Grayson L.
Kirkland, Lane
Kirkpatrick, Jeane J.
Kiser, William S.
Kissinger, Henry A.
Kitchen, Helen
Kitchen, Jeffrey C.
Kleiman, Robert
Klein, David
Klein, Edward
Klurfeld, James
Knight, Robert Huntington
Knoppers, Antonie T.
Knowlton, William A.
Knowlton, Winthrop
Kohler, Foy D.
Kojm, Christopher A.
Kolodziej, Edward A.
Koltai, Steven R.
Komer, Robert W.
Kondracke, Morton
Korb, Lawrence J.
Korbonski, Andrzej
Korry, Edward M.
Kraar, Louis
Kraemer, Lillian E.
Kramer, Helen M.
Kramer, Jane
Kramer, Michael
Kramer, Steven Philip
Kraslow, David
Krasner, Stephen D.
Krasno, Richard M.
Krause, Lawrence B.
Kreidler, Robert N.
Kreisberg, Paul H.

259

260

Melloan, George R.
Melville, Richard A.
Mendlovitz, Saul H.
Menke, John R.
Meron, Theodor
Merow, John E.
Merrill, Philip
Merritt, Jack N.
Merszei, Zoltan
Meselson, Matthew
Messner, William Curtis, Jr.
Metcalf, George R.
Mettler, Ruben F.
Meyer, Cord
Meyer, Edward C.
Meyer, John R.
Meyer, Karl E.
Meyerson, Martin
Mickelson, Sig
Middleton, Drew
Midgley, Elizabeth
Midgley, John J., Jr.
Miller, Charles D.
Miller, David Charles, Jr.
Miller, Franklin C.
Miller, J. Irwin
Miller, Judith
Miller, Paul L.
Miller, William G.
Miller, William J.
Millett, Allan R.
Millington, John A.
Mills, Bradford
Milner, Helen
Minow, Newton N.
Mladek, Jan V.
Mochizuki, Mike
Moe, Sherwood G.
Mondale, Walter F.
Montgomery, Parker G.
Montgomery, Philip O'B.
Moody, Jim
Moody, William S.
Moore, John Norton
Moore, Jonathan
Moore, Paul, Jr.
Moose, Richard M.
Moran, Theodore H.
Morgan, Cecil
Morgan, Thomas E.
Morgenthau,
  Lucinda L. Franks
Morley, James William
Morrell, Gene P.
Morris, Grinnell
Morris, Max K.
Morrisett, Lloyd N.
Morse, David A.
Morse, Edward L.
Morse, F. Bradford
Morse, Kenneth P.
Moses, Alfred H.
Moss, Ambler H., Jr.
Motley, Joel
Moynihan, Daniel P.
Mroz, John Edwin
Mudd, Margaret F.
Mulford, David C.

Mulholland, William D.
Muller, Henry
Muller, Steven
Munger, Edwin S.
Munro, J. Richard
Munroe, George B.
Munroe, Vernon, Jr.
Munyan, Winthrop R.
Murphy, Joseph S.
Murray, Allen E.
Murray, Douglas P.
Murray, Lori Esposito
Muse, Martha T.
Muskie, Edmund S.

N

Nachmanoff, Arnold
Nacht, Michael
Nadiri, M. Ishaq
Nagorski, Zygmunt
Nathan, James A.
Nathan, Robert R.
Natt, Ted M.
Nau, Henry R.
Neal, Alfred C.
Negroponte, John D.
Neier, Aryeh
Nelson, Clifford C.
Nelson, Jack
Nelson, Mark A.
Nelson, Merlin E.
Neustadt, Richard E.
Newberg, Paula R.
Newburg, Andre W. G.
Newell, Barbara W.
Newhouse, John
Newman, Priscilla A.
Newman, Richard T.
Newsom, David D.
Newton, Quigg, Jr.
Newton, Russell B., Jr.
Ney, Edward N
Nichols, Rodney W.
Niehuss, John M.
Niehuss, Rosemary Neaher
Nielsen, Waldemar A.
Nimetz, Matthew
Nitze, Paul H.
Nolan, Janne E.
Nolan, Kimberly
Nolte, Richard H.
Nooter, Robert H.
Norman, William S.
Norstad, Lauris
Norton, Augustus R.
Norton, Eleanor Holmes
Nossiter, Bernard D.
Novak, Michael
Noyes, Charles Phelps
Nugent, Walter
Nye, Joseph S., Jr.

O

Oakes, John B.
Oberdorfer, Don
O'Cleireacain, Carol
O'Connor, Walter F.
Odeen, Philip A.

Odom, William E.
O'Donnell, Kevin
Oettinger, Anthony G.
Offit, Morris W.
O'Flaherty, J. Daniel
Ogden, Alfred
Ogden, William S.
O'Hare, Joseph A.
O'Keefe, Bernard J.
Okimoto, Daniel I.
Oksenberg, Michel
Okun, Herbert
Oliver, Covey T.
Olmstead, Cecil J.
Olsen, Leif H.
Olson, William C.
Olvey, Lee D.
O'Malley, Cormac K. H.
Omestad, Thomas
O'Neill, Michael J.
Opel, John R.
Oppenheimer, Franz M.
Ornstein, Norman J.
Osborn, George K., III
Osborne, Richard de J.
Osmer-McQuade, Margaret
Osnos, Peter
Ostrander, F. Taylor
Overholser, Geneva
Owen, Henry
Owen, Roberts B.
Oxman, Stephen A.
Oxnam, Robert B.
Oye, Kenneth A.

P

Packard, George R.
Page, John H.
Pagels, Heinz R.
Paine, George C., II
Pais, Abraham
Palenberg, John C.
Paley, William S.
Palmer, Mark
Palmer, Norman D.
Palmer, Ronald D.
Palmieri, Victor H.
Panofsky, Wolfgang K. H.
Parker, Daniel
Parker, Maynard
Parkinson, Roger
Parris, Mark Robert
Parsky, Gerald L.
Passin, Herbert
Patrick, Hugh T.
Patterson, Gardner
Patterson, Hugh B., Jr.
Patterson, Robert P., Jr.
Patterson, Torkel L.
Pauker, Guy J.
Paul, Roland A.
Payne, Samuel B.
Peacock, P. Dexter
Pearce, William R.
Pearlstine, Norman
Pearson, John E.
Peck, Michael A.
Pedersen, Richard F.

Pelgrift, Kathryn C.
Pell, Claiborne
Penfield, James K.
Pennoyer, Robert M.
Peretz, Don
Perkins, Edward J.
Perkins, James A.
Perkins, Roswell B.
Perle, Richard N.
Perlmutter, Amos
Perry, Hart
Peters, Arthur King
Peters, Aulana L.
Petersen, Donald E.
Petersen, Gustav H.
Petersen, Howard C.
Peterson, Peter G.
Peterson, Rudolph A.
Petraeus, David H.
Petree, Richard W.
Petschek, Stephen R.
Petty, John R.
Pezzullo, Lawrence A.
Pfaltzgraff, Robert L.
Pfeiffer, Jane Cahill
Pfeiffer, Ralph A., Jr.
Pfeiffer, Steven B.
Phillips, Christopher H.
Phillips, Russell A., Jr.
Picker, Harvey
Picker, Jean
Pickering, Thomas R.
Piel, Gerard
Pierce, William C.
Piercy, George T.
Pierre, Andrew J.
Pifer, Alan
Pigott, Charles M.
Pike, John E.
Pilliod, Charles J., Jr.
Pincus, Lionel I.
Pincus, Walter H.
Pinkerton, W. Stewart
Pino, John A.
Pinola, J. J.
Pipes, Daniel
Pipes, Richard E.
Pitts, Joe W., III
Plank, John N.
Platig, E. Raymond
Platt, Alan A.
Platt, Alexander H.
Platt, Nicholas
Platten, Donald C.
Plimpton, Calvin H.
Podhoretz, Norman
Polk, William R.
Pollack, Gerald A.
Polsby, Nelson W.
Pond, Elizabeth
Poneman, Daniel B.
Poor, J. Sheppard
Portes, Richard D.
Posen, Barry R.
Posner, Michael H.
Posvar, Wesley W.
Potter, Robert S.
Potter, William C.

261

Powell, Colin L.
Powell, Robert
Power, Philip H.
Power, Thomas F., Jr.
Powers, Joshua B.
Powers, Thomas Moore
Powers, William F., Jr.
Pranger, Robert J.
Pratt, Edmund T.
Press, Frank
Pressler, Larry
Preston, Lewis T.
Prewitt, Kenneth
Price, John R., Jr.
Price, Robert
Puchala, Donald J.
Puckett, Allen E.
Pugh, Richard C.
Purcell, Susan Kaufman
Pursley, Robert E.
Pusey, Nathan M.
Pustay, John S.
Putnam, George E., Jr.
Putnam, Robert D.
Pye, Lucian W.
Pyle, Cassandra A.

Q
Quandt, William B.
Quester, George H.
Quigg, Philip W.
Quigley, Leonard V.

R
Rabb, Maxwell M.
Rabinowitch, Victor
Radway, Laurence I.
Ragone, David V.
Ramo, Simon
Ranis, Gustav
Rashish, Myer
Rather, Dan
Rathjens, George W.
Rattner, Steven L.
Rauch, Rudolph S.
Ravenal, Earl C.
Ravenholt, Albert
Ravitch, Richard
Rawl, Lawrence G.
Raymond, Jack
Raymond, Lee R.
Read, Benjamin H.
Reed, Charles B.
Reed, John S.
Reed, Joseph Verner
Reed, Philip D.
Reeves, Jay B. L.
Regan, John M., Jr.
Reichert, William M.
Reid, Ogden
Reid, Whitelaw
Reinhardt, John E.
Reisman, W. M.
Renfrew, Charles B.
Resor, Stanley R.
Reston, James B.
Revelle, Roger
Rey, Nicholas A.

Reynolds, A. William
Rhinelander, John B.
Rhinesmith, Stephen H.
Rhodes, Frank H. T.
Rhodes, John B., Jr.
Rhodes, William R.
Ribicoff, Abraham A.
Rice, Condoleezza
Rice, Donald B.
Rice, Joseph A.
Rich, Frederic C.
Rich, John H., Jr.
Rich, Michael D.
Richardson, David B.
Richardson, Elliot L.
Richardson, John
Richardson, Richard W.
Richardson, William B.
Richardson, William R.
Richman, Joan F.
Rickard, Stephen A.
Riddell, Malcolm
Ridgway, Rozanne L.
Rielly, John E.
Ries, Hans A.
Riesel, Victor
Ripley, S. Dillon, II
Ritch, John B., III
Rivard, Robert
Rivers, Richard R.
Rivkin, David B., Jr.
Rivkin, Donald H.
Rivlin, Alice M.
Robb, Charles S.
Roberts, Chalmers M.
Roberts, Richard W.
Roberts, Walter Orr
Roberts, Walter R.
Robinson, Charles W.
Robinson, James D., III
Robinson, Linda S.
Robinson, Marshall A.
Robinson, Pearl T.
Robinson, Randall
Robison, Olin C.
Roche, John P.
Rockefeller, David
Rockefeller, David, Jr.
Rockefeller, John D., IV
Rockefeller, Rodman C.
Rockwell, Hays H.
Rodman, Peter W.
Rodriguez, Vincent A.
Roett, Riordan
Roff, J. Hugh, Jr.
Rogers, Bernard W.
Rogers, David E.
Rogers, William D.
Rogers, William P.
Rogovin, Mitchell
Rohatyn, Felix G.
Rohlen, Thomas P.
Rohter, William Lawrence
Rokke, Ervin J.
Romberg, Alan D.
Romero-Barcelo, Carlos
Roney, John H.
Roosa, Robert V.

Roosa, Ruth AmEnde
Rosberg, Carl G.
Rose, Daniel
Rose, Elihu
Rose, Frederick P.
Rosecrance, Richard
Rosen, Arthur H.
Rosen, Jane K.
Rosenblith, Walter A.
Rosenblum, Mort
Rosenfeld, Robert A.
Rosenfeld, Stephen S.
Rosenthal, A. M.
Rosenthal, Douglas E.
Rosenthal, Jack
Rosenzweig, Robert M.
Rosin, Axel G.
Rosovsky, Henry
Ross, Arthur
Ross, Dennis B.
Ross, Roger
Ross, Thomas B.
Rosso, David J.
Rostow, C. Nicholas
Rostow, Elspeth Davies
Rostow, Eugene V.
Rostow, Walt W.
Rotberg, Robert I.
Roth, Stanley Owen
Roth, William M.
Roth, William V., Jr.
Rouse, James W.
Rovine, Arthur W.
Rowen, Henry S.
Rowny, Edward L.
Rubin, Seymour J.
Ruckelshaus, William D.
Rudenstine, Neil L.
Rudman, Warren B.
Rudolph, Lloyd I.
Rudolph, Susanne Hoeber
Ruebhausen, Oscar M.
Ruenitz, Robert M.
Ruina, J. P.
Runge, Carlisle Ford
Rush, Kenneth
Rusk, Dean
Russell, Thomas W., Jr.
Rustow, Dankwart A.
Ruth, David A.
Ruttan, Vernon W.
Ryan, Hewson A.
Ryan, John T., Jr.
Ryan, John T., III

S
Sadowski, Yahya
Safran, Nadav
Sagan, Scott
Sage, Mildred D.
Said, Edward
Sakoian, Carol
Salcido, Pablo
Salisbury, Harrison E.
Salk, Jonas
Salomon, Richard E.
Salomon, William R.
Saltzman, Charles E.

Salzman, Herbert
Sample, Steven B.
Samuel, Howard D.
Samuels, Barbara C., II
Samuels, Michael A.
Samuels, Nathaniel
Samuels, Richard J.
Sanchez, Nestor D.
Sanders, Edward G.
Sanford, Charles S., Jr.
Sanford, Terry
Sarro, Dale M.
Saul, Ralph S.
Saunders, Harold H.
Savage, Frank
Sawhill, John C.
Sawyer, Diane
Sawyer, John E.
Saylor, Lynne S.
Scalapino, Robert A.
Scali, John A.
Schacht, Henry B.
Schachter, Oscar
Schaetzel, J. Robert
Schafer, John H.
Schaufele, William E., Jr.
Schecter, Jerrold
Scheffer, David J.
Scheinman, Lawrence
Schiff, Frank W.
Schilling, Warner R.
Schlesinger, Arthur, Jr.
Schlesinger, James R.
Schlosser, Herbert S.
Schmertz, Herbert
Schmidt, Benno, Jr.
Schmoker, John B.
Schmults, Edward C.
Schneider, Jan
Schneider, William
Schneier, Arthur
Schoen, Douglas
Schoettle, Enid C. B.
Schorr, Daniel L.
Schubert, Richard F.
Schuh, G. Edward
Schuyler, C. V. R.
Schwab, William B.
Schwartz, David N.
Schwartz, Harry
Schwartz, Norton A.
Schwarz, Frederick A. O., Jr.
Schwebel, Stephen M.
Sciolino, Elaine F.
Scott, Stuart N.
Scowcroft, Brent
Scranton, William W.
Scrimshaw, Nevin S.
Seaborg, Glenn T.
Seabury, Paul
Seagrave, Norman P.
Seamans, Robert C., Jr.
Sebenius, James K.
Segal, Sheldon J.
Seibold, Frederick C., Jr.
Seidman, Herta Lande
Seigenthaler, John L.
Seigle, John W.

262

Seignious, George M., II
Seitz, Frederick
Selby, Norman C.
Selin, Ivan
Semple, Robert B., Jr.
Setear, John K.
Sewell, John W.
Sexton, William C.
Shafer, Raymond Philip
Shalala, Donna E.
Shannon, James M.
Shapiro, Eli
Shapiro, George M.
Shapiro, Isaac
Sharp, Daniel A.
Shayne, Herbert M.
Shearer, Warren W.
Sheeline, Paul C.
Sheffield, James R.
Sheinkman, Jack
Sheldon, Eleanor Bernert
Shelley, Sally Swing
Shelp, Ronald K.
Shelton-Colby, Sally A.
Shelton, Joanna Reed
Shenk, George H.
Sherry, George L.
Sherwood, Elizabeth D.
Sherwood, Richard E.
Shinn, James J.
Shinn, Richard R.
Shipley, Walter V.
Shirer, William L.
Shoemaker, Alvin V.
Shoemaker, Don
Shriver, Donald W., Jr.
Shriver, Sargent, Jr.
Shubert, Gustave H.
Shulman, Colette
Shulman, Marshall D.
Shultz, George P.
Sick, Gary G.
Siegman, Henry
Sifton, Elisabeth
Sigal, Leon V.
Sigmund, Paul E.
Sihler, William W.
Silas, C. J.
Silberman, Laurence H.
Silk, Leonard S.
Silvers, Robert B.
Simes, Dimitri K.
Simmons, Adele Smith
Simmons, Richard S.
Simon, William E.
Simons, Howard
Sims, Albert G.
Sisco, Joseph J.
Sitrick, James B.
Skidmore, Thomas E.
Skilling, Jeffrey K.
Skinner, Elliott P.
Skolnikoff, Eugene B.
Slade, David R.
Slater, Jacqueline R.
Slater, Joseph E.
Slawson, Paul S.
Sloan, David M.

Sloane, Ann Brownell
Slocombe, Walter B.
Slocum, John J.
Sloss, Leon
Small, Lawrence M.
Smart, S. Bruce, Jr.
Smith, Carleton Sprague
Smith, Datus C., Jr.
Smith, David S.
Smith, DeWitt C., Jr.
Smith, Gaddis
Smith, Gerard C.
Smith, Hedrick
Smith, John T., II
Smith, Larry K
Smith, Malcolm B.
Smith, Michael Joseph
Smith, Perry M.
Smith, Peter B.
Smith, R. Jeffrey
Smith, Richard M.
Smith, Robert F.
Smith, Stephen G.
Smith, Theodore M.
Smith, Tony
Smith, W. Y.
Smythe, Mabel M.
Snipes, James C.
Snow, Robert Anthony
Snyder, Craig
Snyder, Jack L.
Snyder, Jed C.
Sobol, Dorothy Meadow
Soderberg, Nancy E.
Sohn, Louis B.
Solarz, Stephen J.
Solbert, Peter O. A.
Solomon, Anthony M.
Solomon, Peter J.
Solomon, Richard H.
Solomon, Robert
Sonne, Christian R.
Sonnenfeldt, Helmut
Sonnenfeldt, Richard W.
Sorensen, Gillian Martin
Sorensen, Theodore C.
Soros, George
Sovern, Michael I.
Spain, James W.
Spang, Kenneth M.
Spencer, Edson W.
Spencer, John H.
Spencer, William C.
Spencer, William I.
Spero, Joan E.
Speth, James Gustave
Spiers, Ronald I.
Spiro, David E.
Spiro, Herbert J.
Spofford, Charles M.
Sprague, Robert C.
Squadron, Howard M.
Stackpole, Stephen H.
Staley, Eugene
Stalson, Helena
Stamas, Stephen
Stankard, Francis X.
Stanley, Peter W.

Stanley, Timothy W.
Stanton, Frank
Stanton, R. John, Jr.
Staples, Eugene S.
Starobin, Herman
Starr, Jeffrey M.
Starr, S. Frederick
Stassen, Harold E.
Stavridis, James
Steadman, Richard C.
Stebbins, James H.
Steel, Ronald
Steiger, Paul E.
Stein, Eric
Stein, Jonathan B.
Steinberg, David J.
Steinberg, James B.
Steinbruner, John D.
Steiner, Daniel
Stepan, Alfred C.
Stern, Ernest
Stern, Fritz
Stern, H. Peter
Stern, Paula
Sterner, Michael E.
Sternlight, David
Stevens, Charles R.
Stevens, James W.
Stevens, Norton
Stevenson, Adlai E., III
Stevenson, Charles A.
Stevenson, John R.
Stevenson, Ruth Carter
Stewart, Donald M.
Stewart, Patricia Carry
Stewart, Ruth Ann
Sticht, J. Paul
Stiehm, Judith Hicks
Stifel, Laurence D.
Stilwell, Richard G.
Stobaugh, Robert B.
Stoessinger, John G.
Stoga, Alan
Stokes, Bruce
Stokes, Donald E.
Stokes, Louis
Stone, Jeremy J.
Stone, Roger D.
Stone, Shepard
Stookey, John Hoyt
Stratton, Julius A.
Straus, Donald B.
Straus, Oscar S.
Straus, R. Peter
Straus, Ralph I.
Straus, Robert K.
Strauss, Robert S.
Strauss, Simon D.
Strausz-Hupe, Robert
Stremlau, John J.
Stroud, Joe H.
Styron, Rose
Sudarkasa, Niara
Suleiman, Ezra N.
Sullivan, Eugene J.
Sullivan, Leon H.
Sullivan, Roger W.
Sullivan, William H.

Summers, Harry G
Sunderland, Jack I
Surrey, Walter Ste
Suslow, Leo A.
Sutterlin, James S.
Sutton, Francis X.
Sutton, Percy E.
Swank, Emory C.
Swanson, David H.
Swearer, Howard R.
Sweitzer, Brandon W
Swenson, Eric P.
Swigert, James W.
Swing, John Temple
Symington, W. Stuart
Szanton, Peter L.

T

Taber, George M.
Taft, William H., IV
Talbot, Phillips
Talbott, Strobe
Tanham, George K.
Tannenwald, Theodore, .
Tanner, Harold
Tanter, Raymond
Tarnoff, Peter
Taubman, William
Taylor, Arthur R.
Taylor, George E.
Taylor, T. James, Jr.
Taylor, William J., Jr.
Teeters, Nancy H.
Teitelbaum, Michael S.
Tempelsman, Maurice
Tennyson, Leonard B.
Terracciano, Anthony P.
Terry, Sarah M.
Thayer, A. Bronson
Theobald, Thomas C.
Thery, Jane L. Barber
Thoman, G. Richard
Thomas, Barbara S.
Thomas, Brooks
Thomas, Evan W., II
Thomas, Evan W., III
Thomas, Franklin A.
Thomas, Lee B., Jr.
Thomas, Lewis
Thompson, W. Scott
Thompson, William Pratt
Thomson, James A.
Thomson, James C., Jr.
Thornburgh, Dick
Thornell, Richard P.
Thornton, John L.
Thornton, Thomas P.
Thorp, Willard L.
Thorup, Cathryn L.
Thurman, M. R.
Tillinghast, David R.
Tillman, Seth P.
Timothy, Kristen
Tisch, Laurence A.
Todaro, Michael P.
Todman, Terence A. ˙
Tolbert, Kathryn
Toll, Maynard J., Jr.

263

Tomlinson, Alexander C.
Tonelson, Alan
Topping, Seymour
Toth, Robert C.
Train, Harry D., II
Train, Russell E.
Trainor, Bernard E.
Trani, Eugene P.
Travers, Peter J.
Travis, Martin B., Jr.
Treat, John Elting
Tree, Marietta
Treverton, Gregory F.
Trewhitt, Henry L.
Trezise, Philip H.
Triffin, Robert
Trooboff, Peter D.
Trost, C. A. H.
Trowbridge, Alexander B.
Truman, Edwin M.
Tu, Lawrence P.
Tucher, H. Anton
Tuchman, Barbara
Tuck, Edward Hallam
Tucker, Richard F.
Tucker, Robert W.
Tung, Ko-Yung
Turkevich, John
Turner, Stansfield
Turner, William C.
Tuthill, John Wills
Tyrrell, R. Emmett, Jr.
Tyson, Laura D'Andrea

U

Udovitch, A. L.
Uhlig, Mark
Ullman, Richard H.
Ulman, Cornelius M.
Ulmer, Alfred C.
Ungar, Sanford J.
Ungeheuer, Frederick
Unger, Leonard
Urfer, Richard P.
Usher, William R.
Utley, Garrick

V

Vagliano, Alexander M.
Vagliano, Sara
Vaky, Viron P.
Valdez, Abelardo Lopez
Valenta, Jiri
Valentine, Debra A.
Vance, Cyrus R.
van den Haag, Ernest
vanden Heuvel, Katrina
vanden Heuvel, William J.
Van Dusen, Michael H.
Van Fleet, James A.
Van Oudenaren, John
Van Vlierden, Constant M.
van Voorst, L. Bruce
Veit, Lawrence A.
Veliotes, Nicholas A.
Vermilye, Peter H.
Vernon, Raymond
Vessey, John W.

Vila, Adis Maria
Vine, Richard D.
Viscusi, Enzo
Vogel, Ezra F.
Vogelgesang, Sandy
Vojta, George J.
Volcker, Paul A.
Von Klemperer, Alfred H.
von Mehren, Robert B.
Vuono, Carl Edward

W

Wadsworth-Darby, Mary
Wahl, Nicholas
Wakeman, Frederic E., Jr.
Walinsky, Adam
Walker, Charls E.
Walker, G. R.
Walker, Joseph, Jr.
Walker, William N.
Wall, Christopher R.
Wallace, Martha Redfield
Wallich, Christine
Wallich, Henry C.
Wallison, Peter J.
Walt, Stephen M.
Walters, Barbara
Waltz, Kenneth N.
Warburg, Gerald F., II
Ward, F. Champion
Ward, John W.
Warner, Edward L., III
Warner, Rawleigh, Jr.
Warnke, Paul C.
Washburn, Abbott M.
Wasserstein, Bruce
Waterbury, John
Watson, Craig M.
Watson, Thomas J., Jr.
Wattenberg, Ben J.
Watts, Glenn E.
Watts, John H.
Watts, William
Way, Alva O.
Weaver, George L.-P.
Webb, James H., Jr.
Webster, Bethuel M.
Webster, William H.
Wehrle, Leroy S.
Weidenbaum, Murray L.
Weiksner, George B., Jr.
Weil, Frank A.
Weinberg, John L.
Weinberg, Steven
Weinberger, Caspar W.
Weiner, Myron
Weinert, Richard S.
Weinrod, W. Bruce
Weiss, Charles, Jr.
Weiss, Edith Brown
Weiss, S. Ariel
Weiss, Seymour
Weiss, Thomas G.
Welch, Jasper A., Jr.
Welch, John F., Jr.
Welch, Larry D.
Weller, Ralph A.
Wells, Damon, Jr.

Wells, Herman B.
Wells, Louis T., Jr.
Wells, Samuel F., Jr.
Wender, Ira T.
Wertheim, Mitzi M.
Wesely, Edwin J.
Wessell, Nils Y.
West, Robert LeRoy
Weston, Burns H.
Westphal, Albert C. F.
Wexler, Anne
Whalen, Charles W., Jr.
Whalen, Richard J.
Wharton, Clifton R., Jr.
Wheat, Francis M.
Wheeler, John P., III
Wheeler, John K.
Wheeler, Richard W.
Wheelon, Albert D.
Whipple, Taggart
Whitaker, C. S., Jr.
Whitaker, Jennifer Seymour
White, John P.
White, P. Maureen
White, Peter C.
White, Robert J.
White, Robert M.
Whitehead, John C.
Whitehouse, Charles S.
Whiting, Allen S.
Whitman, Marina v.N.
Whitney, Craig R.
Whittemore, Frederick B.
Wiarda, Howard J.
Wickham, John A., Jr.
Wiener, Malcolm H.
Wieseltier, Leon
Wiesner, Jerome B.
Wilbur, Brayton, Jr.
Wildavsky, Aaron
Wilds, Walter
Wiley, Richard A.
Wiley, W. Bradford
Wilhelm, Harry E.
Wilkins, Roger W.
Wilkinson, Dag
Will, George F.
Willey, Fay
Williams, Eddie Nathan
Williams, Franklin H.
Williams, Harold M.
Williams, Haydn
Williams, James B.
Williams, Joseph H.
Williams, Maurice J.
Williamson, Thomas S., Jr.
Willrich, Mason
Wilmers, Robert G.
Wilson, Donald M.
Wilson, Ernest James, III
Wilson, Heather A.
Wilson, James Q.
Wilson, John D.
Wimpfheimer, Jacques D.
Winder, R. Bayly
Wing, Adrien Katherine
Winik, Jay
Winks, Robin W.

Winokur, Herbert S., Jr.
Winship, Thomas
Winslow, Richard S.
Winterer, Philip S.
Winters, Francis X.
Wirth, Timothy E.
Wisner, Frank G., II
Witunski, Michael
Wofford, Harris L.
Wohlstetter, Albert
Wohlstetter, Roberta
Wolf, Charles, Jr.
Wolf, Milton A.
Wolfensohn, James D.
Wolff, Alan Wm.
Wolfowitz, Paul D.
Wolpe, Howard E.
Wood, Richard D.
Woodside, William S.
Woolf, Harry
Woolsey, R. James
Wriggins, W. Howard
Wright, Jerauld
Wriston, Walter B.
Wyman, Thomas H.

Y

Yalman, Nur
Yang, Chen Ning
Yankelovich, Daniel
Yarmolinsky, Adam
Yeo, Edwin H., III
Yergin, Daniel H.
Yoffie, David
Yost, Casimir A.
Young, Alice
Young, Andrew
Young, Edgar B.
Young, Lewis H.
Young, Michael K.
Young, Nancy
Young, Richard
Young, Stephen B.
Youngman, William S.
Yu, Frederick T. C.
Yudkin, Richard A.

Z

Zagoria, Donald S.
Zakheim, Dov S.
Zarb, Frank G.
Zartman, I. William
Zeidenstein, George
Zelnick, C. Robert
Zilkha, Ezra K.
Zimmerman, Edwin M.
Zimmerman, Peter D.
Zimmerman, William
Zimmermann, Warren
Zinberg, Dorothy S.
Zinder, Norton D.
Zorthian, Barry
Zraket, Charles A.
Zuckerman, Mortimer B.
Zumwalt, Elmo R., Jr.
Zwick, Charles J.
Zysman, John